VIRTUAL REALITY
APPLICATIONS and EXPLORATIONS

VIRTUAL REALITY
APPLICATIONS
and EXPLORATIONS

EDITED BY **ALAN WEXELBLAT**

Academic Press Professional
A Division of Harcourt Brace & Company

Boston   San Diego   New York
London   Sydney   Tokyo   Toronto

ACADEMIC PRESS PROFESSIONAL
955 Massachusetts Avenue, Cambridge, MA 02139

An Imprint of ACADEMIC PRESS, INC.
A Division of HARCOURT BRACE & COMPANY

United Kingdom Edition published by
ACADEMIC PRESS LIMITED
24–28 Oval Road, London NW1 7DX

Library of Congress Cataloging-in-Publication Data

Virtual reality : applications and explorations / [edited by] Alan
    Wexelblat.
        p.   cm.
    Includes bibliographical references and index.
    ISBN 0-12-745045-9 (alk. paper)
    I. Wexelblat, Alan, date- .
QA76.9.H85V57   1993
006—dc20   92–9231
                                                               CIP

Printed in the United States of America
93   94   95   96   BB   9   8   7   6   5   4   3   2   1

This book is for my wife,
Jennie Faries

Thanks to: my family; Tamar Amidon; Michael Benedikt;
William Bricken; Pat Cadigan; Tom Furness; Sari Kalin;
Aaron Marcus; Joy Mountford; Lew Shiner; Bruce Sterling; my Voice
of Reason; Space Crafters; Turkey City; and of course my editors
Kathleen Tibbetts, Brian Miller, and the other wonderful folk
at Academic Press.

CONTENTS

Part III   Softwhere in the World

Contributors

Numbers in parentheses indicate the pages on which the authors' contributions begin.

Meredith Bricken (199), University of Washington, Human Interface Technology Laboratory, Mail Stop FJ15, Seattle, WA 98195

Chris M. Byrne (199), University of Washington, Human Interface Laboratory, Mail Stop FJ15, Seattle, WA 98195

Thomas Erickson (1), Apple Computer, Human Interface, Advanced Technology Group, 20525 Mariani Avenue, MS: 76-3H, Cupertino, CA 95014

Kim Michael Fairchild (45), Institute of Systems Science, National University of Singapore, Heng Mui Keng Terrace, Kent Ridge, Singapore, 0511

Brian Gardner (91), Apple Advanced Technology Group, One Infinite Loop, MS: 301-3K, Cupertino, CA 95014

Charles Grantham (219), University of San Francisco, 2130 Fulton Street, San Francisco, CA 94117-1080

Myron Krueger (147), Artificial Reality, P.O. Box 786, Vernon, CT 06066

Michael McGreevy (163), NASA Ames Research Center, Human Interface Research Branch, Aerospace Human Factors Research Division, Moffet Field, CA 94035

Stuart Moulthrop (77), Georgia Institute of Technology, School of Literature, Communication, and Culture, The Ivan Allen College, Atlanta, GA 30332-0165

Vincent John Vincent (123), Vivid Effects, 317 Adelaide Street West, Suite 302, Toronto, Ontario, Canada M5V 1P9

Alan Wexelblat (23), MIT Media Lab, 20 Ames St., E15-4392, Cambridge, MA 02140

Susan Wyshynski (123), Vivid Effects, 317 Adelaide Street West, Suite 302, Toronto, Ontario, Canada M5V 1P9

Foreword

Virtual Reality:
As Real As You Want It To Be

Pat Cadigan

Welcome to one of the oldest forms of Virtual Reality in existence: a book. I should know, as it so happens that I make my living as a writer. It also happens that a good deal of my work is directly concerned with Virtual Reality, so perhaps instead of calling myself a writer, I could start passing myself off as a, um, Virtual Realtor.

Maybe in the future, Virtual Realtor will be one of the growth occupations, though it will probably be nothing like writing books. For one thing, judging from the essays on the following pages, you'll need a lot more hardware (and software), as well as a strong ability to visualize and good organizational reflexes.

Exactly when we'll see the first true Virtual Realtors is as yet undetermined, but there are plenty of informal prototypes around, as you'll know if anyone has tried to sell you beach-front property that turned out to be polluted swampland—figuratively, or even literally, depending on what you were looking for, and how anxious you were to buy in.

What does this have to do with any of the essays in this book, all of which deal with practical issues and problems concerned with the construction of a computer-generated graphic environment for purposes of education, work, and/or recreation? Just this essential truth: we've *always* had Virtual Reality, in many, many forms. We're just now getting around to making it technically literal, via computers.

The truly oldest form of VR is located in a relatively small area stretching roughly between your left ear and your right ear. From here, we produced select pieces and portions of our personal VR to show the world— statues, pictures, music, plays, books, films. And, oh, yes, television.

The pieces and portions we drew from our personal VR became more elaborate, larger and longer in duration. Virtual Reality, as detailed in the following essays, is the next logical step, and the question I've heard most often about it is "What for? What is Virtual Reality good for, what is the purpose?" The authors here will tell you that it's a good place to work and/or to learn; a good way to explore environments too deadly to visit in person; a good way to manage the information deluge; a *great* way to have a good time; and any number of other things.

It is true that VR's potential applications are almost too numerous to list. But how things will really turn out when we move from the potential to the actual—ah, that's a different matter entirely. Because, as William Gibson, one of VR's cultural godfathers, once said, "The street finds its own uses for things." No statement has ever been truer. What it means, friends, is that intent seldom has the same degree of impact as the results . . . or, if you will, consequences. And that includes not only VR, but what we will learn from it, and in it.

So once again: "What for? What's it good for, what's the purpose?"

It's important because we need better, easier ways of managing information or it ceases to be information and simply becomes noise. Because improved educating techniques make for more knowledgeable and more capable people. Because we need places to exercise our curiosity by performing experiments that may be too difficult, if not downright impossible, in the outer world. Because VR has always been with us conceptually anyway. Because whatever we learn in creating VR teaches us something more about *this* reality and how we fit into it. Because it's not time to stop exploring the possibilities. Because it's not time to stop *doing. Anything.*

How many more reasons do you need?

I wrote a book called *Synners,* in which VR was in regular use, commercially and privately, and in the course of the story, some people generated a reality that was a synthesis of the outer world, technological VR, and human perceptions. Because of this, some things happened that were good, and some other things happened that were bad, and in the end, it was as mixed a blessing as any other new development. Ultimately, this is all you can say about VR: Like anything else, it will be a mixed blessing. There are lots of reasons good enough to justify it. There are no reasons good enough to stop it.

As e. e. cummings put it: "There's a hell of a good universe next door; let's go."

Preface

Welcome to an exploration of Virtual Reality. The seed that became this book was planted in 1989 while I interviewed for a new job. As anyone who has ever interviewed knows, you answer the same questions over and over again for each prospective employer. I had been involved in working on virtual reality (VR) and artificial reality (AR) since 1986 and—with my colleagues Kim Fairchild and Greg Meredith—had just published a paper on the topic [1]. So each job interview inevitably came to a discussion of AR and VR.

That year was also the first time that VR came strongly into the eye of the general public, as articles on the subject appeared in several trade magazines as well as in the *New York Times;* Jaron Lanier's likeness had even been seen on the front page of *The Wall Street Journal.*

These articles—and similar efforts in the semitechnical and popular press—tried to acquaint the public with what appeared to be a host of new ideas that were suddenly springing to life. Of course, those of us working in the field knew that the roots of VR and AR went much deeper, back years and even decades to the pioneering work of people like Krueger and Southerland. But by 1989 the public's imagination had begun to be captured, and when people saw "virtual reality" on my resumé the questions quickly started.

It was usually easy to explain to interviewers what AR and VR were. But inevitably they would want to know what I thought it was "good for." What would people "do" with this technology? Over and over again, I found myself trying to convey what I saw as the enormous potential of the ideas of VR and AR to revolutionize the way we interact with computers.

I think it is the ideas behind the gadgets—the goggles and gloves—that will be the most important and longest lasting contribution we will make to the world. Fundamentally, VR overturns a central tenet of computer systems as they have been built to this point.

Since the very beginning of computers, an enormous amount of skill learning has been required of people to use the machines. From programming languages through typing to interface metaphors, every mode of interaction we priests of the computer (programmers) have given to our followers (users) has required that the human adapt to the computer. We require people to use skills they are not born with in ways that are, at best, awkward. Our interfaces do not enable or empower people; despite our best efforts they have become glass barriers between the people and what the people would like to do.

But AR and VR can change that. By making data and programs accessible in the form of three-dimensional (3-D) worlds that are directly present to the senses and to navigation we propose—for the first time—to make the computer adapt to the human. Homo sapiens are inherently three-dimensional creatures: From the moment we first lie on our backs in our cribs we learn to reach and grasp and manipulate objects in a 3-D space. From the moment we first begin to crawl and later walk we learn to navigate and locate things in a vast 3-D space. These interactions are so deeply wired into our brains that we often cannot imagine the world any other way.

Fundamentally, when you look past the computer clothing that usually differentiates AR and VR, at the core each is concerned with the ideas of 3-D spaces, navigation, and location. Places—the *wheres*—assume center stage in this idea, which (as I will argue in my chapter in this book) has the potential to affect every area of purposeful human activity.

Having given this explanation over and over in my job interviews it was inevitable that someone would suggest writing a book on the topic. I do not remember who first gave me the idea, but the 1990 First Conference on Cyberspace [2] inspired me to begin the actual work of trying to make it happen.

After the conference I was sitting with Greg Meredith, trading ideas back and forth, when he used the term "softwhere" to mean software that was primarily concerned with issues of location, navigation, and manipulation of objects—all key elements in making VR useful. I was taken with the neologism and asked if I could use it for my book. Meredith agreed. Then, at a VR conference organized by the Human Interface Technology Lab at the University of Washington, I mentioned to Aaron Marcus my plans for a book about "softwhere."

To my surprise, he pointed out that the word was actually his and had been used by him as a way of describing the effort "to make the

ethereal and ephemeral concrete" [3]. Marcus had actually programmed one of the first virtual landscapes in 1973, in Fortran on a
PDP-10 using an Evans and Southerland LDS-1 graphics display system. His landscapes were displayed in several U.S. art galleries and
museums in the mid-1970s.

Marcus also had published a series of monographs called *Soft
Where, Inc.—The Work of Aaron Marcus.* The cover of the first volume
and its explanation are shown in Figures 1 and 2 (reproduced by permission of the author). These monographs were mentioned by Krueger
in his seminal book *Artificial Reality* and apparently Meredith had
picked up the word from reading or talking about the Krueger book.

Marcus also influenced this book in another important way. I had realized early in the project that it would be foolish of me to simply report on the work done by my friends and colleagues in the field. Rather
than treating you, the reader, to my second-hand interpretations I
wanted a volume that allowed the people working in the field to speak
for themselves, to express their vision of what they saw as the future of
their own work. So I began asking people who had done seminal work
to contribute chapters to the book.

When I mentioned to Marcus that I had asked Krueger and McGreevy
to contribute he pointed out to me these people were well known and
well published in the field. Their vision would be conveyed regardless
of what I did. Weren't there also people, he challenged me, who I knew
of who had important things to say on this topic who had not yet been
heard from?

As you can see from looking at the table of contents, I took his advice. I went in search of people who were doing work in this area but
who had not yet been exposed to the public eye; some had never published on this topic before. I offered them a spot next to a couple of the
"Big Names" of the field if they would put their ideas into a form anyone with a little computer knowledge and a little understanding of VR
or AR could read.

In contributing to this book, the authors and I agreed that it was important to talk about areas of application rather than specific systems.
You can read technical reports galore about the details of particular artificial worlds being built, but nothing on the larger visions that cause
people to build these worlds. I wanted my book to have more explanatory power than a simple series of "this is what I built" papers could

give. The "Applications" of the title therefore refers to *areas* of application. I also encouraged people to be a little far-out, to reach into the next decade and explore the implications of the ideas we all felt were important; thus "Explorations" refers to their attempt to explore some aspect of the near future with this technology.

To make the book easier to use I have divided it into three major areas: Computer Science, The Arts, and The World. Each begins with a small explanation of why I think VR is important to the area and a description of the chapters in that section. Each chapter also begins with a brief piece to introduce you to the authors and their ideas. I hope this will encourage you to read this book as a nonlinear text, skipping from chapter to chapter as different interests take your fancy.

I am grateful to my authors—without them this book could not exist. We have all worked hard to meet the goals laid out above, and the result is what you hold in your hands. We hope that you are a person like the ones we keep meeting: You have heard or read about VR, but wonder what it's good for. You understand that computers are important but you sense that they are not fulfilling their potential. You want to glimpse the future.

Presented here are our visions of what that future might look like. We hope that this volume will inspire you enough that you will want to become involved, enough that you will begin thinking about how VR and AR might be used in the areas that you know about.

And I hope you enjoy the book.

Alan Wexelblat
Reality Hacker, Cyberspace Bard
Cambridge, MA

REFERENCES

[1] Fairchild, Kim, L. Greg Meredith, and Alan Wexelblat, "The Tourist Artificial Reality," in *CHI'89: The Proceedings of the 1989 Conference on Computer-Human Interaction,* Austin, Texas, May 1989, New York: ACM Press, 1989.

[2] Benedikt, M. (Ed.), *Cyberspace: First Steps,* Cambridge, MA: MIT Press, 1991.

[3] Marcus, Aaron, "Cybernetic Environments," *Soft Where, Inc.,* Vol. 1, West Coast Poetry Review, 1975.

Soft Where, Inc.

The Work of Aaron Marcus

West Coast Poetry Review

Reno

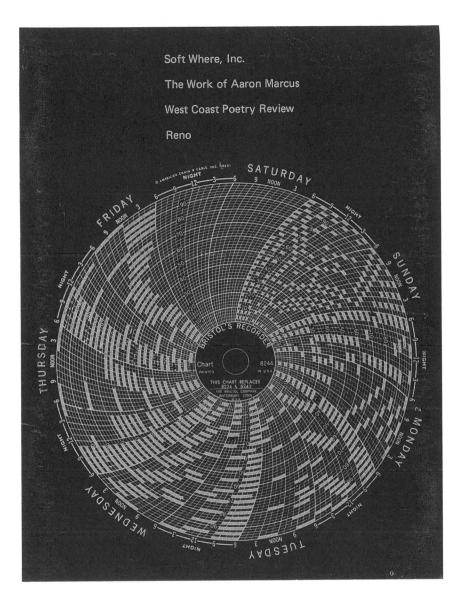

Fig. 1.

Genesis 1 and 2

Copyright ©1975
by West Coast Poetry Review
ISBN 0-915596-07-5

All rights reserved. Reproduction of the contents of this publication except for review is prohibited without permission of West Coast Poetry Review.

West Coast Poetry Reveiw
1127 Codel Way
Reno, Nevada 89503

This publication has been produced in a limited edition of 1000 copies. The typography is set in IBM Selectric Composer Univers. The printing by Dave's Printing & Publishing has been done on Vintage Velvet text paper and on Springfield Durakote cover paper.

This project is supported by a grant from the National Endowment for the Arts in Washington, D.C., a Federal agency.

On the cover is a reproduction from the score for *Genesis 1 and 2:* a ritual chant, original diagram on paper, 8-1/2" x 14", 1973. The instructions for the performance of the work are as follows:

Assemble 26 people where day and night meet, where earth, sky, water, and fire meet.

Facing a center, 24 people from a circle standing or sitting within touching distance (extra people are in single file in back of these 24 people and also face the center). Number 24 is at the north, 12 at the south, 6 at the east, and 18 at the west.

Number 25 is near the center facing east. The 26th person, the Timer, is near the center facing west. Both are along the east-west axis.

Number 25 selects a high note and an octave lower a low note. They should be comfortable and resonant. The low note is sung as BA, as in 'baw'; the high note is sung as ME, as in 'meet'.

Each of the 25 persons (or extra people in a radial line) finds the appropriate concentric band in the time chart, beginning with Number 1 near the center of the chart. Empty spaces indicate silence. Filled spaces represent sound. A short breath may be taken between continued spaces.

The Timer will clap every 5 seconds (this may be determined by the rhythm of slow breathing) for the first time through the sequence of marks and every 1 second (this may be determined by the rhythm of heartbeats) for the second time through the sequence. Each clap signals to the 25 people the beginning of a new time-space, and each person should begin to chant or to be silent according to the chart. The syllables should be alternated each time-space that a person is to sing. The person should begin by first singing the low or high note according to whether the person is male or female.

The chart sequence begins at 6 pm Saturday evening on the chart and all singing ends at 6 pm Friday evening. During all of Saturday, the Timer will continue to clap the time intervals. With a little practice and a moment of silence before each of the two sequences, begin the event.

The two sequences will actually require only about twelve minutes and about two and one-half minutes respectively to complete.

FIG. 2.

Part I
Softwhere in Computer Science

I am often asked to give lectures or teach courses on virtual reality. These introductory talks try to explain to the audience not only what VR is, but try to ground the work in its long tradition. I feel it is important to see VR not as some totally new technology unconnected to anything else, but rather as a natural extension of ideas that have been in the computer science community for more than 25 years.

In this section I present three chapters that relate to traditional computer science activities and discuss how current hard problems in computer science can be addressed with VR ideas and technology.

Chapter 1

Artificial Realities as Data Visualization Environments: Problems and Prospects

Thomas Erickson
Apple Computer
Human Interface, Advanced Technology Group
Cupertino, California

Tom Erickson is one of the "finds" in this book—people whose names I expect you've never heard, especially in connection with VR. When I first set out to do the book I asked my friend Joy Mountford to tell me who within Apple was doing interesting work in this area. She immediately pointed me to Tom and I am delighted to have him as a contributor. He shares with me the view that data—especially its presentation to users in a comprehensible form—are the prime challenge for computer science in the coming decade. Here he talks about how VR can help answer that challenge.

—A.W.

Introduction

In the popular press, artificial reality sounds wonderful. It's just like real reality, except better: a wave of the hand, a simple, natural gesture, and a new world opens up. No longer will users have to struggle with arcane and cumbersome user interfaces. Everything will be intuitive. Unfortunately, it's really not that simple. A recurring theme of this chapter is that while some aspects of artificial realities are easy and natural to use, other aspects present a host of new design problems.

One of the critical problems we face is accessing, managing, interpreting, and sharing the ever-increasing amounts of information that are being generated by our society. Artificial reality environments, in tandem with a number of other developments, are likely to have an immense impact on our ability to deal with information. I begin by providing some background, and describing ways in which artificial realities can enable us to deal more effectively with data. However, I want to avoid presenting a sugar-coated picture of artificial reality: As it stands today, artificial reality has far to go before it becomes a useful tool. To this end, I describe my experience using one of today's artificial reality systems to visualize data, paying particular attention to the various problems that arose. Once we understand where artificial reality is today, I turn to the future, discussing potential application scenarios, as well as some of the problems they raise. I conclude by focusing on artificial realities as environments that support interaction and suggest that there is much knowledge from the domains of architecture and urban design that might be profitably applied to the design of artificial realities. Ultimately, work from a variety of design disciplines will be necessary if artificial reality is to evolve from a laboratory curiosity and expensive form of entertainment into an environment that can be of use to those who do not love technology for its own sake.

Data and Visualization

Data

When I speak of data, I mean not only data generated by scientific experiments, but any sort of information ranging from news stories to maps to stock quotes. Regardless of the definition, no one will dispute that overwhelming amounts of data are being generated every day. Much of what we read in newspapers and magazines is already available in electronic form, and there are thousands of databases of specialized information ranging from legal cases to potato futures. Nontextual data are also abundant. For decades NASA has been collecting immense stores of digital images of the solar system. The Human Genome project, the ambitious attempt to decode human DNA, is generating massive amounts of data. Earth-orbiting satellites transmit detailed images of the earth's surface, enabling digital maps of the earth's surface to be updated every 16 to 20 days. Closer to home, the U.S. Census Bureau has released its TIGER (Topologically Integrated Geographic Encoding and Referencing) system, a digitized map of the entire United States, down to the level of individual streets. Market research firms and credit bureaus have been collecting demographic information for decades, and new products—collectively known as Geographic Information Systems—are springing up to support the integration of geographic and demographic information. There is no sign that this torrent of data will do anything but accelerate.

But these data are of little use unless people can easily access them. Fortunately, several trends promise to lay the foundations for more effective use of data. Increasing amounts of data are being generated in digital, and thus computer-accessible, form. More and more data are becoming accessible through on-line databases. The recent passage of the High Performance Computing and Communications Initiative by the U.S. Congress will facilitate the development of the National Research and Education Network (NREN), a gigabit network that will make it possible to transport and share much more data much more quickly. While there is far to go before any person can readily access any information, we are taking steps in the right direction. This leads to the next question: Once we have access to all this data, how are we to use it efficiently?

Visualization

Visualization is one of our best hopes for making more effective use of data. It is no coincidence that visual terms are used as a pervasive metaphor for understanding: "I *see* what you mean," "Let me *shed some light* on the subject," "Let's take a *closer look* at that argument," "I have a different *view*," as well as terms such as *insight, foresight,* and *overview.* Although visualization is often associated with the colorful representations of exotic scientific phenomena such as the galactic jets, enzymes, or brain scans that frequently adorn the covers of magazines, it is important to recognize that visualization can be usefully applied to the most prosaic data. The goal of visualization is to represent data in ways that make them perceptible, and thus able to engage human sensory systems. The three, nonexclusive ways in which visualization can help us in using and interpreting data are selective emphasis, transformation, and contextualization.

Selective emphasis allows the detection of previously hidden patterns by highlighting certain features of the data and suppressing others. One example, described in Perlman and Erickson [1], is a

```
1.  ____,____.
2.  _____:__,___,__,__,& _____.
3.  _____&___.
4.  ____.
5.  _,_____.
6.  ____;_-____--__-_____--___& __,__;___.
```

FIG. 1.1. A punctuation graph of a paragraph. Selective emphasis of punctuation allows the writer to detect potentially overly complex sentences such as #6, as well as recognize familiar patterns (e.g., the list in #2).

visualization program that can assist technical writers in eliminating long, complicated sentences from their documentation. The program is quite simple: It reads a document and produces a "punctuation graph" by leaving the punctuation intact, replacing "and" with "&," other words with underscore characters, and beginning each sentence on its own line (see Figure 1.1 for a partial example).

The Figure 1.1 representation, by selectively emphasizing punctuation, makes it easy for writers to analyze their work. Writers can look over a punctuation graph of a document to see whether they have adhered to such basic rules as "vary the length of sentences." They can also pick out overly complex sentences (sentence 6), and recognize such common patterns as lists (sentence 2) much more easily than when looking at a full text representation.

Another way in which visualization can facilitate the interpretation of data is through transformation. Nonvisual data can be transformed into a visual image by mapping its values into visual characteristics. Data thus represented can draw on our extensive experience in interpreting such visual images and on our facility for pattern recognition. An example of the power of visually transforming data may be seen by trying to solve the following problem:

> One morning a monk awoke and decided to make a pilgrimage to the top of a nearby mountain. At 6 A.M. he began climbing a path that led from the foot of the mountain to its peak. After spending the night on the mountain top, he arose at 6 A.M. and began retracing his steps, following the path back to its beginning. The question: Was there any point on the path where the monk was at the same time on each day?

Most people find this problem difficult to solve if they try to think about it verbally or mathematically. However, if the problem is transformed into visual terms, it is easy to solve. Draw a graph, with the vertical axis representing distance along the path from the bottom, and the horizontal axis being the time of day, beginning with 6 A.M.. The journey of the monk up the mountain, regardless of its speed, is represented by a continuous line from the lower left toward the upper right; the line for the journey back down is from the upper left toward the lower right. Clearly the lines must necessarily cross at some point, which represents the position on the path the monk was at on the same time each day (Figure 1.2).

The third way in which visualization may facilitate the effective use of data is through contextualization, that is, by providing a visual context or framework within which the data may be displayed. Imagine a system that provided real-time access to news stories coming across the UPI wire. One possible representation is simply to display a list in which each story is represented by an icon and a line of text containing its title and point of origin. However, if stories are coming in rapidly, it is likely that the user will be overwhelmed by the quantity of information. An alternative representation is to position the stories on a world map, locating them according to their point of origin. Such a representation would enable users to deal more effectively with the influx of data. Stories originating in particular areas could be focused on; patterns of activity, such as a flurry of new stories appearing in an unusual place, might signal newsworthy events such as earthquakes, riots, or

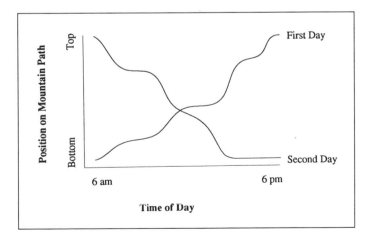

FIG. 1.2. The monk on the mountain problem. The problem becomes easy to solve when it is transformed into visual terms: regardless of the speed of travel, or of when the monk begins, it is clear that the two lines always intersect at some point.

other catastrophes. Note that the representation of each story is unchanged; the value added arises from providing a visual context within which the data can be interpreted.

Although each of the examples has focused on one way in which visualization assists us in interpreting data, most visualizations work in multiple ways. Transformation of data may facilitate selective emphasis or work hand in hand with contextualization. Geographic information systems are a burgeoning new application area that support transformation and selective emphasis of data within a geographical framework. For example, a geographic information system could permit business owners to analyze possible sites for new locations. Such an analysis might involve displaying points representing households making more than fifty thousand dollars a year on a city map showing major traffic patterns, exit ramps, natural patterns, and the locations of competitors. The reader interested in the finer points of data visualization will find many subtler examples in Edward Tufte's seminal work, *Envisioning Information* [2].

Although there is much we do not understand about visualization—deciding how to transform numeric data into a useful visual representation is still very much an art—it is a very active area of research. Much recent work has been spurred by the development of scientific visualization, a new domain of computer science forming at the boundaries of computer graphics, supercomputing, and human computer interaction (see [3] for a survey). Scientific visualization is aimed at creating tools for generating and manipulating visual representations of data from fields such as astrophysics, molecular biology, geophysics, fluid dynamics, and so on. As a National Science Foundation report on visualization in scientific computing stated, "The ability of scientists to visualize complex computations and simulations is absolutely essential to insure the integrity of analyses, to provoke insights and to communicate those insights to others" [4]. It is likely that tools and discoveries from scientific visualization will have broader applicability.

Finally, note that the word "visualization" is really too narrow. "Perceptualization" is probably more apropos, although it doesn't roll readily off the tongue. Sound and touch, as well as visual appearance, may be profitably used to represent data. For example, Gaver, Smith, and O'Shea [5] have demonstrated that people can use changes in "textures" of sound to detect problems in a computer simulation of a bottling plant. Similarly, Brooks and his colleagues [6] have used force feedback to represent bump and electrostatic forces in a system for exploring molecular docking. Users of the system can feel resistance as they try to maneuver a substrate molecule into the active site of a protein. Although the use of sonic and force feedback by visualization systems has lagged behind visual feedback, rapid strides are being made in both domains. The key to visualization is in representing information in ways that can engage any of our sensory systems and thus draw on our vast experience in organizing and interpreting sensory input.

Artificial Reality

In my view, artificial reality is not a radically new thing; rather it differs only in degree from previous systems. A system takes on the aura of artificial reality as it exhibits an increasingly tight coupling between an expanded range of input and a broader range of feedback options. In conventional graphic user interfaces, users are restricted to a keyboard and a single-point input device such as a mouse, with visual feedback, and generally no sonic feedback beyond that of a system beep or two. Typically, the user can only move one thing at a time, and that only in two dimensions; to move an item in a third dimension, or to rotate it, the user must go into a different mode.

New position-sensitive interface devices such as computer-interfaced gloves and head-mounted displays greatly increase the coupling between user input and system feedback: Motion of the hand, the head, and the body can be tracked and used to adjust the view and other system characteristics appropriately. Alternatively, more conventional input devices such as 3-D mice or six degree-of-freedom "space balls" may be used to broaden input bandwidth, or input devices may be removed from the body altogether, with remote edge-detecting cameras interpreting hand and body movement taking their place. Similarly, an increase in the range of feedback options—3-D graphics, perhaps augmented with 3-D sound and force feedback—especially when tightly coupled with increased input bandwidth, also moves a system toward the artificial reality arena.

Artificial Reality and Visualization

Artificial reality can enhance visualization in several ways. Most immediately, artificial reality makes it easier to interact with visualizations. In conventional computer systems, interacting with data, particularly 3-D data, is often difficult. How is the user to obliquely rotate a 3-D object given only a 2-D image and a mouse? How is the user to change the scale of data? How is the user to change the perspective from which the data are viewed? While a variety of methods exist, they range from the unintuitive (obscure commands and icons) to the cumbersome (knob boxes for rotating each separate axis). Such methods require all but the most expert user to stop thinking about the data, and to instead think about how to use the interface to manipulate the data.

In an artificial reality where the user has a presence in a 3-D space, there are more natural possibilities for manipulating 3-D images. Images can be rotated in the same way as a corresponding object in the real world: by grabbing it, and moving the hands appropriately. Users can change their viewpoints simply by walking around the object. And so on. The power of artificial reality is that it makes part of the interface invisible: The user no longer has to manipulate the interface to manipulate the data; the user need only manipulate the data directly.

There are two other ways in which artificial realities can enhance visualization. First, artificial realities allow multiple users to interact simultaneously with the same visualization. Several people looking at a visualization (or listening to it, or touching it) can do so from precisely the same perspective, thus easing problems of reference. Second, although this benefit lies somewhat farther out in the future, artificial realities can serve as environments for supporting human/human interaction. After all, visualization is not an end in itself—it's just a tool for interpreting data. Ultimately, whether the data are scientific or mundane, they are being interpreted so they can be communicated to others. Before pursuing this in more depth, it is best to look at an example of artificial reality as it is today, and examine its benefits and shortcomings as a visualization environment.

An Artificial Reality for Visualizing the Brain

In the fall of 1989, a colleague and I visited a leading supplier of artificial reality interface hardware and conducted an informal experiment with a head-mounted display and computer-interfaced glove. The goal was to assess the value of artificial realities for interactive scientific visualization (see [7] for a full account). Although we had previously tried similar systems, our trials were with relatively simple data sets (typically rooms or buildings) created by vendors for demonstrations. We felt a more telling evaluation would be to use an existing data set created for scientific use, a 3-D contour map of a human brain [8]. While the data set had to be simplified by two orders of magnitude to be displayed within the prototype artificial reality system we were using, it retained three characteristics not usually found in demonstration artificial realities: It was extremely complex, it was opaque, and it lacked expanses of empty space.

The artificial reality system allowed its users to navigate through the data set in two ways, by moving physically and by gesture-controlled virtual movement. Physical movement was quite simple: As the user's body moved in physical space, the image displayed by the head-mounted display was appropriately adjusted. As the user walked toward the image of the brain, it would get bigger, generating the illusion that the user was walking toward an image of a constant size. The user could walk right up to the brain, pass through its surface, and could walk around inside it. To view the brain from a different perspective, the user could walk around it or crouch to view its underside. Users also needed to move virtually through the data (without corresponding physical movement), because the constraints of the physical environment—walls and the length of cords tethering interface devices to computers—could prevent the user from approaching parts of the model. Virtual movement was by gesture-controlled "flying." Pointing with a forefinger allowed to user to "fly" forward; pointing with two fingers permitted backward flight. The system also displayed an image of a hand whenever the user's gloved hand was in his "virtual field of vision" (what would have been his field of vision had the head-mounted display not occluded the view of the real world). This permitted the user to reach out and grasp virtual objects, which could then be manipulated by moving the arm or body.

Experiencing the Brain Visualization.   When users donned the head gear and "entered" the visualization environment, they could see a brain floating in otherwise empty space. Since the brain had been scaled up in size by a factor of 10, it was initially difficult to tell how far away the brain was, and thus whether a few steps would take the user into the brain or whether it would be necessary to move virtually to enter it. The only other image present was the image of a hand, which appeared whenever the user's gloved hand passed in front of his or her face.

Although the resolution was poor and the image boxy, the stereopsis and interactivity greatly enhanced the reality of the brain image. The correspondence between real-world movement and the movement with respect to the data set was accurate and natural; there was no need to consider consciously which physical actions were required to achieve which effects. Virtual movement through the data set required a bit more thought. However, with a few minutes of practice, both users were able to "fly" through the data effectively, in spite of the problems noted below.

Interface Problems. A number of minor pragmatic and technical problems resulted. The headgear was heavy, the cable that tethered the user to the equipment could get wrapped around the legs, the system would fail if the user got too close to the position tracking receiver, and in spite of the simplified data set, the updating of the display in synchrony with head movements was a bit jerky. In addition, users required constant supervision to avoid walking into equipment, walls, and too close to or far from the position tracking receiver. Some of these problems have been addressed in the current version of the system, and all of them are likely to be ameliorated by increases in the power and portability of the technology.

There were other problems that are more thought provoking. The system used gestures to control virtual movement through the data space. The pointing gesture used to fly was a relatively natural one. However, both users accidentally flew several times when trying to point at something while describing it. (Even though the users were aware that no one else could see what they were pointing at, it was still natural to point.) Although users quickly learned that they ought not to point at things, this was easier to realize than to achieve. At moments of particular interest or excitement, the user would forget, point, and go flying off, losing sight of the area of interest. The flying gesture also mapped into habitual gestures (e.g., placing a finger on the chin), again causing inadvertent flight.

An obvious solution to the "accidental flight" problem is to make the flying gesture a bit less common and natural. However, this creates a new problem. With only a few, natural gestures, learning is not a problem; but as the number of gestures increases, and as they are made "narrower" to prevent accidental invocation, they become more difficult to learn and remember. Gestures are particularly difficult because they can vary along so many dimensions. If a user makes a gesture that fails to work as expected, there are many possibilities for what went wrong. A gesture may vary in its starting position, size, speed, form, and ending position, as well as in its position relative to objects in the virtual environment. There is no magic solution here: The more natural a gesture is, and the more variations the system will tolerate in recognizing it, the easier it will be to do accidentally; the less natural a gesture is, and the more stringent the system is in recognizing it, the more difficult the gesture will be to perform.

Another problem is the use of "flying" as a metaphor for virtual movement. While "flying" is a provocative and engaging concept, the fact is that it does not feel like flying. When the user is flying toward an object, it feels instead as though the object is approaching the user. Presumably this is because users have kinesthetic feedback regarding whether or not their bodies are moving. And although users can suspend their disbelief and ignore their kinesthetic feedback, in a very short time they'll be paying attention to such feedback as they walk around and through the object, or grab it to reposition it. A system that requires users to alternate between attending and not attending to a particular channel of feedback is probably not a good idea.

Another difficulty with "flying" is that people do not actually know how to fly. Flying suggests nothing about what gesture should be used to do it, and it suggests nothing about how to control speed or direction. Since the purpose of an interface metaphor is to leverage people's understanding of the real thing to facilitate their use of the interface, flying is not a particularly apt metaphor. An example of a better metaphor is pushing and pulling. Besides avoiding the inconsistent kinesthetic feedback, pushing-pulling also suggests natural gestures for doing it: palm open and fingers together for pushing; clenched fingers for pulling. The direction and speed of the push or pull obviously determine the direction and speed of the motion imparted to the object. As in the physical world, objects might be given momentum, so that an object would coast until it was grabbed. The pushing-pulling metaphor also has the virtue of extensibility: With two-handed input, the user could stretch or compress the data set, thus providing a natural way to scale the image as well. The point here is not that pushing-pulling is the best metaphor for virtual movement; other investigators have suggested a variety of promising metaphors (e.g., [6]). Rather, the point is that metaphors need to be carefully chosen so as to make the nonobvious parts of a system understandable to the system's users [9].

A final problem resulted from the data set itself: In contrast to the landscapes or buildings generally favored for demonstrations of artificial reality, this data set was dense and opaque. It is one thing to fly through an architectural space, or over a 3-D map, but quite another to move through an opaque brain. This was not a major problem because the brain structures had been color coded ahead of time, and the users were familiar with their relative sizes and forms. Nevertheless, had the brain data set had more detail, or had the users been unfamiliar with neuroanatomy, orientation and navigation difficulties could have made use of the data set impossible. Making the brain structures translucent would help, but it would not solve the density problem: Users would see a montage of superimposed colored shapes. It would probably be necessary to add a map-like overview to provide a third-person view of the user's position in the data space.

Summary. In this section we've looked at the use of an artificial reality as a visualization environment. As suggested, artificial reality did enhance the ease of interacting with the visualization. The users were able to interact quickly and naturally with the data, with only a very short period of trial and error. However, even in an environment that consisted of only one coherent data set, with a small number of commands, a number of problems occurred. Gestures used as a means of control were sufficiently natural that commands were unintentionally triggered. There is no ideal solution for this problem: The narrower a gesture is made in an effort to prevent accidental invocation, the less natural, memorable, and learnable it becomes. It was also noted that the "flying" metaphor for virtual movement may not be the most apt, in that it does not fit either the user's experience or provide guidance in how to navigate in the artificial environment. Finally, it was noted that although the direct, first-person experience is of clear importance and value, there is still a need for abstract, third-person representations to prevent users from becoming lost or disoriented in virtual space.

These problems are raised not as insurmountable obstacles—clearly, there are many possible solutions—but to make the oft-neglected point that virtual realities do not eliminate the difficult problem of user interface design, but rather raise new design issues. This point is worth keeping in mind as we look at possible directions for the development of visualization environments.

Artificial Reality Tomorrow: Some Visualization Scenarios

In this section I present three scenarios involving visualization and artificial reality. The goal is to explore a number of directions in which artificial reality and visualization may evolve, while remaining aware of the problems that will need to be addressed.

The following scenarios are based on assumptions that appear reasonably likely in the next decade:

- vastly increased computational power, disk space, data transmission speed, and graphics resolution
- computer support for multiple users from the level of the operating system to the human interface
- the ability to move about unencumbered by heavy displays, cables, or limitations in transmission distance.

Probably the most radical assumption embodied in the following scenarios is that the variety of data depicted will be cheaply and quickly accessible, and will be easily integrated with data from different sources. This assumption is radical only in that it requires changes in infrastructure and the development of standards that may take some time to achieve.

The Brain, II

We begin by expanding on the example of the brain visualization just described. An obvious use for this artificial reality environment is in planning a surgical operation. Imagine a team of neurosurgeons donning headgear and gloves and entering into the brain artificial reality to consult on removal of a brain tumor. The surgeons could explore various options, rotating, scaling, and showing cross sections of the brain image as appropriate. Perhaps each surgeon has a pointer to highlight areas being discussed; perhaps the other surgeons can adopt the speaker's perspective and get precisely the same view (and sound, and feel) of the data; such an ability would greatly ease problems of reference.

This scenario suggests other desirable attributes of the brain artificial reality. It is likely that surgeons are going to want to take notes, perhaps by capturing and annotating particular views of the brain data set. If there is a neurosurgery database of other cases, it would be valuable to superimpose different brain images to find those with similar tumors. Once similar cases are identified, proposed procedures can be evaluated in the context of success or failure of previous operations. As has been suggested, if the brain images are of sufficiently high resolution, navigation through opaque or even translucent images may be quite difficult. It would be desirable to have a means of traversing particular paths or jumping to particular locations: Finding a small structure like the red nucleus might be quite time consuming in a high-resolution brain database.

While it is easy to think about the possibilities of such a scenario, it is wise to remain aware of the various problems that will arise in such an environment. The real world provides physical constraints that simplify interactions; but in an artificial reality, if two surgeons grab the brain and move it in different directions, what should happen? Should it tear, stretch, or should one surgeon be given automatic priority? While operating in the artificial reality will be reasonably simple, as long as the operations have real-world analogs (e.g., rotating and translating the brain), many of the operations that make the artificial reality such a powerful tool will lack analogs. Methods for allowing users to adopt identical viewpoints, isolating neuroanatomical structures for independent observation, and jumping to particular points in a large data space will have to be invented, and when the number of such nonanalogous operations becomes large, the user interface problem becomes nontrivial. Some of these functions can be represented as analogs of real-world artifacts: a map for navigating the brain, a pointer for highlighting portions of the data set, recording devices, and annotation tools for the students. But even here, a need will still exist for users to somehow obtain the artifacts when they are not present and to store them when they are no longer needed.

Satellites and Wheat Fields

An interesting experiment involving satellite-based remote sensing and the control of semiautomated, position-sensing fertilizer spreaders has been taking place in Montana [10, 11]. The experiment involves the analysis of satellite images of wheat fields for minute changes in color that indicate particular types of nutrient deficiencies in the wheat. On the ground, semiautomated fertilizer spreaders use global positioning satellite technology to determine their positions within the wheat fields, and use the information on the particular nutrient deficiencies for their current position to control the mix of nutrients in the fertilizer applied to that part of the field. It is hoped that this will result in increased quantities of wheat (better nutrition, thus higher yields), decreased cost of production (less fertilizer is used), and decreased environmental pollution (from runoff of excess fertilizer).

At first glance, this seems a long way from artificial reality: no head-mounted display, no gloves, no user. Nevertheless, there are several elements of an artificial reality. The artificial reality environment is constructed from the satellite image; the position of the fertilizer spreader rather than the user is tracked; and, rather than updating a display image based on the user's position, the fertilizer mix is adjusted relative to the spreader's position. True there is no visual artificial reality, nor user to perceive it, but it is not much of a step to imagine such a system.

An artificial reality based on remotely sensed, satellite-gathered imagery would have a variety of uses. Remote sensing can detect a variety of environmental conditions, ranging from drought and disease, to nutritional deficiency, to the paths of animal migrations. Processing and transformation of the image could make these conditions readily detectable, particularly given the unmatched facility of humans at pattern detection. Being able to enter an artificial reality and get an overview of a large land area could be of considerable use in managing farm and range land, controlling the spread of disease, or making decisions about resource allocation in times of drought or other environmental crises. While ranchers could probably not count their cows or look for fence breaks, since the current resolution of satellite images is limited to about 4 meters, they could still do quite a lot. Another limitation is that satellite flight paths provide complete coverage of the entire earth's surface only every 16 to 20 days. Thus, one would not necessarily be able to track a fire or a rapidly spreading disease. On the other hand, a much more frequently updated image could be generated from aerial photos of a particular area, albeit probably at a greater cost. Obviously, aerial photographs would also offer better resolution, so that ranchers who cared could, in fact, count their cows.

Again, as with the brain visualization environment, there are a number of design problems. If such an artificial reality consisted of imagery derived from a mix of aerial and satellite photographs, how are the differences in scale to be represented? The images will also have been taken at different times, something which may be crucial in certain analyses—how is that to be represented? An image transformed to make evidence of a crop blight visible may not show evidence of drought or a Caribou migration—how will users be allowed to switch between different views or image transformations, or even find out what different transformations are possible? Will artificial realities come with pop-up menus?

Site Simulation

"Location, location, location"; thus goes the old saw about what's important for a business. Today business people in search of a new site can superimpose demographic information on top of geographic information: Commercially available systems and data allow users to get answers to questions such as "Show me married couples with children who live on a major road within five miles of the site, and have an income over $40,000."

Translate such functionality into an artificial reality environment, combine it with satellite imagery or aerial photography, and the user cannot only make decisions in terms of the demographics, but can take the physical appearance of the site into account. Add basic information about the surrounding buildings and the location and orientation of the site, and the user can see whether a cafe's patio will get full sun in the winter. Combine data about traffic flow rates and the type of construction of the building with the ability to do acoustic modeling, and the user can evaluate the impact of the traffic noise at rush hour. Not only can the owner do all this, but financial backers, employees, and consultants can also evaluate and confer on the sites being considered. Assume a high-band-width optical network, and various parties need not travel to do any of this.

As before, new problems arise as new functionality is added. Simulations and modeling capacities require means of controlling them. It seems unlikely that most users will have either the knowledge or the inclination to simulate the effect of the sun during winter by shrinking the artificial reality way down, and adjusting the tilt of the earth.

Artificial Reality as an Environment: Design for Interaction

The scenarios described in the previous section were focused around visualization. People were depicted as entering artificial reality environments to view, interpret, interact with, and operate on data.

However, I believe that artificial reality environments will become more than sophisticated, interactive, 3-D movie theaters. The real promise of artificial reality is that it can provide a framework for human/human interaction, a stimulating and engaging environment that people will enter for a variety of reasons and purposes. Yet, with the exception of the seminal work of Myron Krueger and his colleagues [12], most designers of artificial reality systems have neglected the question of how to make an artificial reality a rich and engaging place.

Although there is no fixed set of rules for achieving this, we are not without useful knowledge. Significant bodies of work are available from urban designers, landscape architects, and architectural theorists on how environments affect the interactions that occur within their bounds. In what follows, I describe some ways in which environments can promote interaction and suggest some guidelines, and warning signs, that designers of artificial realities may do well to heed.

Christopher Alexander, noted architect and design theorist, writes of the corner of Hearst and Euclid, in Berkeley, in the context of discussing the design of cities [13]. It is quite an ordinary corner: sidewalks, a stoplight, a drugstore, and a news rack in the entrance to the drugstore. As pedestrians wait for the light to change, they browse the news rack, and perhaps buy a paper: traffic flows, coins move from pockets to the news rack's coin slot, and papers from rack to hands. In a real sense, the traffic light helps sell papers. Alexander argues that the corner functions as a coherent, interactive system, a unit of the city.

Note that what makes the news rack–stoplight system function effectively is a variety of constraints. Most obviously, physical constraints are operative: Pedestrians do not want to get run over crossing against the light, and most would prefer to avoid a dash across the street. But there are also social constraints. While flagrant violations of traffic lights by pedestrians are not uncommon, neither is it uncommon to watch a pedestrian wait patiently for a light when no cars are in sight. Such social constraints are the reason—although it is a much subtler effect—it is accurate to say that the news rack helps people obey the traffic light: If there is something of interest, people are less likely to transgress the relatively weak social constraints on obeying traffic lights. From this description, I propose the following conjecture: Constraints generate interactions. Will designers of artificial realities want to build in constraints? Perhaps. However, people who have struggled to realize the potentials of a technology are often unwilling to place artificial constraints on it, regardless of their utility.

Note that constraints may have nonlocal effects: for example, the effects of the news rack–traffic light system are not simply confined to the system itself. The news rack, situated in the entrance to a drugstore, overlaps with another system: the news rack–entrance–drugstore system. William Whyte, a researcher of interactions in urban spaces, notes that entrances that contain things of interest are more likely to draw people into a store, even though the things of interest may be totally unrelated to the content of the store. "Pauses lead to successive pauses. When a person has stopped to look at one attraction, he is more likely to be responsive to other stimuli in the same vicinity." Pedestrians who pause to look at the news may see something of interest within the store, or recall a need for some sundry item, and be drawn within, into yet another system. Whyte also points out that traffic lights, because they cause pedestrians to bunch up, create a rhythm in the flow of people, which may have an impact at some distance away. For example, "Window shoppers attract window shoppers. One person stops, another stops, then a couple. They attract others" [14].

It is likely that other phenomena occur at the corner of Hearst and Euclid. Perhaps one stranger asks another if she has change for a dollar; or a particularly outrageous headline may cause one pedestrian to exclaim in disgust, prompting a bystander to agree. Whyte calls this phenomenon *triangulation,* the tendency of an environment to encourage spontaneous interactions between strangers. Whyte has described examples of triangulation provoked by things ranging from inanimate objects (e.g., large sculptures in urban squares) to eccentric pedestrians. What sort of factors might encourage triangulation in an artificial reality?

Finally, it is worthwhile to note that even minor features of the physical environment can structure behavior in subtle ways. In a study of ATM use [15], the observation was made that people waiting to use an automated teller station typically left an area of open space between the head of the line and the person using the machine. This in itself is not surprising: Entering a secret code to withdraw cash is an activity widely regarded as private. What is surprising is that the lines of users usually formed behind a crack in the pavement, which happened to be at a reasonable distance from the ATM. An obviously accidental environmental feature served to structure the behavior of ATM users. This type of phenomenon is apparently well known to building contractors. Don Norman, a cognitive scientist who has done extensive work on human interface design, reports that he recently had a section of his driveway repoured, and that the contractor suggested putting in a colored border between the old and new sections. The contractor explained that it would act as a natural boundary that people who used the driveway to turn around in would not venture beyond. Norman lives on a dead-end, popular beach street, and gets about ten turn-arounds a day; he reports that it works. On telling this story to his neighbor across the street, his neighbor reported being told the same thing by *his* contractor, and pointed to the cement entryway to his brick driveway [16].

It is instructive to speculate about what might happen if someone were to try to incorporate the corner of Hearst and Euclid into an artificial reality. It would be easy for designers to go wrong. There would be strong pressure for relaxing constraints in the artificial reality version of Hearst and Euclid. Clearly, no one really likes to wait for traffic lights. Why not just allow users (and our virtual autos on both streets) to traverse the intersection magically without regard for one another? On first glance this would seem to improve things. No need for pedestrians to wait. No need for a stoplight. No need for cars to stop. No (virtual) traffic accidents. Very efficient. But it is an efficiency that is likely to lead to sterility. With an uninterrupted flow of pedestrians, it is less likely that people would stop to browse and buy, or fall into a chance conversation. And if an automatic teller shows up (and you see them everywhere these days), will there be cracks in the pavement for people to line up behind?

I would like to close with a description that captures some of the richness and changeability that characterizes a good environment. Kevin Lynch, an environmental and urban design theorist, is writing of cities, but he might just as easily be writing of a large data set or a well-designed artificial reality:

> At every instant, there is more than the eye can see, more than the ear can hear, a setting or a view waiting to be explored. Nothing is experienced by itself, but always in relation to its surroundings, the sequences of events leading up to it, the memory of past experiences. . . . While it may be stable in general outlines for some time, it is ever changing in detail. Only partial control can be exercised over its growth and form. There is no final result, only a continuous succession of phases. [17]

Acknowledgments

The brain visualization assessment was carried out in collaboration with Phil Mercurio. Thanks to Dave Tyler for information on applications of remote sensing to agriculture, Ed Hutchins for the paper on the ATM study, and to Frank Leahy and Alan Wexelblat for comments on an earlier draft of this paper.

REFERENCES

[1] Perlman, G., and T. D. Erickson, "Graphical Abstractions of Technical Documents," *Visible Language, 23* (4), Autumn 1983.

[2] Tufte, E., *Envisioning Information,* Cheshire, CT: Graphics Press, 1990.

[3] Friedhoff, R. M., and W. Benzon, *Visualization: The Second Computer Revolution.* New York: Harry N. Abrams, 1989.

[4] McCormick, B. H., T. A. DeFanti, and M. D. Brown, "Visualization in Scientific Computing," *Computer Graphics, 21* (6), 1987.

[5] Gaver, W. W., R. B. Smith, and T. O'Shea, "Effective Sounds in Complex Situations: The ARKola Simulation," *CHI '91 Proceedings: Human Factors in Computing Systems,* New Orleans, April 1991, p. 85, New York: ACM Press, 1991 (available from Addison-Wesley).

[6] Brooks, F. P., "Grasping Reality Through Illusion—Interactive Graphics Serving Science," in *CHI '88 Proceedings: Human Factors in Computing Systems,* Washington, D. C., May 1988, p. 1, New York: ACM Press, 1988 (available from Addison-Wesley).

[7] Mercurio, P. J., and T. Erickson, "Interactive Scientific Visualization: An Assessment of a Virtual Reality Environment," in *Human-Computer Interaction: Interact '90,* D. Diaper, D. Gilmore, G. Cockton, B. Shackel, Eds., p. 741, New York: Elsevier Science Publishing Company, 1990.

[8] Livingston, R. B., and K. R. Wilson, "The Human Brain: A Dynamic View of its Structures and Organization," film, 28 minutes. Presented by Roche Laboratories; made by Wexler Films; distributed by Wexler Film Productions. (1976)

[9] Erickson, T., "Working with Interface Metaphors," in *The Art of Human Computer Interface Design,* Brenda Laurel, Ed., p. 65, Reading, MA: Addison-Wesley, 1990.

[10] Larsen, W. E., D. A. Tyler, and G. A. Nielsen, "Using the GPS Satellites for Precision Navigation," in *Automated Agriculture for the 21st Century: Proceedings of the 1991 Symposium, 16–17,* p. 201, St. Joseph, MI: American Society of Agricultural Engineers, 1991.

[11] Petersen, C., "Precision GPS Navigation for Improving Agricultural Productivity," *GPS World,* p. 38, January 1991.

[12] Krueger, M. W., *Artificial Reality II,* Reading, MA: Addison-Wesley, 1991.

[13] Alexander, C., "A City Is Not a Tree," in *Design After Modernism,* John Thackara, Ed., New York: Thames and Hudson, 1988.

[14] Whyte, W. H., *City: Return to the Center.* New York: Doubleday, 1988.

[15] Marine, L., "Study of the Opportunistic Use of Environmental Structure to Organize Behavior," unpublished manuscript, 1990.

[16] Norman, D. A., personal communication, 1991.

[17] Lynch, K., *The Image of the City,* Cambridge, MA: The MIT Press, 1990.

Chapter 2

The Reality of Cooperation: Virtual Reality and CSCW

Alan Wexelblat

MIT Media Lab
Cambridge, Massachusetts
wex@media.mit.edu

It's awkward to write your own introduction. I've been working in and around VR and AR for seven years now but really have a different agenda than those who want to build virtual worlds. My deep belief is that for too long computer scientists and systems builders have acted as though there only was one user. I see worlds of users working together, and I see a critical need for computer science to pay much more attention to this. VR, as discussed in my chapter, can serve as an enabling technology. I hope to open some doors through my VR work and bring in many more people through those doors.

Introduction

Virtual reality (VR) can be used to support almost any human activity. Or, stated another way, virtual reality can be applied to almost any domain. Some applications of VR technology—such as three-dimensional walkthroughs and entertainment—are beginning to see widespread use. Others, such as the idea of organizational modeling discussed in this book, will take longer to develop. In this chapter I argue that as virtual reality applications begin to spread, the technology could potentially touch almost every purposeful activity we undertake in a technological civilization.

I begin by laying out some assertions about computers and about human activity. I then go on to explore how computers and virtual reality can affect that activity. This path runs through the area of computing science called *CSCW*, or computer-supported cooperative work. Ultimately, I will spend very little time talking about the gadgets normally associated with virtual or artificial reality (AR). Instead, I argue that important principles found in AR and VR can be applied to computer-supported cooperative work. This argument will, I hope, show you that the potential applications of virtual reality are as broad as our imaginations and our social needs can make them.

Requisite Assumptions

Two assertions I take as given. I will not defend these principles in depth, because that would take me far outside the scope of this chapter.

My first assertion is that the purpose of computers is to support human activity. While it is true that computers are used in esoteric areas, such as computing the digits of pi, as well as practical mundane areas such as controlling the flight of aircraft, ultimately all this activity is for the benefit or pleasure of humanity. In some cases, such as in the American banking system, the computer has become indispensable. We simply could not handle our money as we do today without them. In other cases, such as pocket personal assistant schedulers such as the Sharp Wizard and the new Apple palmtop, the computer is a more sophisticated replacement for paper and pencil. In any event, the *point* of using the computers is to support what people do or what they want to do. Computers extend the range of human activity, and they support and augment existing activities.

My second assertion is that human activity is inherently cooperative. This assertion runs counter to popular myth, especially in America. We Americans are born and raised on the legends of lone heroes. From the explorers who "discovered" the New World, to the lone cowboys riding into the sunset, to intellectual heroes such as Edison or Einstein, we learn about the actions of the individual. The fact is that each of these people worked in and with organizations without whose resources and help the hero would never have been able to survive let alone achieve his or her goals. But this fact is glossed over, if it is mentioned at all, in our culture of the individual. Even our supposed team activities have their individual stars, from sports to the stage.

Of course, we know from everyday experience that this is really a myth. The reality is that almost nothing gets done solely by one person.

We are social animals and we cooperate in everything we do, from work to play to family. Most importantly, when we want to get something done, we seek out the people who can help us. This is the first "reality of cooperation."

This intuition is supported by any number of studies of real-world working conditions. For example, Heath and Luff's study of the London Underground showed that cooperation occurred through simple informal mechanisms such as controllers raising their voices so that coworkers could overhear important parts of conversations [1].

If you believe these two assertions—that computers should support the activities of people and that people's activities are inherently cooperative—then it is natural to investigate the area of CSCW. Before turning to an in-depth examination of that area, I should note that because I believe in these assertions, I also believe in the use of VR technologies by more than one person, often at the same time.

This belief is contrary to most sample VR systems I have seen. The prototype and demonstration worlds of the past few years have almost all been single-user systems. Although VPL has been offering RB2 (Reality Built for Two) systems for years, famous systems like UNC's Molecular Docker and the Seattle, Washington, Human Interface Technology Laboratory's (HITLab) Virtual Seattle are single-person systems. Because many of the early applications of virtual reality—such as architectural building walkthroughs—are simple retrofits of virtual reality technology into the interfaces of preexisting single-user applications, the virtual worlds so constructed are also single-user oriented. I think that this trend is an aberration that will disappear as the ideas CSCW begin to filter into the heads of VR workers.

Computer-Supported Cooperative Work

CSCW is a relatively new discipline within computing science. The first official conference on CSCW was held in 1986, in Austin, Texas. When we organized that conference, we had real doubt that anyone would be interested enough in the ideas to attend a conference. Although a discussion group on the topic organized by Irene Grief at MIT had been attracting 20 or so participants, we hoped to get 100 people to attend. As it turned out, we got more than twice that number and started a series of conferences, which is still continuing (the most recent meeting was in Toronto in 1992). The Europeans, often ahead of North America in this area, organized their own counterpart conference, which meets in the odd-numbered years.

CSCW draws its participants from a number of computing science disciplines. Its strongest overlap is with the area of human/computer interaction (HCI). This discipline contributes people interested in building, using, and studying systems interacting with groups of people. In addition, CSCW attracts people interested in office automation, since the office is one of the most heavily cooperative workplaces in today's society. Psychologists, sociologists, organizational theorists, and anthropologists are familiar with the study of group dynamics already and participate in CSCW conferences, research, and system-building.

Last, there is a subgroup of implementors in which I count myself. We system builders are particularly intrigued by the challenges of constructing systems for groups of people. The products of our efforts are often dubbed "groupware"—an occasionally hot marketing term. The challenge of implementing CSCW systems is that it is largely untrod ground. The number of such systems on the market is minuscule. We define the field by our acts of creation. Similarly, the areas of application are as broad as we can imagine them to be. In these respects, building CSCW systems is like building virtual realities.

Principles of CSCW

I feel two principles of CSCW are important to understand. The first is that cooperation is not a separable activity, like "compiling a program" or "writing a letter" that has definite start and end times. I confess that this principle seems to have eluded many of my fellow developers of groupware. They continue to build special-purpose CSCW systems that do not connect to users' normal work activities and wonder why their systems are not used. In my article "Groups Without Groupware" [2], I challenge this trend, which is slowly changing in the CSCW field.

A study of the experiences of the CSCW field, such as that undertaken by Jonathan Grudin [3, 4], shows that the most common failures occur because the computer system does not match the work patterns of the intended users. For example, in a famous panel discussion [5], Terry Winograd reluctantly admitted that he did not make much use of the Coordinator system in his office, even though he is one of the strongest proponents of the benefits of the system.

The Coordinator is a structured conversation tool, based on the conversation-for-action paradigm discussed in Winograd's book [6]. The Coordinator helps people have purposeful conversations by adding structure to e-mail messages and categorizing the replies made to messages. For example, one user may make a Request, to which the only possible replies are Acceptance, Rejection, or an offer to Negotiate.

The conversation is structured according to specific rules with the goal of reducing wasted effort and leaving a clear record of what people have agreed to do—what actions they have agreed to perform.

Winograd's given reason for not using the Coordinator in his normal daily work was because it did not connect to his normal electronic mail flow on the usual Stanford computers. Most people he communicated with were not using the Coordinator and so the system, for all its benefits, did not fit into his normal work pattern.

This sort of group behavior versus system behavior has worked against group calendar systems, which sit unused (aptly named "shelfware") despite promises of improved efficiency. What happens is that people do not enter their events into the group calendar, and so the quality of information in the system is low, which discourages people from using the system, which in turn leads to people not putting information into the system, and so on. This failure is so ubiquitous that Grudin chose it as the first illustrative example in his "Why CSCW Applications Fail" paper [3].

The second principle of CSCW is that successful groupware systems should allow people to cooperate by overcoming barriers of space and time that are imposed on people. For people to cooperate in a non-computer-supported environment, they must usually either be present in the same location or be working at the same time. But this is not always convenient or even possible. Computers, by carrying information over distances or storing information over time, allow people to transcend these boundaries to some degree.

This time-space distinction is often used to categorize groupware systems, which we discuss next.

Types of Groupware—The Time-Space Distinctions

Groupware, the common name for computer-supported cooperative work systems, is often categorized according to the type of interaction it

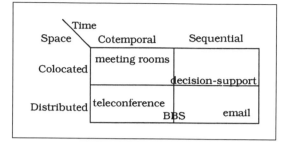

FIG. 2.1. TYPES OF GROUPWARE.

supports. The distinct axes reflect degrees of separation in time and space, as shown in Figure 2.1. The space axis reflects the degree of spatial distribution versus colocation and the time axis reflects the degree of sequentiality versus synchronousness (often called "real time") in a system. The example groupware systems shown in Figure 2.1 are as follows:

- *Meeting rooms* are specialized spaces in one physical location, which are customized with special computer systems to support the collaborative activities that happen during meetings. Because of the nature of the activity they support, they tend toward the upper-left corner of the diagram, being both highly cotemporal and highly colocated.

  These meeting rooms support several kinds of meetings, from brainstorming meetings where the goal is to generate, organize, and evaluate ideas, to group decision-support rooms, which provide support for group voting, action-item recording, and production of meeting minutes. Because meetings are still a subject of much research, some meeting rooms provide tools for observers to record and analyze the meeting process.

- *Decision-support systems* are often not sold specifically as "groupware," but end up being used by several people, usually at the same time. Because they are often run on one computer, the input to them tends to be sequential, even when there are several people working on generating the decision factors; thus, these systems tend toward the upper-right corner of the diagram.

  Many more kinds of decision-support systems exist than can be enumerated here. In general, they help the user input and arrange factors that may positively or negatively affect a decision. The system then displays a sum, weighted average, or other combination of the factors. This is intended to show the user(s) what the decision should be, assuming that the input factors and weights are correct.

- *Teleconference systems* are usually enhancements on video-conferencing systems. They are used to conduct meetings or joint activities, much as might be done in a meeting room. The goal of the "tele" part, though, is to allow participants to be physically far apart from one another.

  In addition to the computer-enhanced conferencing systems such as BBN's Slate [7], which shows a document or set of slides to a group of participants at the same time, a large number of specialized "tele" systems are available. These special systems allow multiple people in remote locations to cooperate on a specific task. For example, a large number of "chat" or "talk" programs allow typed conversations in real time. There are also several "shared drawing" programs, which present multiple users with one virtual surface onto which they can draw or write.

  Also in this category are a large number of simulations (many of which have characteristics of VR) with physically distributed participants. These range from serious—such as the Army's SIMNET [8], which provides realistic simulations of tanks, helicopters, and other war-fighting equipment—to fun—such as the networked games popular both on PCs and workstations.

- *BBS* (Bulletin-Board Systems) are computerized equivalents of paper and pushpin boards. People compose and leave (post) notes; other users read these notes and follow up with notes of their own. Many BBSs also support the storage and retrieval of files, both text and software, and serve as information exchanges. Modern BBSs support more than one user logged in at the same time. Frequently, though, users are unaware of each other's presence even if they are both writing replies to the same note. Thus they sit in the middle of the cotemporal-sequential axis. Their users are definitely distributed, though. Often only the operator or owner of the computer on which the BBS runs ever sees that machine.

  Also in this category are a number of commercial information providers such as CompuServe and GEnie. These services go beyond the traditional BBS and supply real-time "chat" programs, large archives of information, access to games, news services, and so forth.

- *E-mail* (for electronic mail) is probably the oldest and most widespread CSCW system. Most BBS and information services provide electronic mail in some form. In addition, there are dozens of e-mail programs running on PCs and Macs. Most often, these are used within one company or organization. Thanks originally to the efforts of DARPA's (the DoD's Defense Advanced Research Projects Agency) ARPAnet and later to the effort of hundreds of companies and universities and thousands of individuals, e-mail has become worldwide. These e-mail and similar links form what is informally known as the Net, the closest thing we have today to Gibson's vision of cyberspace [9]. It is estimated that today the Net reaches more than 4 million people on six continents [10].

E-mail has been extensively studied (for example, [11]), and its use is as varied as its users. But generally it involves the sequential exchange of messages, usually composed primarily of text, over large distances. Users receive e-mail and compose replies, which are usually returned by e-mail.

E-mail has become so ubiquitous that some researchers are beginning to describe applications which use e-mail for communication as "e-mail enabled."

This section gives you a feel for how groupware applications can be categorized, based on their use. Another way to categorize applications is based on important factors of their design. We will look at one such factor in the next section.

Types of Groupware—The Collaboration Awareness Question

One of the major factors affecting groupware today is the degree to which it is "collaboration aware." That is, the degree to which knowledge of, and support for, the cooperative activity has been designed specifically into the tool. Collaboration awareness often cannot be precisely judged. Generally, it ranges from systems that are completely collaboration-ignorant to ones in which all activity is performed in a collaboration-aware manner.

This can best be illustrated by a number of examples, as shown in Figure 2.2. Beginning at the collaboration-ignorant end, we have programs such as compilers. These are solely single-user applications; two people can be compiling exactly the same program at exactly the same time on the same machine, but all the work will be duplicated and neither will be aware that the other is doing the same work.

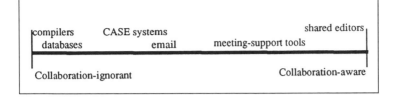

FIG. 2.2.   APPLICATIONS ON AN AWARENESS SCALE.

Databases, surprisingly, are also almost totally collaboration-ignorant. They usually provide some form of record locking, which prevents users from overwriting each other's work, but they do not help users get a task done together. Records locked by one user are often totally unavailable to other users. In addition, users have no way to know what other people are doing in their interactions with the database. Two people could be making exactly the same query against the database at the same time and would have no way of knowing that they were duplicating their efforts.

CASE (Computer-Aided Software Engineering) systems are generally built with the explicit or implicit understanding that software engineering is done by a team of people. Many such systems are simply built on top of a database or revision control system, which provides for locking of objects so that two developers do not accidentally overwrite each other's work. Other CASE systems support management of software projects by allowing users to track the work being done in the system at any given time and by allowing developers to pass objects around among themselves. This is similar to the functionality provided by workflow systems.

E-mail systems, as discussed above, are somewhat collaboration-aware. Usually users compose messages individually and then send them to other users. Thus the collaboration awareness is built into the parts of the system that understand how to deliver mail from one user to another and handle user conveniences such as automatic replies and aliases.

Meeting-support tools come in two major varieties, each with a high degree of collaboration awareness. The first variety supports "distributed" meetings where all the participants are not necessarily in the same physical location. These kinds of tools range from simple video- and teleconference tools to sophisticated computer-based voice-, video-, and text-transfer systems.

The other kind of system is often called a computer-supported meeting room. As the name implies, it involves a specially crafted room in which the meeting participants gather. In the room are a number of computers, usually at least one per person. Often some form of shared display such as a computer-controlled whiteboard is also present. In these meeting rooms, users take advantage of software to help manage the meeting agenda, take votes, record action items, and similar meeting activities. In addition, some meeting-support systems offer tools to help facilitate the meeting, such as mood indicators, and possibly to capture the meeting (on video and disk) for later playback and analysis.

Note that the meeting-support tools found in the augmented meeting rooms are not necessarily restricted to such rooms. They can also be incorporated into distributed meeting-support tools that participants use in their homes or offices.

Shared editors are often found as components of meeting-support systems, and rarely as part of CASE systems. Shared editors generally allow more than one person at a time to view and possibly manipulate a document or drawing. In some shared editors, the users can cooperatively create or revise the body of the document; in other cases, users are restricted to adding annotations or other marks, such as proofreader's marks, which are not directly part of the original document but instead form a kind of second layer of information in the system.

Problems to be Solved

Builders of CSCW systems must solve a number of difficult problems, making choices that can enhance the ability of the system to support cooperative work, but usually at the expense of a more complex system. Among the issues that must be addressed are the following:

- How much data will be shared?
- Who will have control over input and output and for how long?
- How will users communicate with each other?
- How will users know what other users are doing?
- What parts of the system will users see at any one time?
- How will a user know what other users are seeing and how does what others see compare to what he sees?

A great deal of effort goes into solving these problems because they affect the usability of the system as much or more than the specific functionality provided. In essence, a CSCW system must work to help its users gain a shared understanding of the material that is the subject of the collaboration. Users must be able to answer questions such as "Do you see what I see?" before they can communicate the information necessary for them to complete their task cooperatively.

At this point, it is wise to step back and examine whether or not building the answers to these types of questions is the right thing for collaborative-systems people to be doing. I assert that it is not, for two major reasons:

1. It seems "unnatural" to solve these problems only for CSCW systems when in fact they are problems that should be solved for most kinds of systems. If we believe the assertions I stated at the beginning of the chapter—that work is cooperative and computers should support work—then it is odd to have special-purpose "groupware" or "collaborative systems" at all. If cooperation is not a separable activity, then why should cooperative tools be separate?

2. It seems to lead to a great deal of duplicated effort. Each CSCW system reinvents key components and re-solves difficult problems. A particularly egregious example of this is the proliferation of graphical browsers and editors (used for displaying, navigating, and editing various sorts of box-and-line representations). Everyone writes his or her own browsers and object editors, no two of which work exactly alike. Some even implement whole new hypertext-ish systems; for example, gIBIS [12] and SIBYL [13] run on the same hardware and even use the same basic conversational paradigm, yet have separate and different ways of linking their nodes and allowing users to navigate.

Components such as editors, browsers, database interfaces, and so on are largely orthogonal to the problem the groupware implementor is trying to solve, but they are created anew each time. This is partly because work done for one application is not available to other implementors, and partly because the existing, underlying system does not support a rich enough collaboration environment. If sophisticated editors, browsers, and so on were available as part of the environment, groupware developers would be encouraged to share and reuse them, eliminating duplication.

Where to Go Next

In the preceding sections I have provided a brief introduction to the field of CSCW and outlined why cooperation is so important and useful in the computer world. However, these systems have a long way to go before they become as commonplace and natural as I would like them to be. Improvements need to be made.

There are two areas related to virtual reality where improvements can be made that would be beneficial to builders and users of collaborative systems. Both would make system building easier and system use more natural. They are direct enhancements to the underlying systems and new interaction media. Not coincidentally, virtual reality offers approaches and technologies that can affect both these areas. In this section I examine each of these areas briefly and suggest some ways that virtual reality can be used as an enabling technology.

Underlying Systems

Underlying systems are being enhanced all the time. Parallel machines and new operating systems such as Mach and operating-system components such as the Andrew File System offer some promise in terms of enhanced performance. Increased hardware speed and improved system functionality will allow the computer to perform more complex tasks faster for more users. Even today's "low-end" virtual reality systems often benefit from specialized hardware. For example, the W Industries Virtuality system—which runs primarily on standard Amiga 3000 hardware—uses two custom graphics boards to render images for each eye. Similarly, the Sense8 toolkit, which runs on any PC hardware, takes advantage of a special Intel graphics board, which provides quick texture-mapping of polygons. This is not to say that specialized hardware is a bad thing, nor that these people are using "tricks" in marketing their systems. Rather, they serve as commercially viable examples of cases where the underlying standard hardware platform has been enhanced specifically to support the demands of virtual reality.

Underlying operating systems are harder to speed up. One cannot simply "add a board" to existing operating systems to enhance their performance. Improved operating systems (or operating environments) are usually designed from the ground up. Two major efforts, PCTE (Portable Common Tool Environment) [14] and OSF's DCE (Distributed

Computing Environment), promise to raise the ante by providing a much more sophisticated, yet general-purpose, platform on which development can be based. Other efforts, such as the Object Management Group's effort to standardize object server technology, may allow us to break some of the bonds holding users to particular machines by creating machine-independent storage and retrieval technologies. In such an environment, developers and users could simply "hand over" their objects—data files, documents, programs—and depend on them to be reliably stored and retrieved later as desired. This sort of reliability is essential if we are to build VR systems that can share virtual objects between themselves.

Some efforts, such as the HITLab's VEOS (Virtual Environment Operating System) and the Atherton Backplane, offer new ways to connect our tools to underlying system supports such as data storage and retrieval. The VEOS architecture seeks to address specifically the problems of sharing of object information by incorporating higher level concepts such as a "world" object that can receive messages about any object in the virtual world and can coordinate interactions between objects. With a system architecture model that takes interobject coordination as a primary concern, it is easy to build systems and virtual worlds to support multiple users. Similarly, W Industries wrote a special-purpose operating system called Animette that is optimized to handle real-time input and output to peripheral devices—a property essential to most VR products but lacking in most general-purpose operating systems.

However, each of these approaches suffers from various drawbacks, not the least of which is a mutual incompatibility, which discourages developers from committing to one or the other system unless required to do so. The question is "How can we improve on this situation?"

An exhaustive catalog of features and suggested improvements for each system would not add much to the discussion. Instead, I use a general approach to evaluate the potential of an underlying technology for CSCW development. We can classify underlying systems along three dimensions of utility to cooperative-system implementors: *communication, coordination,* and *notification.* Systems that provide greater capability along these dimensions will be more conducive to building groupware and will provide better support for groups in general.

Note that this should not be confused with the blanket assertion that "more is better." Clearly—to take just one example—more raw communication would just lead to more user overload and confusion if

"more" were taken to mean "a larger amount of data." Rather, systems
that provide more possibilities for communication, coordination, and
notification will allow developers to build better CSCW systems. We
still must bear the burden of wisely selecting from, and making use of,
these capabilities.

Dimensions of Underlying Systems.

Communication is the ability to send information among agents (where
agents are objects, programs, or users). Almost all systems provide
some form of communication, including primitives such as message-
passing or shared memory, and output to and input from storage media such as disks and file systems. Higher level communication is
often achieved through specified interfaces—graphical user interfaces
(GUIs) to talk to users, application program interfaces (APIs) to talk
to other programs—and multiple media such as combined audio
and video.

In general, this emphasis on higher-level communication and multiple media is headed in the right direction for building better virtual
worlds. ECSCW '92 featured a workshop in which participants discussed various means of opening up CSCW systems. Most of the presentations in the workshop spoke of implementations that involved
adding more sophisticated APIs or additional communication channels to existing systems. For example, Kaplan [15] promoted the use of
his message-bus architecture, a simple system built on top of UNIX
sockets to which arbitrary programs can be connected to send information to other programs. Unfortunately, because the message bus resides
outside the base system on which it runs (most UNIX computers) it requires additional work on the part of the programmers to connect their
groupware to something like the message bus. This kind of capability
should be built into systems at the same level as, for example, file I/O is
today. No special coding would be needed beyond making calls to a
standard, well-defined library.

In addition to making simple generic program-to-program capabilities available, we can enhance communication by moving to a "higher"
level, allowing us to communicate objects rather than simple data.
CSCW programs should be able to exchange objects such as windows,
database records, and views of information. A preliminary experiment
in this direction was the view manager component of the DELI grapher
[16]. Unfortunately, this experiment has not been followed up in the

open literature. The only similar (though independently derived) work I can find is Ralph Hill's work on ALV [17].

With advanced communication facilities sending normally private objects among agents, the underlying system would need to keep track of copies and versions as well as controlling simultaneous access. This leads us to consider the second property, *coordination,* the ability to arrange rendezvous or other interactions between agents as well as the ability to schedule activities and allocate resources so that agents' actions do not conflict.

Current systems provide only the lowest level coordination facilities such as file locking and serialization of input events. A database system may implement slightly more sophisticated coordination control. However, most databases actually hamper collaboration by establishing only mutually exclusive coordination. We can improve on this by implementing ideas such as soft locks (which can be broken under predetermined conditions). An important step in this direction was recently taken by Rodden and Blair [18] who have begun considering how the ideas and mechanisms of traditional distributed systems can be applied to groupware.

In general, improved coordination can be achieved by externalizing agents' states. That is, the more an agent can find out about other agents present in the system and what they are doing, the more coordinated activity can be arranged, either by the users or their computer agents, assuming that artificial intelligence problems of plan abduction can be solved. Thus, it is important that groupware developers include in their systems some representations of users.

Some current CSCW systems do include such representations. Most use a simple object called a *telepointer* [19]. Telepointers track the position of other users' mouse cursors, moving whenever other users move their mice. This allows users to show each other where on the screen their attention is focused. In some cases, the representation is anthropomorphic, such as a graphic representation of a human hand. Randy Smith used hands in the Artificial Reality Kit (ARK) [20]—an AR system aimed at teaching basic physics—so users could watch each other grab and throw objects, flip switches, pull levers, and so on.

Video-equipped systems can transmit actual pictures of the users. The EuroPARC multimedia environment [21] includes a facility where users' video pictures are directly manipulable—moving your picture next to that of another user opens a video link between the two offices [22]. The importance of such avatars goes beyond enabling casual interaction. By making users present-to-hand within the system, group-ware developers allow their users to engage in more sophisticated coordination than is possible purely through machine interactions. Simply put: It is easier to avoid conflicts than to resolve them after they occur, and users can coordinate to avoid conflicts with these new systems.

Having an avatar or an actual presence makes such coordination possible by allowing users to find and observe each other, but to know that coordination is needed requires a facility-like notification.

Just as coordination deals with synchronous activity, *notification* deals with asynchronous activity. This facility is very weak in most current systems, usually limited to text-only warning messages or event signals generated from within an application. A general notification facility improves on this slightly by making notification windows a part of the computational environment. An example of such a facility is Zephyr [23], the message notification service developed at MIT's Athena project. Zephyr allows users, and programs built with the Zephyr library, to pop up message windows on other users' workstations. Several different kinds of notification messages can be sent and Zephyr handles issues of security and authentication to make sure that the correct messages appear on the correct screens. Unfortunately, Zephyr notifications are still limited to simple textual messages.

A more sophisticated set of notifications can be created by using audio. Audio has the advantage of using a different cognitive channel than the usual visual/physical interactions. Plus, audio notifications can be customized to give quick information on the event for which the notification is meant. For example, the Khronika system of audio notifications [24] contains special sounds for "meeting is taking place" and "tea time." These sounds are recorded from the users' environments and thus are heard as natural sounds and do not intrude.

Other sounds (such as a thunderclap) can be made deliberately intrusive because they serve to warn users (in this case to go outside and make sure their car windows are rolled up). There is some evidence that sound in general can be used to enhance collaboration [25, 26] and the U.S. Air Force has also investigated for more than 25 years the use of sound notifications in airplane cockpit situations [27].

Unfortunately, all these notifications are one way. They appear to the user and the user is expected to react with some form of independent action. The notification is usually separate from the context in which the user is expected to react. To improve this, notifications should be made active, able not only to carry information but able to take action on behalf of the user. The support of a number of these running concurrently requires the sort of sophisticated process control promised by the advanced computation environments mentioned earlier.

Astute readers have no doubt been judging as they read how virtual reality systems can address these underlying needs. Communication in virtual worlds is still quite primitive. Users can communicate through objects they manipulate and by some gestures, although it is hard to separate communicative gestures from the command and control gestures used in most VR systems.

Direct communication between users is even harder. At best, users are given a microphone with which to speak to other participants who are in the world at the same time. However, this communication path is given at the expense of all the communication media we have available in traditional computer systems. In today's VR worlds we cannot even leave each other written notes. This significantly limits the utility of most virtual worlds.

Given that users are present simultaneously, the potential for coordination in a virtual world is much greater than with conventional simultaneous interaction. In virtual worlds, users can directly observe each other's behavior and interactions. Objects to be shared can be passed directly between users or can be left by one user for another. As noted earlier, the ability to externalize users' states in the system is much greater in a virtual world where users have explicit representations. Coordination in the real world is often done by simply observing others and reacting to what they do. In most CSCW systems this is not possible, but in virtual worlds it is the most natural means of interaction.

Notification can be similarly direct in the virtual world. Users can point out objects and give gestural or verbal messages. However, the inherently asynchronous nature of notifications means that the restriction to instantaneous, real-time notifications imposed by current technology is too stringent. We need ways to leave notifications for future users, either by communication means (such as modifying objects in the virtual world) or through the introduction of active agents, which can carry our messages for us.

New Media

Another direction that can be profitably pursued is the emerging interaction media. First, voice and video are becoming more and more available as everyday media for computer users. Some machines, such as the NeXT, come equipped with special-purpose digital signal processors (DSPs) suited for manipulating high-speed or real-time voice and video. Numerous add-in DSP boards are available for PCs, Macintoshes, and UNIX workstations.

Although real-time service in either medium frequently requires additional computational power and bandwidth, simple storage and retrieval of data in these media is now becoming almost routine. For Apple recently introduced its QuickTime facilities, which allow Mac programmers to include short video clips in their programs. Limited video-editing capabilities are also provided.

The availability of these media means that it is more practical to build artificial realities similar to ARK. While these systems are not immersive experiences in the sense that they do not replace the user's sight and sound of the real world with that of the virtual, they have many of the same properties as virtual realities. Thus they can avoid many of the weaknesses of fully immersive virtual worlds by drawing on conventional system abilities such as text entry, pull-down menus, and so on.

The one major previous foray of collaborative-systems developers into this arena—video conferencing—has been a relative failure as a replacement for face-to-face conferencing [28]. However, attempts to provide video as an additional channel continue to enjoy early success. CSCW '90 contained three papers demonstrating successes with prototype video systems [29–31].

Audio, although long neglected, has also begun to emerge as an important tool for interfaces in general and for collaborative interfaces in particular. As mentioned earlier, sound shows promise not only in the special realm of notification, but as a general-purpose means for enhancing cooperation of all kinds. An exciting example of this is contained in [26], wherein Bill Gaver and coauthors show how users attempting to complete a cooperative task (run a cola-bottling plant simulation) were better able to complete the task with ambient audio feedback. Audio channels for transmission of users' voices have also begun to be accepted.

Generally speaking, new media such as audio and video have been used to broaden the bandwidth of information flowing between users of cooperative systems. As noted before, this broadening of the communication band is necessary for systems to support the rich interactions required by groupware systems. Virtual reality systems bring a rich graphical environment, but too often neglect these other media.

Do You See What I See?

The last area of overlap between CSCW and virtual reality is the ability of VR to be useful in solving one of the most important, long-standing problems in CSCW: figuring out who sees what. As far back as 1986, issues surrounding what-you-see-is-what-I-see (WYSIWIS) were identified as important to groupware development and successful use [32]. Since then, a great deal of work has gone in to making systems that provide more or less tightly coupled WYSIWIS views of information to users.

Almost every groupware system involves some means of putting up the same information on multiple displays and keeping these displays as synchronized as possible within the constraints of the hardware, the task, and the users' preferences. Failure to do this leads to user confusion and frustration with the system. A particularly difficult problem in using cooperative systems occurs when users realize that they are not seeing the same thing. It is often not obvious or completely impossible in today's groupware to know how to change things so that users do all see the same thing.

Virtual reality allows groupware developers to avoid these issues by having users inhabit a common world. This mode of interaction models our natural experience in the day-to-day world. In real life, we rarely have to worry about whether other people can see the same things we see. If they can't, it's easy to move ourselves or the object so that we all see the same thing. For example, if you are on the other side of an object in the virtual world, it is immediately obvious to me both that you do not see what I see and how to change the situation so we can both see the same thing.

A related problem is the focus of users' attention. In normal conversation we often use shorthand phrases like "that paragraph" or "this task." In a face-to-face situation, we can use ostention (gesturing, pointing, etc.) to clarify which object we mean. In a cooperative system, though, there are often only indirect means of showing the other person what thing we mean, such as by description (e.g. "the third paragraph on page four"). Virtual reality offers the ability to go back to directly indicating objects when needed, thus making our interactions as smooth and efficient as they are in the real world.

This is not always an easy task, but virtual reality offers developers the possibility of removing artificial barriers introduced by our workstation- and personal-computer-based technology.

Conclusion

As noted in the introduction, there are two realities of cooperation. The first is that cooperative work is the mode most people use when getting things done. Individual effort almost always takes place in the context of a group of people with similar or related goals. This reality led us to an examination of the young field of CSCW, which looks to support cooperative activities by building specialized collaborative systems.

These systems suffer from significant weaknesses, not the least of which is the problem that collaborative systems must make up for weaknesses in the underlying computational environment. This, in turn, led to an examination of the second, "virtual" reality of cooperation, which showed that virtual reality ideas and technology can be used to help overcome some of the problems facing CSCW system developers.

In this context we can consider virtual reality to be an enabling technology for CSCW, and because CSCW is applicable to most domains of human work, we can open up whole new areas of application for virtual reality.

REFERENCES

[1] Heath, Christian, and Paul Luff, "Collaborative Activity and Technological Design: Task Coordination in London Underground Control Rooms," in *ECSCW '91, Proceedings of the 2nd European Conference on Computer-Supported Cooperative Work*, Amsterdam, Netherlands, September 1991.

[2] Wexelblat, Alan, "Groups Without Groupware: A Critique of CSCW Implementation," to appear in *Interacting With Computers*.

[3] Grudin, Jonathan, "Why CSCW Applications Fail: Problems in the Design and Evaluation of Organizational Interfaces," in *CSCW '88: Proceedings of the Conference on Computer-Supported Cooperative Work*, Portland, Oregon, September 1988, New York: ACM Press, 1988.

[4] Grudin, Jonathan, "interface," *CSCW '90: Proceedings of the Conference on Computer-Supported Cooperative Work*, Los Angeles, CA, New York: ACM Press, 1990.

[5] Bikson, Tora, James H. Blair, Richard E. Barry, Charles E. Grantham, and Terry Winograd, "Communication, Coordination, and Group Performance," panel discussion at CSCW '88, Portland, Oregon, September 1988.

[6] Winograd, Terry, and Fernando Flores, *Computers and Communication*, Norwood, NJ: Ablex Publishing, 1986.

[7] Lison, B., and T. Crowley, "Sight and Sound," *UNIX Review*, October 1989.

[8] Thorpe, Jack A., "The New Technology of Large Scale Simulator Networking: Implications for Mastering the Art of Warfighting," in *Proceedings of the Ninth Interservice Industry Training Systems Conference*, November 1987.

[9] Gibson, William, *Neuromancer*, New York: Bantam Spectra, 1984.

[10] Rutkowski, Anthony M., editor of *Internet Society News*, quoted in *Computer Underground Digest*, **4** (18), April 1992.

[11] Sproull, Lee, and Sara Kiesler, "Reducing Social Context Cues: Electronic Mail in Organizational Communication," in *Computer-Supported Cooperative Work*, I. Greif, Ed., San Mateo: Morgan-Kaufmann, 1988.

[12] Conklin, J., and M. Begeman, "gIBIS: A Hypertext Tool for Exploratory Policy Discussion," in *CSCW '88: Proceedings of the Conference on Computer-Supported Cooperative Work*, Portland, Oregon, September 1988, New York: ACM Press, 1988.

[13] Lee, Jintae, "SIBYL: A Tool for Managing Group Design Rationale," in *CSCW '90: Proceedings of the Conference on Computer-Supported Cooperative Work*, Los Angeles, California, October 1990, New York: ACM Press, 1990.

[14] Boudier *et al.*, "An Overview of PCTE and PCTE+," in *Proceedings of the 3rd Annual ACM Symposium on Practical Software Development Environments*, Boston, Massachusetts, 1988.

[15] Kaplan, Simon, "ConversationBuilder: An Open System for Collaborative Work," presented at ECSCW '91 Developers' Workshop, Amsterdam, Netherlands, September, 1991.

[16] Fairchild, Kim, G. Meredith, and A. Wexelblat, "The Tourist Artificial Reality," in *CHI '89: Proceedings of the Conference on Human Factors in Computing Systems*, Austin, Texas, May 1989, New York: ACM Press, 1989.

[17] Hill, Ralph D., "The Abstraction-Link-View Paradigm: Using Constraints to Connect User Interfaces to Applications," in *CHI '92: Proceedings of the Conference on Human Factors in Computing Systems*. Monterey, California, May 1993.

[18] Rodden, Tom, and Gordon Blair, "CSCW and Distributed Systems: The Problem of Control," in *ECSCW '91, Proceedings of the 2nd European Conference on Computer-Supported Cooperative Work*, Amsterdam, Netherlands, September 1991, Boston: Kluwer Academic Publishers, 1991.

[19] Foster, Gregg, and Mark Stefik, "Cognoter, Theory and Practice of a Colab-orative Tool," in *CSCW '86: Proceedings of the Conference on Computer-Supported Cooperative Work*, Austin, Texas, December 1986, Austin: MCC, 1986.

[20] Smith, Randall, "The Alternate Reality Kit: an example of the tension between literalism and magic," in *CHI+GI '87, Proceedings of the Conference on Human Factors in Computing Systems*, Toronto, 1987, New York: ACM Press, 1987.

[21] Buxton, William, and Tom Moran, "EuroPARC's Integrated Interactive Intermedia Facility (iiif): Early Experiences," in *Proceedings of the IFIP WG8.4 Conference on Multi-User Interfaces and Applications*, Heraklion, Crete, September 1990.

[22] Travers, Michael, and Alan Borning, "Informal Interaction in Virtual Spaces," in *Proceedings of the Second International Conference on Cyberspace*, Santa Cruz, California, April 1991, Group for the Study of Virtual Systems, Center for Cultural Studies, University of California at Santa Cruz.

[23] DellaFera, C. Anthony (DEC/MIT Project Athena), Mark W. Eichin, Robert S. French, David C. Jedlinksy, John T. Kohl, and William E. Sommerfeld (MIT Project Athena). "The *Zephyr* Notification Service," in *Usenix Conference Proceedings*, Winter 1988, Dallas, TX © 1988, The USENIX Association.

[24] Lovstrand, Lennart, "Being Selectively Aware with the Khronika System," in *ECSCW '91, Proceedings of the 2nd European Conference on Computer-Supported Cooperative Work*, Amsterdam, Netherlands, September 1991.

[25] Gaver, William, and Randy Smith, "Auditory Icons in Large-Scale Collaborative Environments," in *Human-Computer Interaction—Interact 90*, D. Diaper, *et al.*, eds., New York: Elsevier, North-Holland, 1990.

[26] Gaver, W. W., R. B. Smith, and T. O'Shea, "Effective Sound in Complex Systems: the ARKola Simulation," in *CHI '91: Proceedings of the Conference on Human Factors in Computing Systems*, New Orleans, Louisiana, May 1991, New York: ACM Press, 1991.

[27] Furness, Tom, "The Virtual Reality Interface," keynote address delivered at CHI '91.

[28] Egido, Carmen, "Videoconferencing as a Technology to Support Group Work: A Review of its Failures," in *CSCW '88: Proceedings of the Conference on Computer-Supported Cooperative Work,* Portland, Oregon, September 1988, New York: ACM Press, 1988.

[29] Fish, Kraut, and Chalfonte, "The VideoWindow System in Informal Communication," in *CSCW '90: Proceedings of the Conference on Computer-Supported Cooperative Work,* Los Angeles, California, October 1990, New York: ACM Press, 1988.

[30] Ishii, Hiroshi, "Team WorkStation: Towards a Seamless Shared Workspace," in *CSCW '90: Proceedings of the Conference on Computer-Supported Cooperative Work,* Los Angeles, California, October 1990.

[31] Watabe, Kazuo, Shiro Sakata, Kazutushi Maeno, Hideyuki Fukuoka, and Toyoka Ohmori, "Distributed Multiparty Desktop Conferencing System: MERMAID," in *CSCW '90: Proceedings of the Conference on Computer-Supported Cooperative Work,* Los Angeles, California, October 1990, New York: ACM Press, 1990.

[32] Stefik, Mark, Greg Foster, Stan Lanning, and Deborah Tatar, "WYSIWIS Revised: Early Experiences with Multi-User Interfaces," in *CSCW '86: Proceedings of the Conference on Computer-Supported Cooperative Work,* Austin, Texas, December 1986, Austin: MCC, 1986.

Chapter 3

Information Management Using Virtual Reality-Based Visualizations

Kim Michael Fairchild
Institute of Systems Science
National University of Singapore
Kent Ridge, Singapore
fair@iss.nus.sg.

Kim Fairchild is the only person in this book who has been with me on this whole trip. We started together at MCC, we've cowritten papers, given talks together, argued, fought, and had immense amounts of fun. Kim has always had a visionary approach to VR—he sees global-size problems and imagines global-size solutions. Here he addresses a theme similar to Erickson's—the use of VR to manage and present to users information that cannot otherwise be comprehended—but applied to a different context, exploring a different "where."

—A.W.

Introduction

Professionals who manipulate information are suffering from too much success. Computers have made it possible to manipulate larger and larger amounts of information but humans are cognitively ill-suited for understanding the resulting complexity. The information is all readily available but users are unable to efficiently access individual items or maintain a global context of how the information fits together.

Recent advances in virtual reality (VR) technology suggest that encoding subsets of the information using multimedia techniques and placing the resulting visualizations into a perceptual three-dimensional space increase the amount of information that people can meaningfully manage [1, 2].

Extending this work, an appropriate approach would be the creation of a visualization engine that could easily take just about any collection of abstract information and create a VR-based visualization. This space, containing the visualized objects, would be available for one or more users to navigate, examining individual objects and clusters of objects in more detail. If a particular visualization is not appropriate for a particular user on a particular task, the user could immediately create a more suitable visualization.

If this approach is to be successful, three basic problems must be addressed. First, how should individual pieces of information be encoded into visualizations? Second, assuming that reasonable visualizations exist for single pieces, how do these visualizations extend to large collections of these individual pieces? Third, since all the pieces of information in large information bases cannot be shown to information professionals at one time, techniques must be available to allow user control of subsets of the entire amount of information presented.

This chapter further describes the problems that must be addressed in order to exploit VR technology for information management. It first describes the problems and solutions from a theoretical standpoint, and then describes how the solutions have been implemented in research prototypes.

Requirements

The central problem to be addressed is what can be done when there is just too much information with which to deal. With some collections of information, the traditional node-link graph structure visualization can be used, but for modern realworld problems, which require users to understand large collections of information, solutions must be found for managing the large amounts of complex information. This problem can be decomposed into three subproblems: How to make meaningful visualizations of single objects, how to make meaningful visualizations of collections of objects, and how to allow the users to control the selection of the visualizations efficiently.

Visualization of a Single Complex Object

Users are cognitively limited in their ability to understand multimedia encodings of the semantic information of objects.

For example, the x-y-z position of an object might encode the object's creation date, importance, and complexity. The shape and color might encode the type and creator of the object. Although a rich variety of additional encoding schemes is possible (i.e., sound, video, bitmaps, multiple shapes, texture, text), humans are cognitively ill-suited for readily understanding much more complex encodings [3].

Therefore, the requirement is for a model that can encode any type of semantic information into any of the available multimedia techniques. Since each object may have too much information to visualize in a single visualization, only subsets of the semantic information can be encoded at any one time. Since all or any part of the semantic information might be required for particular tasks, the visualization must be able to change dynamically to use different subsets of information.

Visualization of a Large Collection of Complex Objects

Even if appropriate visualizations can be found for individual elements, just too many pieces of information are available to be able to see all at once. The general solution to this problem is to develop models of *degrees of interest* (DOI) [4] or *fish-eye views.* Fish-eye views contain a mixture of objects with high and low levels of detail.

The DOI model associates two values with each object, *semantic distance* and *a priori importance* (API). The semantic distance is a measure of how far the viewpoint is away from the object. The API is a measure of how important an object is to the user.

The "New Yorker's View of the World" is one of the most famous fish-eye views. In this famous *New Yorker* cover, the mailbox in front of a New Yorker's house is shown in high-detail, as well as some of the stores. Next the Hudson River and Brooklyn are shown in less detail. All the states between New York and California are skipped and the visualization ends with just labels demarcating Japan and China.

Perspective in our real world is another example of a limited fish-eye view. It is limited in the sense that all objects have the same DOI value. As the euclidean distance to objects increases, their apparent size decreases. If the objects had different DOI values, similar physically sized objects seen at the same distance would not necessarily appear the same size.

Therefore the requirement is for a model that allows the automatic assignment of semantic distance and API to all objects in a visual scene, resulting in objects being displayed in different *information fidelity*, that is, some objects are shown with higher information content than other objects.

User Definition of Visualizations

Despite the promise of *natural interaction*, perhaps due to the immature state of VR devices, VR interfaces have yet to advance from the "you can pick things up" and "point the way you want to go" interface styles.

In addition to overcoming these limitations in user interaction in VRs, development of VR space for information management requires two additional interaction methods. As described earlier, users must be able to both efficiently define the encodings of subsets of the individual object semantics to visualizations, and define the subsets of objects that should be shown in higher information fidelity.

Specifications

From these requirements come specifications that define a flexible object visualization model, a complexity management model, and a new interaction style suitable for virtual reality applications.

Visualizations of a Single Complex Object

The problem is shown in Figure 3.1. Complex objects such as information about a person contain a large collection of semantic properties. This information can be encoded using many of the multimedia primitives now available on modern computers, but the particular encodings used depend on the user and the tasks that user wishes to perform with the information.

A mechanism is needed to select a coherent subset of semantic properties and encode them into a multimedia shape. Each of the multimedia properties of the icon thus represents and reflects some combination of the semantic values of the original object.

For instance, if a visualization of the information in a typical hierarchical file system is required, the data available might include information on the size of the file, the person who created the file, the type (text, source code, executable, etc.), how often the file has been

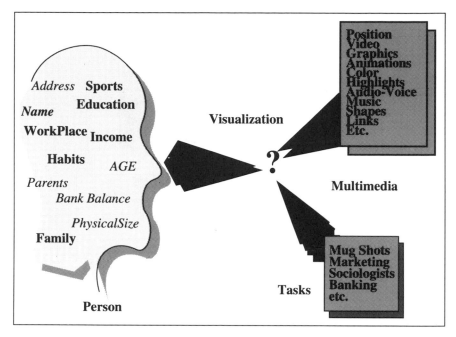

FIG. 3.1. VISUALIZATION OF A SINGLE COMPLEX OBJECT.   The problem is that we have a complex abstract object, such as the information about a person in a database. Depending on what the needs are for the application and the person interacting with the information, the possibilities for encoding the information are virtually infinite. For instance, for a mug shot application, pieces of information such as facial images, height, weight, and eye color are important. If a loan officer wants to visualize the same information, completely different sets of information such as income, habits, and workplace are needed.

What is needed then is a model for nonrestrictive mapping from the semantic space of the information to be multimedia encodings. All the useful possible mappings cannot be determined beforehand by programmers because users themselves might suddenly decide a new mapping would allow them to understand particular relationships in the information more clearly. This requires the development of an editor that end-users can use to define their own mappings.

referenced by various people, where the file is located, etc. Semantic values obtainable from these data could be a measure of the file's importance to a particular person, its relationship to other files, a measure of completeness or usefulness, etc. A visualization of the file might associate color with its importance (red meaning very important), completeness with the size of the icon, and usefulness might determine the position on the display.

Since preparing encoded representations of abstract information has traditionally been difficult and since users vary greatly in their needs for visualizations, the *AutoIcon model* [5] is used for allowing end-user

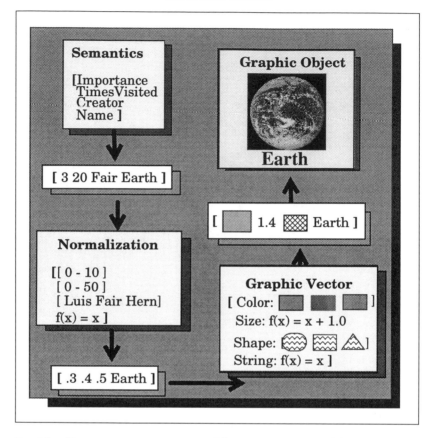

FIG 3.2. THE AUTOMATIC ICON MODEL. The automatic icon model takes some collection of semantic information about an object and works through four transformations, which results in a multimedia encoded visualization of the current state of the object. In the example above, four values, *importance, times visited,* the object's *creator,* and *name* of the object, are used to construct a visualization containing a particular image of a certain size with a text message of a certain color.

In the example, we can see that the importance of the object determined the final color of the graphic object; the times visited determined the size; the creator determined the shape; and the name determined the bitmap and the text string.

control of the mapping between the semantic space of objects and a multimedia visualization. The AutoIcon model defines a representation and a user editing paradigm to allow the mapping of semantic information into multimedia visualizations.

The AutoIcons components shown in Figure 3.2 consist of four subparts: *semantics, normalization, graphic vector,* and *graphic object.* The semantics subpart identifies the data fields or semantics of the information object that is to be represented in the final multimedia encoded representation. The output of this subpart is a vector of data values.

The data values are input into the normalization subpart, which typically normalizes the values to the range of 0 to 1. The particular normalization used might be anything from its alphabetical order to size.

This normalized vector is used as input to the graphic vector subpart. This subpart maps the normalized value onto vectors of graphic properties. For instance, a graphic property vector might be a set of colors, shapes, sizes, sounds, etc.

The output from the graphic vector consists of a vector of *desires* (i.e., color: red, shape: square). These desires are input into the graphic object subpart, which interprets them according to existing procedurally defined graphic object templates. The output is a multimedia encoded information object.

Notice that the output from each component is a vector and the functions within each component are defined as a vector of vectors. The implementation of the AutoIcon model intentionally relies heavily on the manipulation of vectors. This allows the development of an editor focused on vector manipulation and allows the same functionality to be useful for user editing of all the components of AutoIcons.

The user may apply different AutoIcons consecutively to collections of information to produce dramatically different views. For instance, changing the AutoIcon may produce views similar to the SemNet [6], Cone Tree [1], and Perspective Wall [7] views.

Visualizations of Large Collections of Complex Objects

If objects are placed into a three-dimensional display as opposed to a two-dimensional display, the perceived complexity of the information is reduced. This can be further reduced by the use of a head-mounted display to create a virtual space.

This spatial metaphor allows users to see part of the information within a restricted viewing angle when looking in a particular direction from the viewpoint. The user is able to concentrate on the subset of objects within this viewing angle. Moreover, the perspective view makes objects nearer the viewpoint appear larger, helping the user to examine local neighborhoods more effectively [Figure 3.3(a)].

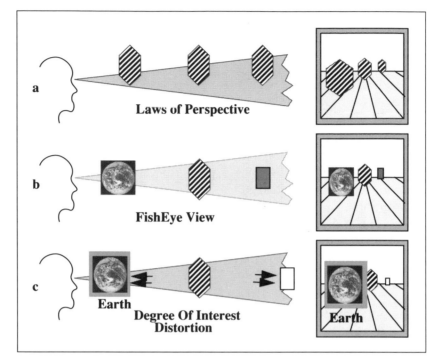

FIG. 3.3. TOO MANY OBJECTS TO DISPLAY. Three techniques that can be used to reduce the preceived complexity of a large collection of objects. In (a), the technique used
in real life is shown. The laws of perspective cause objects that are close to the observer
to be shown in larger size. If users want to find out more about a particular object, they
move toward it.

An improvement on reality is achieved with fish-eye views as shown in (b). Objects
that are considered to have more importance are shown larger with more detail than objects with lesser importance.

With DOI distortion shown in (c), instead of just growing in size, the information content increases for objects closer to the observer. Additionally objects that have greater importance distort their position, basically trying to follow the user around in the virtual
space, while less important objects avoid the user. The user has tools for influencing the
relative importance of objects.

These local neighborhoods will be understandable only if related
elements are within the same neighborhood. In other words, proximity
in semantic space should correspond to proximity in euclidean space.
In general, however, it is not mathematically possible to achieve perfect correspondence between proximity in arbitrary graph structures
and proximity in three-dimensional euclidean space, so AutoIcons provide for the initial placement of the objects in the virtual space and a

DOI function provides for the distortion of the original space to reflect design task requirements of the users. The DOI function provides a fish-eye view [Figure 3.3(b)]; instead of just growing larger as an object gets closer to the user, the object increases in information fidelity as well. The total amount of information encoded into the iconic shape increases as the object becomes more important to the observer. When an object is currently not close to the observer's viewing location and when the object is not considered very important, only a small set of the semantic information about the object is encoded. But when this is not true, the object is either important or close to the viewing location, more of the semantic information is encoded in the iconic shape.

The DOI_{index} value is used to index into a vector of AutoIcons to determine which AutoIcon to use for the visualizations. For instance, in the simple example (Figure 3.3), the vector of AutoIcons (Figure 3.4) has five members: The first AutoIcon produces a bitmap with a label and a color coding, the second produces a bitmap, the third produces a textured shape, the fourth produces a square with color information, and the fifth merely shows that something is there. Assuming a constant API value for all three shapes and the semantic distance (SD) that corresponds to euclidean distance, a formula such as the following determines the AutoIcon used:

$$DOI_{index} = \text{Integer} ((SD + (0.5 - API) \times 2) \times VectorLength)$$

where the API and semantic distance (SD) are normalized [0..1]. Vector length is the length of the AutoIcon vector. For example, if an object is of SD=0.5 and API=0.5 (the default values), then the middle index of the AutoIcon vector is used. If the API=1.0, no matter what the semantic distance from the observer, the lowest index (i.e., 0, typically the highest information fidelity) will be used.

FIG. 3.4.   Vector of automatic icons as used in Figure 3.3.

An improvement of fish-eye views can be achieved by distorting the positions of the object in a space [Figure 3.3(c)]. Objects with a high DOI move toward the user, while objects with a low DOI move away from the user.

The amount of distortion or movement can be given by this simple formula:

$$Distortion = (DOI - 0.5) \times Degree\ Of\ Distortion$$

Finding the correct distortion gets more complicated when considering objects that have a high DOI but are not currently in the line of sight. Instead of just moving in a straight line toward the viewpoint, they first move toward the viewing pyramid to get into the user's view.

User Definition of Visualizations

Two important interaction tasks need to be accomplished in an information management virtual space.

First, the user must be able to *navigate* within the virtual space to define areas of interest dynamically. Several navigation methods were described and evaluated in [6] and are listed in Table 3.1. Many such methods exist but none are generally useful so new ones must be developed.

The second task is to allow end-users to develop their task specific visualizations efficiently. Earlier information management prototypes like SemNet and Cone Tree views concentrated on finding appropriate positions for objects and then providing tools for moving the viewpoint.[1]

As described in the previous section, the problems of complexity management require the definition of multiple encodings of information. For a given task domain, all of the required encodings might be predefined by programmers, but to allow the system to be more flexible and extendible, methods must exist for allowing end-user definition of new visualizations.

In general, this would provide the users with an interactive style in which they have control over the positioning of the information objects in space, allowing them to move the viewing location dynamically in space and select any function defined for modifying the space. Additionally, the AutoIcon-based models used for encoding the semantic

---

[1] Actually the Cone Tree approach keeps the viewer location static but rotates the objects to bring them toward the viewing location.

TABLE 3.1

SURVEY OF NAVIGATION TECHNIQUES

Name	Method	Evaluation
Relative	Sequence of small steps.	This is the method we use in reality, this was found to be the WORST movement method.
Absolute	Pointing on a map where we want to go.	Very fast method, but not very accurate.
Teleportation	Once a position can be named, go to it.	Very fast, but need to have been there before.
Hyperspace	Follow the links between objects.	Useful when the relationships between objects is important for the task domain.
Transformation	Instead of moving the viewpoint, move the objects desired to the viewpoint.	Potentially very powerful, especially to query by reformation. This method is not well understood as of yet.

information into the icon shapes can either be switched to entirely new models or iteratively modified from the current model.

What is needed is a new navigation paradigm that allows end-users to describe automatic icons efficiently. The interface paradigm that shows promise for modifying automatic icons as well as accomplishing other user interaction tasks in VR systems is called *gesture sequence navigation.*

Gesture Sequence Navigation   Gesture sequence navigation, based on sequences of a small set of gestures, takes advantage of the human ability to respond rapidly to recognized stimuli.

Gestures, specific to each user, allow users to traverse a semantic network rapidly. When the user arrives at a leaf node of the network, a stored function is evaluated. This function, depending on the task domain, might do anything from copying a VR object, moving the viewpoint, to changing a visualization.

The initial production and learning of the gesture sequences is supported by automatically generating visualizations (stimuli) that describe the current user location in the network and what the next possible input gestures would accomplish.

After the gesture sequences have been learned, the visualizations are no longer needed. This reserves scarce VR display space solely for encoded information objects.

Gesture sequence navigation consists of three parts (shown in Figure 3.5): *response, stimulus,* and *semantic paths.*

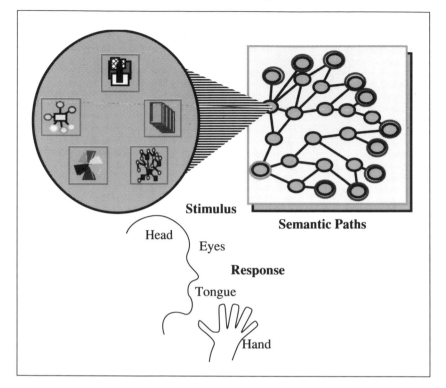

FIG. 3.5. GESTURE SEQUENCE NAVIGATION. Current VR technology makes it very difficult to operate traditional input devices such as mice and keyboards. Therefore, this navigation technique recognizes a wide variety of gesture types. The important thing is that the user is able to make some small number of distinct gestures. The system provides stimulus to the user as to what will happen if any of the gestures are made.

Sequences of gestures navigate the users through a semantic network. Arriving at a leaf node causes a function to execute. While within any internal node, the user may navigate in a three-dimensional space to cause three scaler values to be input into an arbitrary function. For instance, a terminal node might cause a song to play and navigating in an internal mode might cause the volume, balance, and bass to be changed.

1. *Limited Set of Gestures (response):* The interface only requires the user to input a limited number of gestures. Many input devices can be used to make gestures. The only requirement is that the devices distinguish between some small number of user actions. These devices could include a limited key keyboard, a Polhemus six-degree-of-freedom positioning device, an eyetracker [8], a tongue controller [9], or a dataglove [10]. The devices essentially make an *n-way button choice* [11].

2. *Representation of Gestures Sequences (semantic paths):* Sequences

of gestures are represented as a semantic network. The user effectively navigates between connected nodes on this network by performing a gesture sequence. To create new gestures or to make existing gestures easier to perform (by shortening them, for instance), the user modifies the network itself using gesture sequences. In essence, the input language is regular and the network is a virtual finite state machine parsing it.

3. *Dynamic Visualization of Gesture State (stimulus):* Visualizations represent the current state and results of gestures. Since visualizations are the stimuli for the user response, the user may customize and create new visualizations to enhance the recognizability of the stimuli. Additionally, since users are notoriously poor customizers [12], the system is set up to modify the visualizations systematically as it is used. For instance, paths the user has followed before are annotated with appropriate graphics.

Types of Gestures   Three types of gestures can be used to produce user input: *position, dynamic,* and *coordinated* gestures.

Position gestures are the easiest to learn for novices. They rely solely on the input device being in a certain state. For instance, a particular key on a keyboard was pressed or a foot was positioned in a certain spot. This type of gesture could easily be produced by disabled users with devices such as tongue controllers.

Dynamic gestures are tracked in time. For instance, using a two-dimensional mouse, a new node would be selected just because the user has moved toward it for a "significant" amount of time. As a user learns a sequence of position gestures to get to a desired place, the sequence of position gestures becomes chunked into a single dynamic gesture.

Coordinated gestures use multiple sensors and it is the interaction between the states of the individual sensors over time that defines the gesture input. The dataglove is a device that has been used this way to recognize the American Sign Language [13] for the deaf.

The user typically moves through a sequence of nodes or *way-points*[2] using gestures until a desired object or function is found. A real-time three-dimensional animation shows the movement between way-points, which aids in the learning of the gesture sequences. The stimulus takes the form of a visualization of each node, which shows the

---

[2]Originally a term in aviation, a waypoint is the point on an aviation map that serves as a navigational aid.

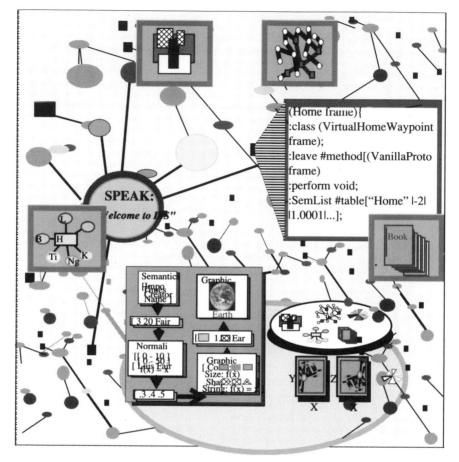

FIG. 3.6. VISUALIZATION OF AN INFORMATION VISUALIZATION SPACE. This is a visualization of what VR-based interface implementing the theories described in this chapter might look like. The visualized information is shown in the background with the interconnected shapes. As shapes get closer to the viewpoint, they increase both in size and information fidelity. Notice the prominent text shape on the right side. If the user moved away from this shape, it would turn into one of the small black shapes in the background.

The collection of control objects shown in the foreground at the bottom allows the user to choose different visualizations or move the viewpoint. This collection, called the *virtual toolbelt*, moves with the user as the user navigates through the virtual space.

Arranged around the outside of the display, the four squares are nodes in the semantic network and are used as the stimuli for the sequence gesture navigation method.

current status of the gesture and where the user will be after the next gesture. When the user has *chunked* [14] the sequence and produce the required individual gestures in quick succession, the animation speeds up until intermediate waypoints may no longer be perceivable.

The visualization of the waypoint provides the stimulus for the users to know where they are in the gesture sequence and where they will be next with the various gesture options.

The waypoint visualization (examples are shown arranged around the edge of Figure 3.6) consists of the visualization of several subparts: the links or *branchpoints* to the next waypoints, the contents of the waypoint, and any action that will execute when the user arrives at the waypoint.

The branchpoints in the current waypoint present information as to what waypoint or context the user will be in if that branch is taken. The branchpoints are visualized by taking a subset of the semantic information about that waypoint and encoding it into an iconic form.

Combining the Theoretical Solutions

These specifications and their associated requirements led to the development of a scenario of use and a general architecture for visualizing information from any application domain. In the following two subsections the scenario and architecture are presented.

A Scenari'o: A Visualization of a Visualization System

The solutions to the three requirements described previously are shown together in the sample *visualization* scene shown in Figure 3.6.

The three distinct regions in this figure can easily be distinguished from each other by their behavior when the viewpoint moves.

At the bottom of the figure is an oval containing several tools. This is the *virtual toolbelt,* an object that contains tools for manipulating the visualizations and interacting with the space. This toolbelt is attached to the user's waist. As the user moves through the space, the toolbelt moves as well.

Around the outside of the figure, shown in squares, are the stimuli for the Gesture Sequence Navigation-based interface. These stimuli are fixed in space even when the users move their heads. In a stereo view of the virtual space, they would seem to be two-dimensional overlays on the three-dimensional space. Their appearance changes as users make gesture sequence input. When the user is not making a gesture sequence the stimulus does not appear, thus saving VR display space for other objects.

Finally, the rest of the objects comprise the visualizations of the information. The objects are shown at several degrees of interest. The printout of text on the right side of the figure shows the information in its highest fidelity. It is connected to the highlighted round shape on the left side, which shows somewhat less information. This object in turn is connected to several other objects that are merely larger versions of the unconnected shapes in the background.

As the user moves through the space, the objects change into other higher or lower resolution visualizations. Objects that have been defined by the user to have higher API distort from their assigned positions and follow the user viewpoint.

An Information Visualization Architecture

In this subsection the theoretical solutions for addressing the requirements are integrated in a common architecture. In Figure 3.7, a data flow view of the architecture is presented.

According to the requirements, end-users must be able to adapt the visualization system to new application needs. This requires the system to be able to visualize arbitrary information. For instance, if a corporation wishes to visualize employee records, mechanisms must be in place to allow smooth extension of the system to interact with employee records data types.

To accomplish this extension, the information is decoupled from the visualization system by a layer called *surrogate object classes*. This is an extendable class hierarchy that implements an access protocol for different information types. For each type of information the system visualizes, a class exists in the surrogate object class hierarchy. When a visualization of a new type of information is required, either an existing class *close* to the new type is modified or a completely new class is written and added to the hierarchy.

Using the appropriate surrogate class, for each application object an *instance of composite object* is instantiated. These instances consist of a triple, the original application object, the surrogate object, and an *automatic icon* for generating the encoded presentation of the object. The particular automatic icon used is determined by the semantic distance of the object from observer and is selected from the automatic icon DOI vector. The automatic icon may also be modified by the user in real time.

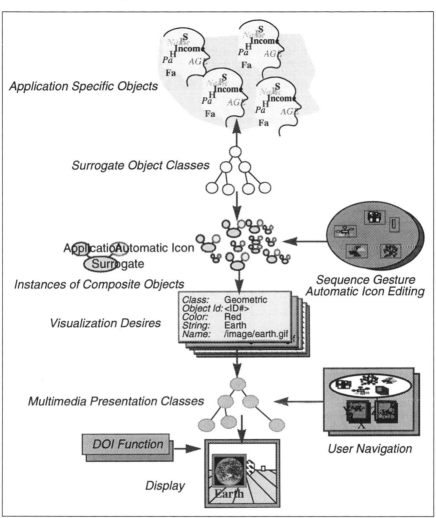

FIG. 3.7. GENERAL INFORMATION VISUALIZATION ARCHITECTURE. The information is decoupled from the visualization system by a layer called *surrogate object classes,* an extendable class hierarchy that implements an access protocol for different application information types. For each application object, an *instance of composite object* is instantiated. These instances consist of a triple, the original application object, the surrogate object, and an automatic icon for generating the encoded presentation of the object. The automatic icon is used for generating a table of slots and values for each composite object. These *visualization desires* are sent to a particular class in the *multimedia presentation class* hierarchy.

Each multimedia presentation class implements a particular type of multimedia object; it might be live video, sound, animation, etc. These are treated as suggestions and may be evaluated differently by different classes.

The automatic icon is used for generating a table of slots and values for each composite object. These are called *visualization desires* and are sent to a particular class in the *multimedia presentation class* hierarchy. At a minimum these desires contain fields for the class in the multimedia presentation class hierarchy and the identification of the composite surrogate object. In the example shown in Figure 3.7, the values for a color, string, and name are supplied as well.

Each multimedia presentation class implements a particular type of multimedia object, for example, live video, animation, voice, a combination, or anything else a designer has defined. The slot and value pairs are treated as suggestions and might be evaluated differently by different classes. Super classes in the hierarchy define default values for any slots not supplied by the visualization desires.

The multimedia encoded representation for each of the original application objects is generated and their positions are modified by the DOI distortion function.

The users interact with the architecture in two ways, by modifying the values of the automatic icons and navigating to different viewing positions in the virtual space.

VR-Based Information Management Systems

Now after discussing information visualization in virtual reality from a theoretical perspective, we examine existing prototype visualization systems. Even though the subfield of using VR to solve information management problems is in its infancy, several interesting approaches and many techniques have been suggested by prototypes.

In this section we present four systems, presented in the order of development. For each we discuss its context (or purpose), describe methodology, and discuss what answers it has for the three basic questions of this chapter: intraobject complexity, interobject complexity, and user interaction.

MCC's SemNet Graph-Based Visualization Prototype

Context   SemNet was an exploratory research project undertaken to advance the understanding of problems facing both users and developers of large knowledge bases (Figure 3.8). The immediate objective of the SemNet project [6] was to identify important problems and a collection of possible solutions to these problems. The problems and solutions that have been investigated, reflecting the disciplines of the authors, derive from the convergence of computer science, measurement and scaling, and cognitive psychology. Because this research explores many alternatives instead of conducting formal evaluations of a few alternatives. A longer term objective was to develop a generic approach to knowledge-base browsing and editing by combining and optimizing the best solutions.

The major problem addressed by the designers of SemNet was how to present large knowledge bases so they can be comprehended by a user. To comprehend a knowledge base, they hypothesize, a user must recognize (1) the identities of individual elements in the knowledge base, (2) the relative position of an element within a hierarchical context, and (3) explicit relationships between elements. Consequently, research was focused on ways to represent elements and their interrelationships within the context of a large knowledge base.

SemNet represents knowledge bases graphically because knowledge bases represent information about relationships between symbolic entities, and graphics are an effective way to communicate relationships among objects. Furthermore, they wanted to exploit the skills that people have already developed for recognizing visual patterns and moving in three-dimensional space.

Methodology. As knowledge bases become larger, more powerful semantic and syntactic techniques will be required for exploring and manipulating the knowledge. SemNet offers a syntactic approach to solving this problem. SemNet's representation of a knowledge base is based entirely on the names and positions of the knowledge elements and the connections among them. SemNet demonstrates how major problems in knowledge base management can be solved, or partially solved, with only this syntactic information. Of course, semantic information available to the application program could be used in conjunction with SemNet's syntactic techniques to achieve a more effective solution.

The positions of the knowledge elements greatly affect comprehension of the knowledge base structure. Positions can be determined by heuristics designed to put knowledge elements close together spatially if they are neighbors in the graph structure formed by their interconnections. These methods for assigning positions become increasingly important and increasingly less effective as the knowledge base increases in size, pointing to the need for further research on this problem.

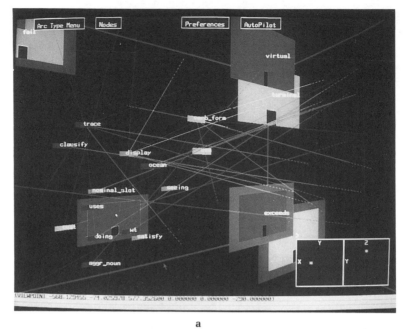

a

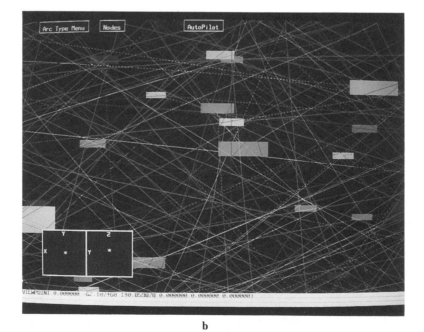

b

An important issue was how, using only syntactic information, SemNet could reduce the displayed information by presenting less information about those knowledge elements unimportant to the user's immediate concern. To some extent, this information reduction is accomplished automatically by the three-dimensional graphic hardware if proximity-based positioning has been used. Objects near the viewpoint, which is assumed to represent the region of immediate interest, are displayed at full size. Object size diminishes as distance from the viewpoint increases, and objects outside the field of view are not displayed at all. The result is a fish-eye view based on three-dimensional perspective. This method was made more effective by combining it with a fish-eye view based on *clustering*. All knowledge elements within local regions of euclidean space were assigned to clusters, neighboring clusters were assigned to higher level clusters, and so on. Only knowledge elements near the viewpoint are presented; further from the viewpoint, cluster objects are displayed that represent all the knowledge elements in a region of the space. The combination of these two methods greatly reduces the displayed information while providing both local detail and global context.

Discussion   The problem of creating intraobject complexity is indirectly handled by SemNet. Merely the name and the connections to other objects are displayed.

Interobject complexity is the focus of SemNet and many techniques for reducing the "perceptual complexity" notably through fish-eye and clustering techniques were demonstrated. The technique that "scales" to enormous knowledge bases is called *clustering*. Basically, once a position for an object is positioned in space, it becomes a member of a hierarchical cluster. The individual objects or an appropriate container cluster object is displayed depending on the location of the viewing point.

FIG. 3.8.   MCC'S SEMNET GRAPH-BASED VISUALIZATION PROTOTYPE.   SemNet displays objects using a fish-eye view, which depends on the position of the viewpoint that the user controls with a mouse. Figure 8a shows the natural fish-eye view that results from placing objects in a three-dimensional space. Figure 8b shows the same objects using SemNet's Cluster-based fish-eye view. In the middle of the display, knowledge-base elements are visible because these elements are in the same subdivision as the viewpoint. The large rectangles are cluster objects that represent the subdivisions adjacent to the subdivision containing the viewpoint. This fish-eye technique of representing the more remote regions in correspondingly larger chunks essentially reduces the number of objects to be displayed on the screen logarithmically, yet preserves a balance of local detail and global context. Reprinted with permission of Microelectronics and Computer Technology Corporation.

Users of SemNet have a rich collection of navigation techniques for moving the eyepoint and techniques for experimenting with different methods and parameters for positioning the knowledge elements.

Xerox PARC's Animated 3-D Visualizations: The Perspective Wall and the Cone Tree

Context   Information access and management is difficult in large information spaces because it is hard to visualize what information exists and how it is related. The SemNet system mentioned in the previous section visualized arbitrary graphs, but the results tended to be cluttered and thus difficult to understand. The Xerox PARC cone tree and perspective wall [17] approaches focus on the visualization of linear and hierarchical information structures.

The graph information space is laid out using three-dimensional visualizations, and the user is provided tools for changing the "area of interest" to cause different parts of the graph to appear closer and thus larger to the user.

Methodology   Two different visualization approaches are used depending on whether the information is linear or hierarchical in nature. For linear information, the perspective wall arranges information left to right on a virtual wall as shown in Figure 3.9(a). This information might typically be arranged by its date.

For hierarchical information, the cone tree view is used. In the cone tree, hierarchies are laid out uniformly in three dimensions. In Figure 3.9(b), a cone tree view of part of a UNIX file system is shown. The tree rotates when the user picks a particular file node to bring that node to the front.

With each of these visualizations, a collection of navigation tools exists to allow the user to influence the presentation of the visualization. For instance, the user might prune or grow particular nodes to influence the number of total nodes presented.

Discussion   The problem of intraobject complexity is not addressed directly by either visualization. Some amount of the information represented by the nodes is represented by its placement, size, color, and connections, but a general mechanism for navigation within the information of a node is not suggested.

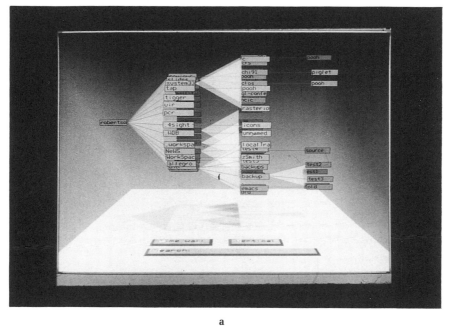

a

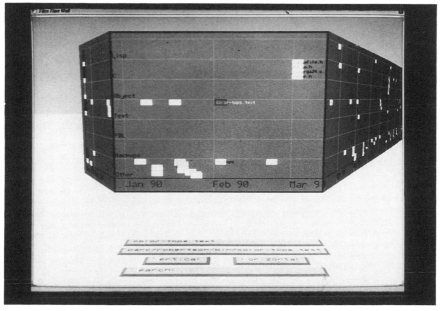

b

FIG. 3.9. XEROX PARC'S (a) PERSPECTIVE WALL VISUALIZATION AND (b) CONE TREE VISUALIZATION.   Copyright © 1991, Association of Computing Machinery, Inc., reprinted by permission.

The strength of the approach is in giving users an understanding of the interobject complexity. As in the fish-eye views used by SemNet, the three-dimensional perspective naturally organizes the information into a global context and local areas of interest.

The graph structure in the cone tree visualization is also very useful in helping users to understand the connections between nodes and how the nodes fit into a global context.

A method is not suggested that would allow "multiple local areas of interest" in that the perspective wall and the cone tree support only one area "close" to the user.

Both visualizations contain an assortment of tools for navigating and thus manipulating the views provided by the visualizations. These tools are within the information space itself. When these tools increase in the future, perhaps the visualizations already demonstrated might be used for handling the tool complexity.

Silicon Graphic's 3-D Information Landscape Prototype

Context   As a result of modern business requirements, users must be able to understand large collections of complex multivariate data. Existing spreadsheets and associated graphics in tools provide narrow bandwidth and limited dimensionality.

To create a paradigm for visualizing large multivariate data sets that exploits the rich visualization capabilities of 3-D, the designers of the *Fusion (Fsn)* [15] system built a system that is based in 3-D charts (Figure 3.10).

Like SemNet, Fsn visualizations transform data into information by mapping visual attributes onto information ones. For data that do not naturally coalesce into distinct object or patterns, the visualization technique supplies its own categories of meaning by collapsing ranges of data into discrete objects (i.e., bar charts).

The Fsn solution is to extend the 3-D bar charts into an extended space for unbounded breadth and add additional containment and structure topology for added dimensionality. This leads to the model of the *information landscape,* in which the 3-D bar charts are connected with each other via some topology on an extended landscape plane.

Methodology   The *Fsn* (pronounced "fusion") prototype is based on a collection of components as follows.

FIG. 3.10.   SILICON GRAPHIC'S 3-D FUSION INFORMATION LANDSCAPE PROTOTYPE.   This
is a Fusion view of a file system. Each cell contains independent data (the files). Users
can examine, print, and move files by manipulating data blocks. The pedestals represent directories with the height mapped into the cumulative size of the contained files.
Notice the surprisingly effective *spotlight* technique, which aids in the identification of
selected cells. Reprinted with permission of Silicon Graphics.

The basic visualization object is called a *data block*. This maps attributes of raw data into graphic attributes such as height, color, saturation, text, and icons. A container object called a *cell* serves as an organizer object for *data blocks* representing a particular relationship among those blocks. *Connectors* are multidirectional connection lines between cells representing contextual relationships between joined cells. The *topology* of the containers is defined by the topology of the connectors between cells.

Using these concepts, a single view of the encoded information is found. A variety of navigational techniques are used for moving the user's viewing position and for selecting a variety of precanned views.

Among the advantages of the information landscape approach is that it is a natural cognitive paradigm for the users; it exploits spatial memory, landmarks, perspective, and neighborhood cues.

Discussion The problem of creating "visualization of a simple complex object" or intraobject complexity is directly handled by the data block component. The data block selects the data (in this chapter we call this the *semantic*) attributes of the object and defines how these data should be mapped into the graphical attributes. This appears similar, at least in spirit, to the AutoIcon model.

The container objects are used to manage interobject complexity. Like SemNet, they can contain any number of simple objects. In Fusion the objects all share some common attribute but in SemNet they were related objects merely because they were positioned close together in virtual space.

Fusion users have many tools for changing the viewing position and selecting prestored views, but they are not able to directly change the visualizations. However, Fusion demonstrates a rich variety of very interesting user interface techniques such as showing objects at different graphical resolutions and "spotlighting" user selections.

Institute of Systems Science's Sphere-Based Visualization

Context VizNet [16] has been implemented using the tools provided by a multimedia authoring environment called *KICK* [17]. KICK is a frame-based multimedia toolkit based on the *Starship* language [18], which includes, among other media objects, modeling and rendering tools for 3-D graphics. VizNet has used these tools to construct its visualizations. At the same time, the internal structures of KICK have been used as testing data for VizNet. The internal structure of KICK is made up of multimedia information nodes linked together into hierarchies (class, part of, etc.) and associations.

Methodology   Associative relationships are visualized by means of the sphere structure. The sphere is used for the visualization of all relationships associated with an object of interest (OOI). The sphere structure can be considered a 3-D version of the 2-D perspective wall [7] in that objects highly related to the node of interest are displayed nearer to it, while objects less related are displayed further away.

In terms of layout structures, the sphere resembles that of an onion, whereby spheres are embedded beneath spheres. This is essential for representing different levels of information. For example, objects directly related to the OOI are displayed in the outermost sphere. Subsequent objects, which are related to the OOI through other objects, are considered as lower level objects and are displayed on the inner spheres. These lower level spheres have darker hemispheres surrounding them, thus giving a visual cue as to how deep within the spheres the user is.

For each sphere layer, objects highly related to the OOI are displayed nearer to the OOI, while objects less related are displayed further away. These later objects drop off at the side of the sphere and thus appear less visible. This provides a natural fish-eye view for the display.

Figures 3.11(a) and (b) show a sphere representation that visualizes the associated links that emanate from a set of images related to an aircraft (sets are represented by an icon with three circles surrounded by a wire-frame fence). In the center of the sphere lies the piece of information under inspection (the set), and around it, arranged radially, are other related items, such as other sets, the fuselage 3-D structure, text, etc. Figure 3.11(b) is a close-up view. There are five sets of images and a link to a 3-D structure. Again, the icons are shown in different degrees of interest.

In terms of manipulation, the sphere resembles the trackball. The user can slide and rotate the sphere, and thus bring a particular node into clear view. In addition, if a node is "walked" over that is linked to lower level nodes, the user "falls" into the inner sphere. Likewise, if the user walks over a node that is linked to higher level nodes, the user will be "transported" up to the outer sphere.

a

b

FIG. 3.11. INSTITUTE OF SYSTEMS SCIENCE'S SPHERE VISUALIZATION. Reprinted with permission of Institute of Systems Science.

Discussion   The problem of handling intraobject complexity is accomplished in VizNet by using a version of the AutoIcon solution proposed earlier. Each object to be visualized is associated with a vector of AutoIcons. Depending on the distance to the user viewpoint, different AutoIcons are used.

Interobject complexity is partially handled by the sphere representation and a version of the conetree representation (not shown). It is difficult to imagine either of these solutions scaling up for enormous databases.

VizNet provides a set of interaction styles for navigating in three dimensional space and semantically within the "onion."

Summary

Three problems in using virtual reality technology to satisfy the needs of information professionals were identified: visualization of a single complex object, visualization of a large collection of complex objects, and user definition of visualizations. Three theoretical solutions were proposed: a model for flexibly encoding the mapping from the semantic space of information objects to the multimedia space of visualizations, a model for managing information complexity using distorted fish-eye views, and a new interface paradigm called gesture sequence navigation useful for controlling the above two models.

How these solutions can be combined into a single visualization system was demonstrated by describing a sample visualization and by presenting a general data flow architecture.

Four existing research prototypes that address the problems of visualizing arbitrary information using virtual reality technology were discussed.

REFERENCES

[1] Robertson, G.G., J. D. Mackinlay and S. K. Card, "Cone Trees: Animated 3D Visualizations of Hierarchical Information," in *CHI '91 Proceedings: Human Factors in Computing Systems,* New York: ACM Press, 189–194, 1991.
[2] Fairchild, K. M., and S. Poltrock, "Soaring through Knowledge Space: SemNet 2.1," videotape presented at ACM-SIG-CHI '87 Human Factors in Computing Systems, and in MCC Technical Report HI-104-86 Rev 1, Austin, Texas, 1987.
[3] Miller, G., "The Magical Number 7 Plus Or Minus 2: Some Limits in our Capacity for Processing Information," *Psychological Review,* 81–97, 1956.

[4] Furnas, G. W., "Generalized Fisheye Views," in *CHI '86 Proceedings: Human Factors in Computing Systems,* New York: ACM 16–23, 1986.

[5] Fairchild, K. M., L. G. Meredith, and A. Wexelblat, "A Formal Structure for Automatic Icons," *Interacting with Computers,* June 1989, and in MCC Technical Report STP-311-88, 1989.

[6] Fairchild, K. M., S. E. Poltrock, and G. W. Furnas, "SemNet: Three-dimensional Graphic Representations of Large Knowledge Bases," in *Cognitive Science and Its Applications for Human-Computer Interaction,* Fairlawn, NJ: Lawrence Erlbaum Associates, 1988.

[7] Mackinlay, J. D., G. G. Robertson, and S. K. Card, "The Perspective Wall: Detail and Context Smoothly Integrated," in *CHI '91 Proceedings: Human Factors in Computing Systems,* New York: ACM Press, pp. 173–179, 1991.

[8] Jacob, R. J., "What You Look At is What You Get: Eye Movement-Based Interaction Techniques," in *CHI '90 Proceedings: Human Factors in Computing Systems,* New York: ACM Press, pp. 11–18, 1990.

[9] Fortune, D., J. E. Ortiz, and R. Barline, "Adaptation of Tongue-touch Keypad and Zofcom System to Educational Applications," in *Proceedings of the Sixth Annual Conference on Technology and Persons with Disabilities,* pp. 249–252, 1991.

[10] Zimmerman, T., J. Lanier, C. Blanchard, S. Bryson, and Y. Harvill, "A Hand Gesture Interface Device," in *CHI'87 Proceedings,* New York:ACM Press, pp. 18–192, 1987.

[11] Foley, J. D., A. Van Dam, S. K. Feiner, and J. F. Hughes, *Computer Graphics, Principles and Practice* 2nd ed., Reading, MA: Addison-Wesley Publishing Company, 1990.

[12] Mackay, W. E., "Triggers and Barriers to Customizing Software," in *CHI '91 Proceedings: Human Factors in Computing Systems,* New York: ACM Press, pp. 153–160, 1991.

[13] Kramer, J., "The Talking Glove in Action," *Communications of the ACM,* p. 515, April 1989.

[14] Wickens, C. D., "Information Processing, Decision-Making, and Cognition," in *Handbook of Human Factors,* New York: John Wiley & Sons, 1987.

[15] Strasnick, S., and J. Tesler, "3D Information Landscapes," software available by anonymous FTP from sgi.sgi.com:~ftp/pub/fsnimages.tar.Z and fsp.tar.Z.

[16] Fairchild, K. M., L. Serra, H. Ng, B. H. Lee, and T. L. Ang, "Dynamic Fisheye Information Visualizations," presented at First British Computer Society Conference on Virtual Reality, 1992.

[17] Loo, P. L., "The Starship Manual (Version 2.0)," Institute of Systems Science, National University of Singapore, *ISS TR#91-54-0,* 1991.

[18] Serra, L., T. S. Chua, and W. S. Teh, "A Model for Integrating Multimedia Information Around 3D Graphics Hierarchies," *The Visual Computer,* **7** (5–6), pp. 326–343, 1991.

Part II
Softwhere in the Arts

One of the most fascinating things about virtual reality is the attention it has attracted in the arts community. I can remember almost a decade ago working with artists who patiently explained to me how badly my drawing program performed and why they would never give up their traditional materials for computers.

Today that is beginning to change; the state of the art in computers has advanced far enough to have an impact and most importantly we have begun listening to the artists. Virtual reality ideas and technologies give artists new freedoms, new means of self-expression, and new ways to bring their skills to bear on the information world.

In this section, I present three chapters by people who are trained as artists as well as being computer-knowledgeable. We welcome their skills and their viewpoints as important contributions in expanding the horizons of VR applications.

Chapter 4

Writing Cyberspace: Literacy in the Age of Simulacra

Stuart Moulthrop
Georgia Institute of Technology
School of Literature, Communication, and Culture
The Ivan Allen College
Atlanta, Georgia
sm51@prism.gatech.edu

It's rare to find someone who has serious credentials both in the computer field and in the literary field, but VR seems to draw those special people. I first met Stuart Moulthrop after he presented a technical paper at the Hypertext '89 conference. We met again at the First Conference on Cyberspace where he presented his literary side. Along the way we began to talk about the evolution of "the story" and what was happening to the narrative form in contemporary society. The original title for this chapter was "The End of the Word as We Know It" but that seemed too fatalistic. Instead, Moulthrop turns to an examination of what literacy means in the cyberspace age.

—A.W.

Their trust in writing, produced by external characters which are no part of themselves, will discourage the use of their own memory within them. You have invented not an elixir of memory, but of reminding; and you offer your pupils the appearance of wisdom, not true wisdom.

—Plato, *Phaedrus*

If the technology makes people more powerful or more smart, then it's an evil technology.

—Jaron Lanier

Introduction

Science fiction as we once knew it no longer exists. And while we're making brash assertions, technological reality has become pretty dubious, too. What we have here is a convergence. Somewhere back in the 1970s or 1980s, the tenuous membrane between these two categories finally shredded away to nothing, and now we find ourselves in an Age of Simulacra where discriminating the virtual from the real is not so easy. This is a time in which a novelist can come up with a catchy concept like "cyberspace" [1] then discover a few years later that a software developer has included the word in the trademark for a future release.

The significance of this event seems clear enough. There is no more science fiction, there is only product development; and to some extent the reverse is also true. Here in the early 1990s, virtual reality as a technology (i.e., a tool for widespread, everyday use) still seems more virtual than real. Important first steps have been taken [2,3], but the systems that support these efforts are as yet too expensive and too much in flux to satisfy a broad market. As in the early days of computing, the number of people significantly engaged with the new technology remains small. This will not be the case for long, but at the moment some of the best thinking about virtual reality, especially about its social implications, consists of speculation. That is, much of what we know about cyberspace comes not from experience or experiment, but from fictions by people like William Gibson, Pat Cadigan, and Bruce Sterling, or social theory by people like Brenda Laurel and Donna Haraway. At the moment, virtual reality and cyberspace are still largely creatures of print.

This state of affairs is decidedly ironic, since some virtual reality boosters portray the technology as a clear antithesis of print. According to Jaron Lanier, one of the pioneers of virtual reality, this medium promises to replace now dominant forms of symbolic communication (speech and writing) with a new, "post-symbolic" paradigm. Symbolic media represent mental events by means of formalized signs, generating what we call information. "Information," Lanier says, "is alienated experience" [4, p. 49]. In Lanier's vision, virtual reality would circumvent representation by directly reproducing experience. If you wanted to understand what goes on inside your car's engine, you would no longer have to wade through obscure texts on automotive mechanics.

You could just strap on an eyephone and data suit and *become a piston!* (Although how much you could learn at 2500 rpm is an open question . . . .)

While it accurately represents Lanier's claims, this view of virtual reality is extreme to the point of caricature (see Figure 4.1), and as such it has drawn down some fairly harsh criticism. Jay Bolter, for instance, dismisses Lanier's concept as "virtual television" [5, p. 230]. Indeed, many researchers and developers, not to mention linguists and psychologists, would reject the assertion that virtual reality marks an end to symbolic communication. But for all its hyperbole, Lanier's notion of unalienated experience does contain an important grain of truth. Like cinema, radio, and television before it, virtual reality articulates information (or experience) in ways that are fundamentally different from those of speech, writing, and print. Virtual reality is hardly nonsymbolic, as we discuss later, but in a sense it truly is *post*-symbolic in that it renders the symbol secondary, silent, or invisible. In his analysis of the cultural impact of writing, Marshall McLuhan [6] contended that writing technologies alter the "ratio" of the senses, privileging vision at the expense of other sensory modes. "Electric technologies" such as

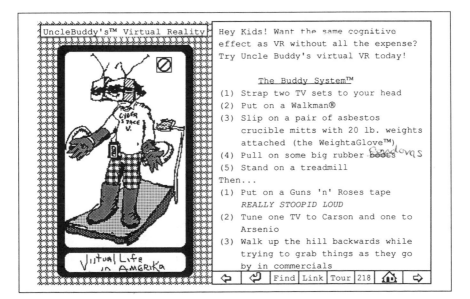

FIG. 4.1. UNCLE BUDDY'S VIRTUAL VR. From *Uncle Buddy's Phantom Funhouse* by John McDaid. © 1992 Eastgate Systems, Inc.

cinema and television readjust the ratio, moving the auditory back into parity with the visual. Presumably virtual reality would carry this revision even further, bringing into balance tactility, proprioception, and potentially all other modes of sensation as well. If symbolism is produced by skewing the ratio of the senses toward the visual, then the omnisensory approach of virtual reality might indeed organize perception in ways that take us beyond the symbol.

But here again we encounter irony. Virtual reality, as we now know it at least, is still very much dependent on eyes-only, symbolic language—it is a creature of print. The symbolic power of writing allows us to extrapolate worlds of social interaction and economic activity, which may some day be made possible by an as-yet emerging technology. Without such symbolic extrapolation, virtual reality would still be something of a laboratory toy. On one level this irony may be trivial, simply an artifact of early development. After all, there was a time when all that people knew about radio or television was what they read in newspapers or pulp magazines. Earlier technologies gestated in print, too, and just as they outgrew their origins, so will virtual reality.

But there is also something nontrivial in this ironic linkage of virtual reality and writing, a deeper sense in which the new post-symbolic technology remains tied to symbolic communication. In some ways, which we need to explore, virtual reality will always be a creature of print—and this is an irony that will not disappear with time. Whenever virtual reality is invoked as "cyberspace," we are reminded of the lingering presence of the symbol even in a post-symbolic context.

What "Cyberspace" Really Means

William Gibson made up the word "cyberspace" for his 1984 novel *Neuromancer,* as a name for a virtual environment or "consensual hallucination" used by information workers in the early twenty-first century. Although the book is science fiction, it has had a significant influence on both theorists and designers of virtual reality systems. As mentioned earlier, the software company Autodesk recently used "cyberspace" in a registered trademark, and a memoir by Gibson features prominently in the first collection of academic essays about virtual reality [2].

Writers of fantasy and science fiction have always had a weakness for Greek-rooted neologisms (e.g., "hyperspace," "psionics," "xeno-morph"), but Gibson's coinage is more thoughtful than most. He apparently based the word on "cybernetics," the name for the science of control and communication, which was itself coined in the 1930s by the discipline's founder, Norbert Wiener. Though cybernetics has come to be identified with computers and information processing in general, Wiener had a different application in mind:

> We have decided to call the entire field of control and communication theory, whether in the machine or in the animal, by the name *Cybernetics,* which we form from the Greek *kybernetos* or *steersman.* In choosing this term, we wish to recognize that the first significant paper on feedback mechanisms is an article on governors, which was published by Clerk Maxwell in 1868, and that *governor* is derived from a Latin corruption of *kybernetos.* We also wish to refer to the fact that the steering engines of a ship are indeed one of the earliest and best-developed forms of feedback mechanisms. [7, pp. 11–12]

Properly speaking, the "cyber" in cybernetics refers not simply to the processing of information, but to the use of information in a feedback system, that is, for purposes of homeostatic control. The archetypal cybernete for Norbert Wiener (as for Maxwell before him) was a primitive automatic pilot, the hydraulic course-correcting mechanism in nineteenth-century steamships. The root sense of cybernetics thus invokes a fundamental conservatism, a commitment to preestablished order. When Wiener was not using the mechanical analogy, he often brought in a social metaphor to describe this function: "a small country community" whose citizens regulate their behavior for the common good [7, p. 160].

By contrast, the "cyber" in Gibson's cyberspace has an altogether different spin. Instead of *control* it seems to indicate *power:*

> A graphic representation of data abstracted from the banks of every computer in the human system. Unthinkable complexity. Lines of light ranged in the nonspace of the mind, clusters and constellations of data. Like city lights, receding . . . [1, p. 51]

The cybernete of Gibson's imagination is neither a course-correcting governor nor a conservative country town: True to its 1980s instantiation, it is an urbanized powerhouse of synthesis and flow, not so much orderly or balanced as dynamic and unthinkably complex. Where Wiener theorizes cybernetic systems in terms of mechanical relays for maintaining a steady course, Gibson seems to have in mind neural networks, parallel processors, artificial intelligences, indeed the microelectronics field itself—systems designed to escape constraints and produce the unexpected. If Wiener's vision features homeostasis and constancy, Gibson seems to prefer the newer concepts of catastrophe and chaos, in which fresh possibilities emerge from the collapse of old orders [8, 9].

Still, to an important extent the older meaning of cybernetics survives even in Gibson's chaotic cyberspace. In its root sense, following Wiener's etymology, "cyberspace" means *the place of steering* or *a domain of control.* In Gibson's world this control seems to belong, at least on first presentation, to the consensual hallucinator: the worker, student, or data pirate who interfaces with the virtual universe in order to manipulate its structures. Were he alive today, Wiener would no doubt see the same vision differently. From a cybernetic perspective, the element of control in cyberspace is actually vested not in the human communicant but in the system itself. (And without giving too much away, this turns out to be the eventual message of Gibson's novel.) That is, the nature and design of the virtual space—how its contents are displayed and arranged, what routes of passage are enabled among them, how they may be transformed—ultimately constrain any individual action within that space.

These constraints constitute what McLuhan called the "environment" of a given medium [10]. Environments are invisible or unacknowledged influences exerted by a medium on the people who use it. Every communication technology generates an environment, along with a form of "antienvironmental" expression (often an artform) by which features of that environment are exposed and interrogated. The environment of alphabetic literacy, as McLuhan and others have described it, is characterized by rationality, abstraction, and indeed an alienation of experience. Writing organizes sense data in regular, linear patterns, disposing those who use it to think in terms of hierarchical structures such as lists, tables, and matrices [11]. On the other hand, cinema and television (so their detractors claim) present a fragmented, decontextualized stream of data characterized by pseudoconjunctions like "Now . . . this," which join unrelated images or events [12]. The media environment of the video age thus emphasizes what one theorist calls "euretics," the creation of form through sampling and collage, as opposed to the analytic method in which new phenomena are tested against established patterns [13].

Literacy teaches us to tabulate and integrate; "videocy" (as Greg Ulmer calls it) encourages us to associate and improvise. What cognitive influence might we expect from the media environment of virtual reality? To answer this question, we must remember that media environments have both positive and negative aspects: They both enable and constrain. As Jaron Lanier sees it, the positive aspect of virtual reality lies in its ability to promote interpersonal relations: "The whole thing with Virtual Reality is that you're breeding reality with other people. You're making shared cooperative dreams all the time . . . . Eventually, you make your imagination external and it blends with other people's. Then you make the world together as a form of communication" [4, p. 46]. If print fosters analysis and video fosters invention, then virtual reality fosters empathy, the ability to engage another person's worldview in a world where views are shared and changeable.

But media environments take away as well as give. Print opens the door to linearity and hierarchy but stifles the irrational, the nonlinear, and the simultaneous. Video gives us a world rich in associations, but may impair our ability to forge rational connections. If virtual reality lets us share a common imaginary space, what conceptual functions does it restrict or circumvent? The answer is not hard to find. If virtual reality is truly a post-symbolic medium, then the price of this new tele-empathy may be our alienation from the symbolic domain of control structures that dictate the nature and form of the new social space. Virtual reality may give us a place to meet mind-to-mind, but in focusing our attention on "making the world together" it may blind us to the fact that on some level, the world is always made to previous order. (For more detailed treatment of this idea, see [14].)

In short, "cyberspace" could be as misleading a name for virtual realities as "Democratic Republic" was for old East Germany. Properly speaking, a cyberspace is a domain of control. If virtual reality truly does become the post-symbolic medium Jaron Lanier dreams of, then it will be not a domain of control but a theater of simulation, a space whose inhabitants are given the illusion of cosmic power while they remain entirely under the influence of their host machine—which brings us back to the salient irony of cyberspace, or post-symbolism's debt to the symbol.

Far from being post-symbolic, the host machine itself will be the highest achievement of symbolic language—a software/hardware aggregate whose design and operation would be unthinkable without technologies of writing, and particularly of print. As the social theorist of science Donna Haraway [15] points out, analogues of writing lie at the heart of all advanced information technologies. The circuitry of computing machines is quite literally *printed* on the surface of micro-chips, and of course digital encoding is among the most powerful forms of symbolic communication yet imagined. Virtual realities will not be able to exist without their enabling cyberspaces; someone, after all, will have to program the world machines. But this programming, being a symbolic transaction or an act of writing, will not be visible or accessible in the post-symbolic environment of Jaron's world. Even more so than cinema and video, a post-symbolic, experiential medium would threaten literacy as we now understand it.

"Informating" Virtual Reality

Clearly this is a scare scenario, and before it turns into some kind of Luddite rant, let me put matters into perspective. Radical post-symbolism is only a tendency in the evolution of virtual reality, not its manifest destiny. As Bolter [5] observes, nothing prevents virtual real-ity from being used semiotically, as a medium for signs. While there will always be a tension between alienated and unalienated experience in this medium, it is by no means likely that one mode will dominate the other. Indeed, historical precedent stands against such an outcome. Television has not yet managed to wipe out print literacy, despite the worst efforts of *USA Today* and *Entertainment Tonight.* The annual de-mand for books has increased, not diminished, since the advent of broadcasting [16]. New media do not displace the old, rather all media are implicated in a continuing process of co-evolution. This is the real-ization that leads Ulmer [13], for instance, to propose a new theory of writing informed by the associative principles of video. It is also what drives much of the recent interest in text/graphic combinations [5] and interactive multimedia systems [17].

Virtual reality will not eradicate reading, writing, or verbal commu-nication of any sort. Rather, like other post-literate technologies, it will influence those practices and be influenced by them in turn. Users of virtual reality systems will no doubt continue to be alphabetically lit-erate in the present meaning of the term, and their designers will surely have to be. However, these builders and users may need types of sym-bolic and textual skills that go far beyond our present sense of literacy, and it is in this regard that virtual reality again presents a problem.

Even if the new technology does not threaten reading and writing, it might still contribute to a dangerous social trend—the attenuation of media expertise. Like cinema, radio, and television, the "electric media" in whose name McLuhan announced the death of the book, virtual reality greatly increases the demands placed on those who would be expert users or designers. This is part of a consistent pattern. Speech, the primal medium, is so fundamental that its acquisition (or some equivalent thereof) is considered part of full human development (etymologically, "infant" means *incapable of speech*). Command over alphabets, ideograms, syllabaries, and other writing systems is quite common but by no means universal; illiterates manage to survive even in so-called "advanced" societies. Mastery of mechanical writing, or print, is considerably less widespread. Until the invention of the typewriter and more recently the word processor, this technology could be used only by a small class of specialists and the people who employed them. Telephone, cinema, and broadcast technologies are still overwhelmingly controlled by these craft and capital elites.

In general, as communications media have grown more powerful, they have also become more complex in their workings, so that their population of expert users has become progressively narrower. We might represent media development in terms of a ziggurat or stepped pyramid, a series of smaller and smaller platforms capable of accommodating fewer high priests, each level consecrated to ever more arcane rituals. Virtual reality would represent the highest and newest level of the pyramid, the preserve of the most exclusive mysteries and the most elite wizards.

This metaphor contrasts sharply with descriptions of virtual reality as a democratic medium—the fantasy of users, in Richard Brautigan's phrase, "watched over by machines of loving grace" [18]. Lanier and other post-symbolists evoke a world where cybernetics clearly means power, not control, an object-oriented universe whose denizens could conjure up images and events at will. But such visions are disingenuous. In fact, any such simulated environment would presume an enormously intricate network of command and data structures—protocols, frames, neural nets, hyperwebs, expert systems—all of which would need, at least initially, to be designed and scripted. The complexity of the scheme increases greatly if we consider more rational projections of virtual reality, like David Gelernter's [19]. Gelernter's virtual world is filled with software agents, programs capable of adapting their structure and function. An agent is not a definite set of instructions, it is a self-reconfiguring executable text whose properties may differ radically over time. In such a bewilderingly complex environment, the cognitive demands of expertise would be staggering. Left to their own devices in a robust virtual universe, it is likely that only a few dedicated information scientists and reality hackers would adequately fathom its workings.

The simplistic, neoconservative response to this troublesome prospect is to reassert old technologies with a vengence. Enough of this post-symbolism, some say, let's return to forms of knowledge we know. They exhort us to restore print literacy as the standard of competence and citizenship (as in [20]). But this kind of blind reaction can be just as misguided as the sunshine scenarios of Jaron Lanier or Timothy Leary. Researchers who come to the problem of attenuated expertise with a broader understanding of technological history cast the problem in a more subtle and revealing light.

According to the sociologist of management Shoshana Zuboff [21], modern communications technologies, including computer-based systems, have been brought into industry primarily to serve the interests of automation. Automation may be thought of as applied cybernetics (in Wiener's sense), the use of information systems to keep processes on a productive course. Automating systems are feedback loops in which informational outputs are routed back into the circuit in order to modify performance. But automation is an old idea. Automating technologies evolved as competitive strategies in the early industrial age, when the volume of production was the most significant factor in business success. By contrast, the current business climate stresses quality over quantity, product development and adaptability rather than sheer numbers.

Studying management problems in this late-industrial context, Zuboff notices something about the feedback loop that Wiener never envisioned: the possibility that information generated by an automated system might be routed outside the system, to a level above the cybernetic circuit of homeostatic control. Zuboff calls this secondary or external flow of data "informating" [21, p. 10]. The difference between automating and informating is easy enough to illustrate in practice. When a tool and die works introduces electronically controlled, self-monitoring presses, it is automating. When managers in the works use performance data generated by the presses to adjust work schedules and production quotas, they are informating. Informating represents an important break with Wiener's old cybernetic paradigm, where control comes before communication and the feedback loop comprising the system and its users remains closed, as in the classical assembly line. In informating strategies, human decision-making is added back into the loop and informationally closed systems are reopened. Thus the attentuation of expertise is to some extent reversed, since equipment operators as well as managers are called on to assimilate and interpret data produced by their automated tools.

Zuboff applies her concept of informating technologies to industrial management, not the development of communications media, but it may be useful to extend her reasoning to this domain as well. If nothing else, the interplay of informating and automating strategies suggests that complex technologies need not always be deployed hieratically, in ways that restrict expertise about the system to a power elite. If some aspects of early virtual reality efforts reflect an automating bias—an inclination toward post-symbolism—there is at least the possibility of other approaches, such as Gelernter's "data parks" and "mirror worlds," in which the terms of the simulation are more open to interrogation.

In fact, a clear precedent exists for the evolution of interactive technologies along an informating rather than an automating path. Consider the case of artificial intelligence and hypertext. I have no interest in wading into the polemics about whether or not artificial intelligence works as promised [22, 23]. (Likewise, I make no special claims here for the utility of hypertext.) However, both sides of the AI debate would probably agree that so-called "strong" artificial intelligences and expert systems fit Zuboff's description of automating technologies. They are designed to manipulate information within a closed system, delivering output to their users without involving them directly in the deliberations. Hypertext systems, on the other hand, are much less ambitious: They simply articulate multiple possibilities for exploration within a textual domain, leaving the actual exploration to the user. In design and structure, hypertexts bear a certain resemblance to artificial intelligence constructs. As H. Van Dyke Parunak notes: "Hypermedia systems offer semantic richness of data storage comparable to that used in expert systems. In fact, a hyperdocument can be viewed as an expert system whose inference engine is not a computer but a human being" [24, p. 388]. In other words, hypertext resembles an AI in which the "I" is you.

An apparent technological regression is at work here, as if one were to build a manlike robot, then remove the insides to accommodate a human operator, turning it into a prosthetic Waldo. But the change here is really more progressive than regressive: The relationship between hypertext and artificial intelligence echoes the evolutionary linkage Zuboff describes between automating and informating technologies. If artificial intelligence was the early-industrial attempt to automate knowledge work, then hypertext represents a late-industrial revision of that strategy, reintroducing human agency into an enterprise that had previously tried to displace it. In at least one area of information technology, the tendency toward homeostatic cybernetic systems has been, if not reversed, then at least joined by an alternative.

Conceivably, a similar alternative might arise in the development of virtual reality; but what would an informating approach to virtual reality be like? Gelernter's ideas about mirror worlds provide a good basis for speculation. These simulated social spaces emphasize real-time dynamism and graphic representation, much like Lanier's consensual reality or Gibson's cyberspace, but in Gelernter's scheme these facilities operate symbolically, not as unanchored simulations. The cellular schematic of the city grid, which is my main window on the mirror world, is driven by data derived from the actual streets outside my actual window: alienated experience at its worst, or best. More to the point, Gelernter's scheme includes *agency,* the ability to create subprograms within the system to gather information, process data, or send messages by proxy. The mirror world is not just a model, it is a medium and a forum for civic discourse. Most important, it is a relatively transparent and reconfigurable medium. Citizens of a mirror(ed) world would be able to interact not just with the social reality beyond the representation, but with the terms of the representation itself—letting them enjoy the benefits of informating as well as automating.

If the development of interactive technologies follows this track, then we might expect a convergence of interests between virtual reality and advanced or "industrial strength" hypermedia development. Both these informating technologies face the same considerable challenge. As a research team from Boeing recently forecast: "A larger role for hypermedia requires eliminating the distinction between authors and readers. We assume that all members of engineering teams will be able to create and access information in a shared, distributed environment" [25, p. 15]. The creation of this environment is, of course, the primary problem for hypermedia as for virtual reality. But the problem of attenuated expertise remains to be solved as well. Our present forms and conventions of communication do not prepare us to dispense with the distinction between author and reader/user, especially when that merger calls on us to master a system as amazingly complex as a virtual world.

One answer to this problem may be found by striking a balance between informating and automating approaches, as in the concept of software agency. Extensions of the system may "know" the system in much greater detail than their users. It will be a great deal easier to act with authority within a complicated system if the system allows its users to delegate authority in some measure. However, users of hypermedia tools or citizens of mirror worlds will also have to function independently of cybernetic assistants, and for this they will need a new kind of intellectual preparation for the demands of these environments. We might call this facility *cybernetic literacy.*

Exactly what this concept could entail is hard to spell out at this early epoch of interactive technology. Certainly it includes "computer literacy" in the fundamental sense: acquaintance with programming languages and operating systems, especially of the object-oriented variety. But cybernetic literacy would also entail a richer understanding of informational control structures and the way they shape our interactions—in McLuhan's terms, a sensitivity to the media environments that surrounds us. McLuhan pointed to art in all its forms as a force acting to destabilize environments; for this reason, the print extrapolations of "cybernetic fiction" will continue to be important. Textual experimentation, as in hypertext and hypermedia, has a part to play as well. Literary theorists like Greg Ulmer and Jay Bolter are probably right to point out that we are much more likely to perceive the limits of current media if we stop thinking of literacy as exclusively an alphabetic or literary domain, taking it instead in the context of multiple, co-evolving technologies.

But above all, cybernetic literacy will have to contain an active and practical component, a willingness to intervene in complex and apparently closed systems. To this end, cybernetic literates will benefit from a solid measure of radical skepticism. They may need to rely on what the sixties called "paranoia," a faculty once defined as a "reflex of seeking other orders behind the visible" [27, p. 219]. Or, we might add, the virtual.

REFERENCES

[1] Gibson, William, *Neuromancer,* New York: Ace, 1984.
[2] Benedikt, Michael, *Cyberspace: The First Steps,* Cambridge, MA: The MIT Press, 1991.
[3] Rheingold, Howard, *Virtual Reality,* New York: Summit, 1991.
[4] Barlow, John Perry, "Scratching Your Eyes Back In: John Perry Barlow Interviews Jaron Lanier," *Mondo 2000* **2**, pp. 44–51, 1990.

[5] Bolter, Jay David, *Writing Space: Hypertext, the Computer, and the History of Writing.* Fairlawn, NJ: Lawrence Erlbaum Associates, 1991.
[6] McLuhan, H. Marshall, *Understanding Media: The Extensions of Man,* New York: McGraw-Hill, 1964.
[7] Wiener, Norbert, *Cybernetics: or Control and Communication in the Animal and the Machine,* Cambridge, MA: The MIT Press, 1948.
[8] Lyotard, Jean-François, *The Postmodern Condition: A Report on Knowledge,* trans. Geoff Bennington and Brian Massumi, Minneapolis: University of Minnesota Press, 1984.
[9] Prigogine, Ilya, and Isabelle Stengers, *Order Out of Chaos: Man's New Alliance with Nature,* New York: Bantam, 1984.
[10] McLuhan, H. Marshall, and Quentin Fiore, *The Medium is the Massage,* New York: McGraw Hill, 1967.
[11] Goody, Jack, *The Interface Between the Written and the Oral,* Cambridge: Cambridge University Press, 1987.
[12] Postman, Neil, *Amusing Ourselves to Death: Public Discourse in the Age of Show Business,* New York: Penguin, 1985.
[13] Ulmer, Gregory, *Teletheory: Grammatology in the Age of Video,* New York: Routledge, 1989.
[14] Cadigan, Pat, *Mindplayers,* New York: Bantam, 1987.
[15] Haraway, Donna, *Simians, Cyborgs, and Women: The Re-invention of Nature,* New York: Routledge, 1991.
[16] Horowitz, Irving Louis, *Communicating Ideas: The Crisis of Publishing in a Post-Industrial Society,* New York: Oxford University Press, 1986.
[17] McDaid, John, Breaking Frames: Hyper Mass-Media," in *The Hypertext-Hypermedia Handbook,* J. Devlin, E. Berk, Eds., New York: McGraw-Hill, pp. 445–58, 1991.
[18] Levy, Steven, *Hackers: Heroes of the Computer Revolution,* New York: Dell, 1984.
[19] Gelernter, David, *Mirror Worlds,* New York: Oxford, 1991.
[20] Hirsch, E. D., *Cultural Literacy: What Every American Needs to Know,* New York: Houghton Mifflin, 1987.
[21] Zuboff, Shoshana, *In the Age of the Smart Machine: The Future of Work and Power,* New York: Basic, Books, 1988.
[22] Bolter, Jay David, *Turing's Man: Western Culture in the Computer Age,* Chapel Hill, NC: University of North Carolina Press, 1984.
[23] Penrose, Roger, *The Emperor's New Mind: Concerning Computers, Minds, and the Laws of Physics,* New York: Oxford University Press, 1989.
[24] Parunak, H. Van Dyke, Toward Industrial-strength Hypermedia," in *The Hypertext-Hypermedia Handbook,* J. Devlin, E. Berk, Eds. New York: McGraw-Hill, pp. 381–396, 1991.
[25] Malcolm, Kathryn, Steven Poltrock, and Douglas Schuler, Industrial-strength Hypermedia: Requirements for a Large Engineering Enterprise," in *Hypertext '91 Proceedings,* P. D. Stotts, R. K. Furuta, Eds. New York: Association for Computing Machinery, pp. 13–25, 1991.
[26] Porush, David, *The Soft Machine: Cybernetic Fiction,* New York: Methuen, 1985.
[27] Pynchon, Thomas, *Gravity's Rainbow,* New York: Viking, 1973.

Chapter 5
The Creator's Toolbox

Brian R. Gardner
Apple Computer, Inc.
Cupertino, California
gardner@apple.com

Brian Gardner is another of that rare breed of artist-technicians. He has exhibited art in galleries on Boston's prestigious Newbury Street; he has worked in film and theater. In addition, he's one of the best hackers with whom I've ever had the pleasure of sharing a keyboard. We worked together a few years back and while we were waiting for those late-night compilations to finish, we often got into discussions of art and the virtually real. Gardner brings his unique viewpoint—that of an artist/creator—to this chapter.

—A.W.

Introduction

The use of artificial worlds in both computer art and virtual reality has suffered the same problems as motion pictures at their inception. Once the technical impressiveness wears off, what does one do? At one time people used to go to the cinemas to be amazed by a railroad train coming at them from the motion picture screen. The impact of the new visual experience was so great people even ran out of the theaters from fright. We see the same sense of amazement and impact today with the infancy of artificial worlds—especially in the goggle-roving of virtual reality landscapes. Soon the novelty of the effect will wear off, as it did in films. The environments will not only have to become more interesting, but they will have to convey things human, such as emotions, feelings, stories, relationships, companionships, and in-depth communications.

In the current generation of artificial worlds, simple artificial intelligence notions are being introduced to computer graphics to make more manipulatable and more interesting environments. Graphic objects called "actors" are introducing behavioral models into artificial worlds. Actors can react to a variety of events and stimuli. As happened in motion pictures, in the next generation of artificial worlds, the actors will have to act. In artificial worlds, however, not only will the "beings" have to act, but acting will be performed by the trees, the sky, and animate and inanimate objects. The "scenery" and "props" will have behaviors and interpretations, rather than being mere decorations.

Decades of artificial intelligence research have taught us that the most important step in problem solving is in the problem's definition and representations. In many ways, exploration of artificial world creation, the ideas involved, and the dilemmas they pose are the keys to computer art and the virtual realities that lie ahead. This chapter attempts to provide some experiences from film, art, perception, and artificial-world building that can help the designers of the next generation of artificial worlds produce environments that are useful as well as decorative.

Making a Good World—Learning from Art

How do you make a good artificial world? Some of the answers can be found in other fields of study.

What objects inside the world can make the environment interesting, can communicate things to people, and can even give emotional feel to the environment? In films such things are lighting, contrast, the composition of the scenes, and construction of scenery.

Many times, other things appearing in the world—for instance, the relationship of one object to another in the world—give a lot of information about the primary object that you would not otherwise obtain. For instance, in the 1771 portrait of Mrs. Ezekiel Goldthwait [1], the painter John Singleton Copley has depicted Mrs. Goldthwait sitting with her hand on a peach in a bowl of fruit. But the fruit is not merely present as a prop for the woman's hand. Rather, it is an icon symbolizing fertility. When the fruit is associated with the woman by tactile proximity, the anthropomorphic properties that people perceive about the fruitfulness are associated by the viewer with the woman, as a gestalt. The silks, satins, and lace of her attire associate her with wealth. The strong side lighting and dim background lighting draw the viewer's attention to her face and hands.

These perceptual associations are not so strange. People pick up a lot of rules as they go through life. Not necessarily hard and fast rules; people use a kind of fuzzy logic. When we see something, we relate it to other things. What we see in the picture is an insinuation that Mrs. Goldthwait is an abundant person—that she probably has much wealth and many children. The bowl of fruit was very popular in Copley's time, as were quill pens, books, flowers, and carefully chosen furnishings.

The same principle will apply if you see a couple of chess pieces or a chess board sitting beside someone. It implies that the person is logical, mathematical, or analytical. It gives a sign of a certain intelligence and logic. That's what the icon "means." If you were to put an icon, such as the chess piece, near other inanimate objects projecting any sort of iconic emotional feel, those emotional feelings will be combined in the image.

Proximity is an important property to take into account when building an artificial world. Gestalt psychology [2, 3] says that there are about five basic laws of *perceptual organization:* proximity, similarity, good continuation, closure, and common fate. Proximity is perhaps the strongest of these for artificial world creation, the others being grouped under the Prägnanz principles [3] governing figure perception. A gestalt is the perception of a whole entity or form, which is more than just the sum of its parts. In a gestalt, the relationships between the elements are more important than the details of the elements themselves. This emphasis on relationships also plays an important role in the rule-based systems of artificial intelligence.

Proximity is part of scene composition—how things are located in a visual presentation. It is important to remember that a person's viewing of the scene will be influenced by cultural factors, such as whether they are used to reading left-to-right or right-to-left, top-to-bottom or bottom-to-top. Studies show that in cultures which read left-to-right, images are also visually scanned in that order.

When I did special effects makeup, one of the effects I had to create was the Hunchback of Notre Dame. The hunchback's face was to be distorted on one side. The question that came up was, which side of Quasimodo's face do you distort? One side looks perfectly normal, the other side is deformed.

It turns out that the answer is "It depends on the image you want the character to project." If you distort the right side of the actor's face then, when projected, it appears on the left side of the screen. When viewing the screen, the first thing our audience sees of this character will be the distorted side of the face. If you want him to be a monstrous type of character, distorting the right side will cause the audience to see the monstrous side of him first, and the human side of him second. This gives him a much more frightening appearance than he would have if the face were done the other way.

On the other hand, if what you are aiming for is a film about human emotions and the injustices that are done to people who are different, then you distort the left side of the actor's face. The American viewer will scan the screen from left-to-right and top-to-bottom. When the hunchback's face is flashed up on the screen, the audience will see the most human side of him first. This perception is then followed by the fact that he's deformed. They will get the sense that this is a human being who is distorted—a disabled person, rather than a human monster. That is a fairly substantial difference.

Lighting in the artificial world is also very important. We pick up a lot of information from the lighting. Current artificial worlds have a pervasive, monotonous glare. Lighting reveals an artistic mastery in the creation of artificial worlds in many media.

In pictorial art, Rembrandt used lighting very effectively in his paint-ings. He used the high contrasts of side lighting, yet with very soft or halo edges, which yielded images that were emotional and striking. He would show a person's soft, sensitive side through the softness of the light, as in his self-portraits and his 1633 depiction of Jesus in "The Storm on the Sea of Galilee" [4]. Yet he was able to direct the viewer's attention though the light's contrast. Through the same spotlight-ing, the less important parts of the scene were left in the dark, deterring distraction.

Many famous filmmakers have used similar techniques. The lighting, particularly in films from the middle part of this century, was a key communicative component. 1930s and 1940s Hollywood used lighting to give a sense of who was a harsh person, who was a sensitive person, and to determine the whole overall tone of a scene. The ambiance and sense of place that Ridley Scott creates through lighting—to accentuate the attributes of decay, beauty, terror, hope, and wonder—are foremost in his films and commercial works. This mastery is largely responsible for winning Scott numerous awards, including the Hugo Award in 1982 for *Blade Runner.*

As an example, whether a scene was supposed to incite fright or not could be determined immediately from the lighting. Darkness provokes suspense and fright in viewers, because they cannot see what's coming next. There is more of a sense of mystery and terror. Alfred Hitchcock is famous for being able to scare people—to convey the sense of suspense and a thriller type of atmosphere—by *not* showing the perpetrator. He shows the victim and he insinuates the attacker, often through the direction of viewer attention. His primary visual tools for this are the camera's position and the scene's lighting.

Many horror and suspense films have used similar techniques. This veils the antagonist in mystery; being intangible to the audience, they cannot assess him. This makes him much more terrifying. If you could define exactly what he was, you could understand him. When people cannot understand something, it becomes the focus of interest and often of fear.

Often what is important in artificial worlds is not what you do put in the scene, but what you *don't* put in the scene. What you omit, but imply, through interrelationships is important. The most important things to include in an artificial world are those things that imply, or cause the direct perception of, the greater gestalt.

Making a Good World—Learning from Doing

Another aspect important to the creation of artificial worlds is acting. At Boston University in the mid-1980s, Marek Holynski, Rafail Ostrovsky, and I built a system called "Puppets' World" [5–8], described in detail in the next section. What we did was attempt to create an artificial world with a number of characters living in it. Our interactions with Puppets' World were managed by reasoning and ruled-based artificial intelligence programs.

When we enter into artificial worlds, it is only for a relatively brief period of time. We don't live in artificial worlds. We go into them from time to time for recreation or business. Whatever our purpose, we go in and we come out a little later. This cycle repeats.

Sometimes it is like a videogame type of situation, in which you really want to freeze time when you leave. That's fine, but at other times you want time to have kept moving while you were gone. If you start the world running and leave it going, it should be able to adapt.

Temporal reasoning should apply. If you leave a scene and come back later, there should be some kind of change to indicate that time has indeed passed.

You can think of an artificial world as a theatrical type of environment, in which you need all the support staff: the directors, the stage managers, the technical people. They can also help you create the artificial world. One of the problems with creating artificial worlds is information overload. It's the same problem as navigating in them. Such an enormous amount of data, programs, objects, and so on, go into the make-up of these artificial worlds that trying to manage all of them becomes very difficult.

One of the things you want to have is actors in the scene that are at the very least behavioral, so that they can take some limited action on their own. But you also want to have some kind of support staff. In my artificial worlds, I like to use actors in the truest possible sense of the word, where the objects are more than just behavioral—they may show some signs of a kind of artificial intelligence.

Puppets' World—The System

Puppets' World was an attempt to use a number of composition techniques from film, theater, and pictorial art in artificial world manipulation. Puppets' World constituted one of the early attempts to link artificial intelligence and computer graphics. It allowed the user to interactively create images of artificial worlds with computer interpretive assistance. The world was comprised of a number of objects in an environment and a knowledge base of abstract relationships between those objects, which could be used to compose a scene dynamically.

Puppets' World was built on top of Graflisp [9,10], a graphics package specifically created for artificial intelligence applications. As the name implies, Graflisp is written in Lisp and it contains a number of routines to do graphical pattern-matching, polygonal and functional rendering, ray tracing, radiosity, solid and surface texture mapping, and interactive and automated drawing facilities by means of a device-independent base. Graflisp was initially used for AI applications in the early 1980s, such as a handwriting generation program. In 1982, the ACM's Boston University chapter published the *Graflisp User's Manual* [9] for its ongoing Cybertoon cartooning project. Revised for Puppets' World in 1984–1985, *GRAFLISP: A Graphics Package Design for Artificial*

Intelligence Applications became my master's thesis [10]. From 1984–1989, Graflisp was further enhanced for perceptual research. The other major preexisting component we used was SNePS [11], the Semantic Network Processing System, which allowed us to hook in small networked knowledge bases, which "ran" Puppets' World.

The original Puppets' World had only one knowledge base. Later, we added knowledge bases to individual objects. We populated the world with a small number of puppets—originally just three: Jane, Bill, and Ron. There were two predefined places: "the house" and "the White House" (Ron being a puppet likeness of then-President Ronald Reagan). The system was also preprogrammed with a number of relationships among the objects in Puppets' World.

I later put a small natural language parser on the front end, which converted sentences into Lisp expressions. This allowed users to give commands like "Show me the home of Bill." Puppets' World worked on the model that the user was the director, or perhaps an artist, and the system was your assistant who had been with you for a while and had some idea of what you wanted.

For example, in response to the above user input, "Show me the home of Bill," the system would set off a chain of reasoning, which would go something like this: I know that a home is a house where a person lives. I know that Bill is a person. Therefore, check to see if Bill has a house. If the system were to find it, it would display that object. But if Bill doesn't have a house, it would extend the reasoning further, for example, to the knowledge that married people live in the same home. Is Bill married? Let's say that yes, Bill is married to Jane. Jane is a person. Does Jane own a house? If, so Bill's home is Jane's house.

Having located the object requested by the user, the system then puts the object into the scene. It then applies its scene composition rules involving positioning, orientation, and visibility. These rules are similar to those used to direct actors in their "blocking," or positioning on a stage. A separate set of rules, called *production rules,* is then carried out by a simple rule-based composition system. The two rule systems would use each other much like we use specialized consultants. Considering these rules, the system will position the house as close as it can to the viewer without cutting off the chimney or the front stairs, for example.

Essential related objects are then placed: perhaps a ground path from the user's point of view to the house, a grassy lawn, and a sky to give the scene the appropriate depth.

Once it has the house well situated, the system then considers the rest of the scene. Imagine that Bill's house is narrow, so the scene might have too much dead space on either side of the house. It then tries to fill the space with related objects. Bill, for instance, since Bill was in the direct initial query. It then checks the time of day—imagine that it is midafternoon when the query is made—and asks "Is Bill home?" If not, Bill cannot be put in the picture. This is a form of *temporal reasoning.*

Derived objects—those that have been used in the chain of reasoning—are considered next. The system uses their proximity to the ends of the chain of reasoning as the ordering for the objects' implied relevance to the scene. For instance, Jane was considered just before, and leading to, the discovery that her house was to be the main object of the scene. The system next considers "Can Jane be put in the picture?" and "Is Jane at home at this time of day?" If so, Jane can be added to the scene. Then the next problem is reasoned: "Where should Jane be placed in the picture: to the left side or right side of the house?"

Puppets' World knows that the people who use the system read left-to-right and top-to-bottom, and that they will read pictures the same way. Whichever object is put on the left will be seen before the one on the right, as discussed earlier.

The system then checks its model of the user who made the query. This model is largely constructed from user-supplied information, though these may be supplemented by inferences derived during an interaction session [12–14]. If it was Rafail—my co-creator, who thinks that architectural structures are very interesting—the system would decide to put the house on the left side. But if I was using the system, my profile indicates that I find people are more interesting than buildings, so it would put Jane to the left of the house.

Having placed a new object, it adjusts the scene, reapplying the rules of composition. So Jane is moved as close to the viewer as possible without moving her out of the house's yard or causing her extremities to be cut off by the edges of the user's field of view. Since the time of day has been determined, it places the sun in the appropriate part of the sky, textures the grass to give the correct appearance for the scene depth [15], applies the appropriate shading and shadows, ray traces any parts of the image necessary, Z-buffers the rest, and renders the 3-D solids into a visual scene.

In later versions, we implemented the ability to lay down other objects that were subordinate to the major objects, such as putting trees into the yard. We added rules about how much of the major objects could be occluded by the subordinate objects. These rules were based on how important the object was in relation to the question the user had asked that had caused the scene to be built.

For example, one rule held that if an object was a key object in a query (such as the house) it should not be occluded at all. Another rule held that a secondary, derived object (such as Jane in the above example) could not be occluded by more than 25%, while objects added purely for appearance's sake (such as the lawn) could be occluded to any percentage necessary.

This allowed the system to add more "frivolous" objects such as trees and shrubbery or streets to give a more realistic appearance to the image, without having to worry about obscuring the important objects. These rules were combined with more sophisticated reasoning about dead space, and use of spatial depth, to allow the system to fill in the background of a scene realistically.

Later versions also added more objects to the world, and more rules about scene composition. This allowed the derivation of more interesting scenes, without requiring the user to increase the complexity of their query. To carry our example one step further, we repeat the same query after 5:00 P.M. the same day. At this time, the knowledge base indicates that Bill would likely be home. Consequentially, the temporal reasoning recommends that the scene's empty space be filled by posing both Bill and Jane with the house. The system uses its new artistic rules about the compositional balance of scenes to place one of the figures on each side of the house.

In summary, Puppets' World emphasized the ability of a system to reason about user preferences, scene composition, temporal reasoning (by considering the time of day of its users), and spatial reasoning. It also allowed us to experiment with tying small knowledge bases directly to graphic objects, with an emphasis in the knowledge base on rules derived from artistic and psychological principles, instead of the usual physical and diagnostic modeling. This is not to say one should ignore scientific or physical modeling, but we felt that if we didn't include the "human factor," or attempt to enable the "artistic aspects," then the world would become boring too quickly. Finally, we were able to generate and compose custom-made artificial scenes, in response to user queries. We did this successfully, even in instances such as "Show me the home of Bill," when the only actual object directly named in the query ("Bill") should not always be displayed. The system can deduce the meaning of the user's query and correctly display the scene's inferred objects.

Puppets' World—Differences from Art

Although Puppets' World used photographic and artistic principles, there were major differences from traditional art because Puppets' World was an interactive artificial world. In films, a scene is typically linear and sequential. A lot of effort is put into the layout of the sequence, because you know that the camera is only going to see things from one particular view. However, in artificial worlds, this is not the case.

Now, instead of the emphasis being on the sequential aspects of the scene, the emphasis is on the environment that is going to be explored. The environment is going to be seen at different points in time, from different points of view. People will be able to move through it and experience it from different angles and different perspectives.

So the construction of the set becomes more important, as do the relationships between the objects. Your "set designer" has to know how to construct scenes for people to go through, rather than just look at. The false fronts used in most movies will not work. Such "crew" members, when implemented as knowledge-based computational mechanisms like the scene composer of Puppets' World, are called *agents.*

Once the scene is built, the user becomes the cameraman. Different users will go through the scenes with different interests. Movies are intended for large audiences, but once computing time becomes cheap enough, we can easily foresee having artificial worlds created for only one person.

It is important, though, to strike a balance between which rules can be broken and which cannot, even for one person. For instance, in art, one can go into fields like impressionism or surrealism, which take "reality" and warp it. They bend or change the rules; they construct new rules. But this works only because the artist is careful about which rules to break and which not to break.

The rules about scene composition and object relationships can be changed. Those that were built into the controlling knowledge base of Puppets' World were derived from general psychological and art-theoretic literature, but any set of consistent composition rules could have been used instead.

However, one must take into account those rules of perception that have evolved into the human genetic pattern or formed by a lifetime of learning. Gravity, or the cues used for depth perception, or the fact that the human retina is more sensitive to vertical and horizontal lines than to diagonal lines are all facts that cannot be ignored. These kinds of factors must influence the building of the artificial world so that people will be able to interact with the scene.

Of course, it is literally possible to ignore these rules, but by doing so you risk reducing your viewer's visual understanding to chaos—rendering him or her unable to have any useful interaction with the world. Worse, the ill effects are generally more strongly felt in the more immersive media than in traditional artistic media. Disorientation, confusion, headaches, mild nausea, and boredom are some of the reactions to artificial world interactions that omit or have conflicting key perceptual information. Indiscriminately breaking rules is seldom wise in artificial world creation or interaction.

One advantage of working in the realm of interactive worlds rather than still art is that the rules about user preferences can be determined on the fly by observing the user's interactions with the system. If the user requested something the system did not know how to construct, it could present a number of alternatives that might under some interpretation fulfill the request. The user could then pick one alternative and indicate if it was sufficiently close or not.

A *rule acquisition* system [12, 13] could observe these choices and record the values for the parameters it had varied to generate the alternatives. Once several values had been noted, the system would begin to generalize user preferences. For example, it could deduce users' favorite colors, favored styles of architecture, favorite angles, preferences for terrain types, preferred rendering styles, and so forth. Moreover, after interacting with many users, it can deduce preferences among groups of users by correlating those responses with the user's occupation, gender, social grouping, or geography. The rule acquisition system will then create new rules, based on its observations and deductions, and add them to the knowledge base. Subsequent new users can then start using the system with an intelligently chosen set of default rules.

Typically, the system will find rules that are generally true, but not true 100% of the time. These rules are stored along with a confidence value. This value is used during the reasoning process, as a weighting factor. The style of inferencing that uses these non-Boolean values is called *fuzzy logic*. A rule acquisition system is a form of learning system, and can be a key piece of technology underlying artificial world manipulation.

The sorts of parameters the system is able to vary—and therefore deduce user preferences about—are largely a function of the world and the objects in it. Today, the more sophisticated the artificial world, the more difficult it becomes to determine which parameters it should represent and analyze. Unfortunately, more research is needed to derive general user preference principles and a standard perceptual parameter set for use across large numbers of different artificial worlds.

The Next Step—Comprehending the Generated World

A major problem with existing artificial worlds is that they can only be experienced from one perspective at a time. In a large, complex world this can mean that many users will never find things of interest to them. The larger the world and the more users in it, the more significant this problem will become. Fortunately, there are solutions to this problem. One such solution is the idea of "invisible cameramen." Remember that we want to view an artificial world as being populated with a kind of theatrical support staff.

Frequently, a creator must travel the artificial world under various stages of construction, trying to figure out what type of world they wish to create or, for that matter, what type of world they've already created (which has happened to me quite a bit.) One often wants to discover what pieces of the world are the interesting bits. "Interesting" may have different meanings for different people or for the same person at different times.

One proposal is that we give the user the ability to create invisible cameramen. You can think of these as people who travel through the environment that has been created and try to analyze it based on what the user is looking for. These agents can also analyze potential environments that are yet to be created by sifting through the parameters that would describe those worlds.

At the same time, you do not want the cameramen who are going through the world to affect that world. You want them to be invisible to the environment and to the occupants of the environment. This ensures that the information they are collecting and analyzing is not corrupted by the analysis process.

These cameramen can also be useful for navigation. The user can send off several invisible cameramen, each with different representations of what "interesting" means. The cameramen can then return images of potentially interesting things, the location of these things, and directions on how to get there.

Exploring Fractal Space—An Implementation of Invisible Cameramen

Fractal geometry [16] is an area of abstract mathematics that focuses on geometries with fractional dimensions. While many people believe our environment to be based on integer dimensions, such as a three-dimensional space and a one-dimensional time, abstract mathematics is not confined to the integer dimensioned euclidean geometry typically used in modeling our world.

Indeed, fractal geometries have been so successful at modeling difficult natural shapes and phenomena that some scientists are now extending the base assumptions about our environment to include fractional dimensions. Some of the natural shapes to be successfully modeled by fractal geometry include coastlines, rivers, lightning, continental shapes, clouds, plants, and mountains [17]. Disregarding the arguments about fractal geometry's applicability to the real world, its success in modeling natural phenomena makes fractal algorithms very important in the creation of many artificial worlds.

In recent years, fractals have become very popular in American computer art. Perhaps the best known fractal imagery is of the *Mandelbrot set.* When depicted, this set has the appearance of a sideways pinched heart-like shape, with extremely complex, rough edges, and is often brightly colored. The colors typically represent both the body of points "in" the set (inside the pinched heart shape), and bands of colored potential energies representing the degree to which a point is "out" of the set.

The Mandelbrot set was discovered by Benoit Mandelbrot in the late 1960s, and can be thought of as a map to an infinite series of *Julia sets.* All of the Julia sets could be collectively thought of as a series of image slices through a fractal space. Like many fractals, both the Mandelbrot and Julia sets create complex shapes and images through the recursion of a very simple equation.

One of the problems with fractal worlds is that there is an infinity of possible things to look through. Some of this infinity is interesting—but only a very small fraction of it. Of course, what is interesting can vary by viewer. However, nearly everyone is interested in features other than an unbroken or slightly broken expanse of empty space, which covers much of the outer range of the Julia sets. Since fractals can be easily parameterized, they are amenable to building visual detectors, like the "interest" detectors discussed earlier. For this reason, fractal space exploration was an ideal testbed for using invisible cameramen.

An invisible cameraman was created to sort through this space. It was limited to an area of Julia space, which would include abstract lightning bolt-like forms, scattered islands, self-similar shapes, or by relatively simple shapes, such as deformed ellipses. The cameraman was given rules about image complexity, scene space, closure, and symmetry. Generally, the more complex the image, the more interesting it was to view. Certain types of symmetry were of interest. Closures roughly correlated to object-ness. The final parameter of interest was the amount of scene space taken up by the set's dominant shape. It is important to remember that this is not an absolute for what is interesting; rather, it is what I wanted this one cameraman to "believe."

Having set a region of space and some rules for interest, the cameraman went through the variations of the Julia sets and collected 50 images. Ten of these were the ones chosen by the cameraman as the most interesting. The extra 40 images served as a control group, for comparison's sake. The result was that the 10 images selected by the cameraman were in fact the most interesting images of the 50. The one downside of this process was that 5 of the 10 best were very similar, but this was due to the natural symmetries in the fractal space of the Julia sets.

It turned out that "interesting" for a Julia set happened to map to the initial complex point as chosen very close to the edge of, but not in, the Mandelbrot set. "Boring" is a point that is inside the Mandelbrot set or very far outside the set. Other factors, such as proximity to the x axis or origin, also correlated interest to the selection of the initial complex point constant. In short, one could predict an interesting Julia set by looking solely as its Mandelbrot set–related parameters.

It was later possible to add rules for the invisible cameraman to look only at the Mandelbrot set–derived parameters, which described each potential Julia set image prior to creation. These invisible cameramen can be especially useful in building an artificial world. They can be sent out before and after some parameter of the world is changed as a feedback mechanism.

In summary, I was able to prove that we can have agents that go out and search through the space—the artificial world—for us. Although I only used 1 invisible cameraman with one set of rules, it is easy to imagine sending out 5 or 10 such cameramen to search an artificial world for you, each with a different idea of what is interesting to them. Then, they will come back with information they deem most interesting to you. This is a useful tool for navigating artificial worlds.

Visual Perception—Making Navigable Worlds

When creating artificial worlds, we wish to enrich them with properties that will be pleasant to view and easy to navigate. But what makes a world easy to navigate? To discover this, we have to look at how people perceive images in real life—better yet, how people perceive the real world in real life. If we look at the psychology of visual perception, there are basically three different theories.

There is the traditional sense of perception, often called *constructivism* [18], which basically holds that light from the world comes in, strikes your retina, and creates a complex mosaic. Out of this chaos, the eye reconstructs the objects and the environment of the world. Traditional "bottom-up" computer science approaches to vision take this approach. It takes an image, the "mosaic," and treats it simply as an array of intensities for processing. Typically, the processing begins with edge detection on the image, and proceeds through a number of indirect representational stages. These usually include parsing the edges, grouping into surfaces, and then attempting to deduce the objects in the scene, often through recognition using object representations stored *a priori*. The object parsing process is called *image segmentation* and sometimes involves an intermediate *2 1/2-D sketch* [19]. When done, it could figure out what was in the environment depicted and try to understand what is happening in the scene. This is always left as an "exercise for the reader."

Early in this century, a new style of perceptual psychology emerged, *Gestalt psychology*. In contrast to constructivism, Gestalt psychology holds that the whole is more than just the sum of its parts. This whole is called the *gestalt*. Gestalt tries to use theories, relating to electro-magnetic field theories of the early 1930s, to group image elements into objects.

Even more recently, in the 1940s and 1950s, a new form of perceptual psychology has emerged, called *ecological optics*. This is also called *Gibsonian theory*, named after its founder James J. Gibson [15, 20, 21]. This theory denies that perception is based on decoding a complex mosaic on the retina; instead, the eye detects things that are invariant in the environment. These *perceptual invariants* are things that hold true over long periods of time. They are features of the environment that our visual system has evolved and attuned to over millions of years.

Some of the biological mechanisms that detect these invariants are innate at birth; others are adaptive mechanisms which attune themselves to the invariants during infancy [22]. It seems likely that similar adaptive mechanisms exist in life-long learning. Many of Gibson's invariants are based on an organism's ability to move and interact with its environment. Gibson even proposed that many of these environmental invariants may be directly perceived, without requiring an image segmentation stage.

Constructivist psychology appears to explain some of the low-level mechanical details of the retina and ganglion, but clearly does not account for human cognitive behavior. In artificial worlds—where we must deal with a moving world that demands action and exploration—Gibsonian theory seems to best explain interactive human perception.

This theory reminds us that it is not necessarily better to throw more graphics techniques, more rendering power, or more artificial intelligence into a scene. These are not necessarily going to give us a better artificial world. The quantity of what goes into your artificial world is not what makes it better or more interesting—it is the quality of what goes into it.

What defines quality for this activity are these environmental invariants, which drive the human perceptual system. We can think of it as though the levels of detail had a weighting system attached, telling us how important that *type* of detail is or that *level* of detail. If these details are not associated with perceptual invariants, then the weighting factor is small. Often you can remove certain kinds of detail from an image and people cannot perceive the difference.

On the other hand, if the detail has a tight link to some kind of perceptual invariant, then the weighting factor is high. For example, if you are standing in a room (which you very well may be as you are reading this) on some flat, level surface, take a look around. How do you judge the distance from where you are to any other point on the floor, or any other object standing on the floor? How far away is it?

Conventional perceptual psychology asserts that you determine that by *stereopsis*. Stereopsis uses the visual disparity between the images reaching each of your eyes as a depth cue. However, stereopsis is only good over relatively small distances [23]. So if the object is at a distance, stereopsis will not help. In addition, a small percentage of the population is *stereoblind*—they cannot fuse the two images from their eyes at all, often caused by amblyopia or early binocular deprivation. According to studies on stereoblindness, about 30% of the population has some kind of stereo incapacity [19, 24–26]. In virtual reality, these problems are compounded by aliasing artifacts of raster imaging [27,28] and the limited image resolution used to present the disparity information, both of which have only been addressed for the monocular case by present computer graphics research.

Stereopsis does not account for distance perception. A vast number of animals have little or no binocular overlap, and hence have not developed stereopsis. People experience depth when viewing most movies without stereoscopic imaging. Using elliptical projection movie screens, theme park viewers can even experience VR-style immersion by using only monoptic cues. In addition, stereopsis is known to be a *relative depth* cue. For stereo vision to be used for *distance perception* would require a metric, such as the distance between the eyes, for which the human body does not provide a sensor. As a quick experiment, try walking around, actively moving and grabbing with one eye covered— the more you move, the less relevant is your lack of stereo vision. So, even though stereopsis may be important, it is only an optional compliment to many other important depth cues [29].

What are the key cues to put into an artificial world to make it more navigable and perceptually rich for depth and distance? Gibsonian psychology points to perceptual invariants that enrich our depth and distance perception. Many of the invariants relate to the ever-existent, textured, ground surface of our environment. For example, you can see that the floor is textured. It may be a very structured texture, such as you see on a rug or tiles, or it may be stochastically textured. Human eyes have great acuity, and can even see the microtexture in monochrome floors. This *ground theory* reveals how much of our perception of depth and distance in our environment relates to the textured ground surface, through texture gradients, texture flow fields, texture accretion and deletion, texture motion parallax, texture perspective, and invariants relating to the horizon line.

The ground surface has a *texture gradient.* If you examine a region of the visual field when viewing the ground, the number of texture elements projected into the region increases as you view the ground further away. In fact, there is an invariant ratio for the number of texture elements per projected area to their distance. Under simple projective geometry, when a texture element's distance is doubled, its projected height is halved. This results in a continuous gradient of ground texture, by which distances can be perceived. At the point where an object touches the ground, the ground's texture yields direct perceptual information about its distance to the viewer. Geometrically, a subsequent comparison of an object's texture gradients to the ground's texture gradient can yield information about the object's surface orientations.

Looking straight down, one can see the number of texture elements per human "foot," one of the calibration metrics people have available in their visual world. Gibson describes in some detail other self-supplied calibration metrics used in visual perception for *egoloco-motion,* such as the nose, head, and limbs [21]. These exemplify the usefulness of a visual sense of self when creating interfaces to artificial worlds. Currently, most virtual reality interfaces represent only the hands, if anything, for visual representation of self. To the best of my knowledge, no one has represented the user's feet for calibrating ground texture or even the user's own nose (arguably, the most viewed object in a person's visual experience) for self-perception in a virtual reality interface. This distinguishes *immersion* from *inclusion,* which, respectively, give the feelings of being surrounded by the other world and being part of its environment.

Texture gradient transformations caused by egolocomotion are also a source of invariants. When you move forward, all the texture flows away from the point towards which you are moving. This directly perceived stable point and *texture flow* patterns in the visual field enables extremely accurate goal-based navigation. Closer objects and textures move faster than those further away. This *motion parallax* offers the same invariant perspective-based ratio as before, but for flow speed. This allows direct information about the slants of the surfaces, deformations of the ground plane, and depth.

The motion parallax of objects in the world also offers a strong perception of depth, surface shape, and scene layout. Motion parallax is of particular importance, especially in current VR worlds lacking in texture. Even simple objects offer enough motion parallax for good navigation. Optical flow is a key issue for artificial world navigation. In VR, unlike in the real world, self-controlled human flight is a very common means of transportation. The invariants of optical flow patterns are a key means of visual navigation of birds and pilots, particularly during take-off and landing.

Due to the lag time of many current VR head position sensors and the low-end rendering systems, the user sees the stable point and optical flow lagging behind during head turns and course corrections. This forces the user to move slowly in current VR systems to minimize confusion and avoid motion sickness. After completing a virtual reality session, the user often exhibits the aftereffects of this adapted behavior for several minutes.

The key to navigating artificial worlds is in the ecological invariance that the creator implants in the environment. The strongest invariants are the ratios, gradients, calibration references, and optical flows tied to motion parallax, surface texture, the ground plane, and ego perception. By enabling the same perceptual invariants that people use to navigate the real world, the creator can construct a world that encourages exploration.

Ecological Optics—Getting Inanimate Objects to Act

Enabling objects in motion to portray human emotional traits is not too difficult. There are texts on human acting [30] and animation texts [31, 32] on getting objects to act—most of which have to do with anthropomorphizing the objects and their physics. But there is also the question "How do you get inanimate objects to act?" In an artificial world, you want the objects, like the actors, to have acting capabilities. To achieve that, you have to consider what it is that makes something look a certain way. In other words, how can you tell the internal state of an object based on its outside? For example, what makes an object "honest looking"?

There are many invariants used by the visual system. Many of these are based on forces such as gravity, growth, animal motion, fluid flow, wind, and weather. Others are based on other ecological properties of the environment, such as light and heat from the sun, inter- and intraobject relationships, air content, water content, and soil content.

These forces and properties cause transformations in our environment. For each of these transformations, there are mathematical relationships that remain invariant to these transforms, some of which are used by our perceptual system.

Many of these perceptual invariants relate to the *affordances* of objects. Affordances have direct meaning for us as to the uses an object may have [21]. For example, the resistance of a surface to deformation, its *viscosity,* tells us if the surface will support our standing on it, be difficult to run on, encourage falling into, allow sitting in, disallow biting into, or enable drinking. An object's resistance to disintegration, dependent on its *cohesion,* can tell us if the object is useful for building with, how long it may last, or give an estimate of its current age. It is possible that the affordances of nature may be recognized by an invariant similar to the Hausdorff measure [16] for fractals, roughness, and hue (color) distributions.

It is extremely common in daily life to perceive objects and their affordances correctly, without knowing or perceiving their physical components. You can see a barrier and recognize it as a picket fence, but not know how many pickets you are viewing. One can recognize a forest and the shelter it provides, yet not know the many subspecies, shapes, or number of trees in view. When asked questions like "How many desks and chairs are in this classroom?," "How many wooden panels on that wall?," and "How many letters in this paragraph?"—the initial answers are usually "Many," "A lot," "I don't know," and "Who cares!" Even after exerting effort, many people either still do not know, or come up with conflicting answers. However, the recognition of these things and what they afford us is instantly obtained, even at a quick glance.

Using perceptual invariants, we are directly perceiving the greater gestalt, bypassing the traditionally assumed object-segmentation of its components. For artificial world creation, this makes simulation of real-life physics less important than the ecological- and perceptual-based representations for communication of affordances. This implies that the impact, and even the perceived realism, of objects in an artificial world is not necessarily tied to computing time. Computational-saving alternative physics may be used successfully in artificial world generation.

The affordances communicated by perceptual invariants, however, surpass just the physical affordances of objects. Consider that emotions, behaviors, and personal actions may be viewed by others as social affordances. These social affordances may be visually communicated through their associated perceptual invariants. When these socially related invariants are imposed on an inanimate object, we anthropomorphize that object and associate those social affordances with it.

Remember that we began this section with questions of how to get inanimate objects to "act." In theater, the fields of acting, make-up, lighting, props, and directing are all focused on changing the audience's perception of the actor to that of perceiving the character. This is achieved by the actor projecting perceptual information that communicates the character's social affordances over time, such as their emotional state, trustworthiness, naivete, age, class and personality. Applying Gibson's theories, acting is really the process of an actor re-presenting the perceptual invariants that communicate the essence of the character being portrayed.

For example, caricatures and cartoons are an effort to take all the detail in an image that is not communicating, throw it away, and emphasize the detailing that is relevant. You can exaggerate different aspects of a cartoon in order to bring out some perceptual invariant, which is in turn going to bring out some human trait.

The inanimate objects of artificial worlds can be made to act by representing and displaying the same perceptual invariants associated with traits to be portrayed. For instance, you may want your trees to look happy, sad, honest, naive, embittered, stark, or young. These parameters are not those represented in a typical physically based simulation. For inanimate objects to act, they must first have an internal representation that supports *associations* among their physically based parameters and their related perceptual invariants. Second, they must be able to access and utilize these relationships under somewhat autonomous action to be considered "acting."

Using Ecological Optics—The GenWorld System

To a large extent, the use of perceptual invariants can be programmed into the system. Textures, texture gradients, linear perspective, aerial perspective, motion parallax, ego modeling, physical modeling, and fractal algorithms can be part of the graphics and animation system. While this enables the techniques, there are still the issues of acting and knowledge representation. How would we go about using the knowledge of perceptual invariants to create scenes? How would we represent such knowledge for objects to act autonomously?

To try and address this question, I built the GenWorld system, which was very similar to the semantic-network-based system used in Puppets' World. GenWorld was also built on top of Graflisp. It used deductive rule retrieval on its knowledge bases and an object-based system to store its knowledge. This allowed knowledge to be inherited through subclassing, similar to the way in which initialized class variables are inherited in current object-oriented systems.

The system was organized into trees of knowledge. These hierarchies were supported by an object-oriented system called ASK, which had the usual *class-based inheritance.* You could classify types of objects and inherit rules about those types of objects. For example, humans would inherit all the rules that were associated with sapiens, which inherited all the rules associated with animals.

ASK also allowed *instance-based inheritance,* which was more isomerous with the hierarchical objects and scene structures of computer graphics. Objects related to each other as instances of a particular system might inherit aspects of that system, such as knowledge bases and preferences. For example, your hand is attached to your wrist, which is attached to your forearm, and so on; all often share common colors, goals, personality, and body language characteristics. These traits and general rules can either be specific to an object, or can be shared with all of that object's subobjects. This inheritance could be controlled so that the traits would be inherited for only a limited number of subobjects in the hierarchy. Additionally, by means of a kind of fuzzy logic, rules could fade over distances.

In a scene, each tree, rock, mountain, or landscape might be part of the object hierarchy of that place. Using ASK, these subobjects could be subject to a controlled sharing of traits, which could govern the perceptual impact of the environment. This allows the creator to specify the mood, artistic style, and chromatic energy of a scene. This inheritance was controlled at the instance level rather than the class level.

The ASK system was able to handle both types of inheritance and was able to handle rules in the same way. For example, you could assign rules to either abstract objects or specific graphical objects. An abstract object could be a thought or series of thoughts. Certain types of thoughts could be classified. Graphical objects were things like wrists, hands, forearms, sky, and mountains. Rules could also be assigned to classes of objects, such as animals, plants, minerals, mammals, reptiles, grasses, rocks, and trees. Forces, constraints, and properties could also be classified and there could be instances of each.

You could associate rule-based knowledge with each of these objects. This was tied to a small expert system, based on a system called Otto [33]. An artificial expert would operate in conjunction with a constraint-based system. In a *constraint-based system,* the creator specifies relationships between objects by imposing constraints between them that the system will attempt to maintain automatically. When a problem was underconstrained, the artificial expert was used to add appropriate constraints to the situation until it was solvable.

This expert system was initially used in a colorizing system I wrote and later ported to GenWorld for use in creating artificial worlds. To generate objects automatically, whether simple things like page layouts or complicated things like artificial worlds, you also want to pick colors automatically to generate a visual effect, such as scariness, ugliness, or pleasantness. These effects have a lot to do with colors and how colors are combined.

One could add constraints such as "this object's color is related to that object's color" by a relationship like "opposites." Or you could add a constraint to say that a color was "pastel" by constraining the amount of saturation a color could have. By using classes of constraining tools, one could control the ranges and relationships between colors of objects. These constraining tools behaved like strings, nails, force-fields, paths, slide-planes, rods, and springs. The system used *hill-climbing* and *simulated annealing* to resolve the set of constraints and yield the optimal set of colors.

Hill-climbing involves taking each of the parameters and moving it in each possible direction to see which is best. This is similar to climbing a hill while blindfolded. You take a test step in each direction, then take whichever direction seems to bring you closer to the top. You repeat this procedure until you get to the top of the hill. In artificial intelligence, hill-climbing is much the same, but the steps are taken along some parametric dimension.

Annealing is a chemical process that occurs when a crystaloid is heated then cooled to form crystals. During real annealing, the molecules converge on the optimal crystal formation by moving around in decreasingly smaller amounts. Simulated annealing is like annealing, but jiggles parameter values rather than molecule locations. Unlike hill-climbing, annealing uses variable step sizes.

The system used these techniques to try to resolve the imposed constraints. The creator and the semantic network would impose the initial constraints. If the problem turned out to be underconstrained and it was not possible to come up with a direct answer, the expert system would come in and tame the situation by adding artistically compatible constraints until it was solvable.

Even during automatic object creation, the rules and constraints governing objects, the relationships among their colors, and the user's preferences could be taken into account. For example, for locations in the artificial world of interest to a particular user, his or her known favorite color could be used as the base color for a scene. The other objects would then change themselves to colors that relate to that base color, or that relate to other objects' colors that relate to the base color. Similarly, during artificial world creation, an object created in a gloomy location would assimilate gloomy colors.

This expert system was carried over into GenWorld and combined with the object-inheritance subsystem and the constraint-based subsystem. With a knowledge of colors and their psychological impacts, objects could colorize themselves to affect their perceived persona. Objects that used these semiautomatic, knowledge-based, self alterations were called SABs (Semiautonomous Beings). SABs were a first technological step in getting graphical objects to "act."

Lessons for Artificial Worlds

Knowledge inheritance turns out to be very useful in creating artificial worlds and is tied strongly to perceptual invariants. For instance, the strongest relevant perceptual invariant for artificial worlds is gravity. Humans have grown up with gravity—it's a fact of life that we experience with all physical objects. Humans are constrained to walking on surfaces because of gravity. Objects are in part positioned, oriented, and shaped by the effects of gravity, submitting to it or fighting against it. The shapes of growing things are altered by gravity. Object extremities may droop from its pull. Fluids will level under it. Gravity's effects are ecologically pervasive, as are the invariants it spawns.

Consider some of the perceptual appearances related to gravity. Age is an obvious one. If you want something to appear older (or younger) you can do this by changing the way gravity appears to affect it. While this is true for realworld actors, it is even more so for the highly malleable actors of artificial worlds. It is also the key to enabling inanimate artificial objects to act.

Perceptual studies by James Todd and his colleagues found that the perception of craniofacial aging, specifically of the bone structure of the face, could be mathematically determined through what was known as a *cardioidal strain* [34]. It is called cardioidal strain because of the heart-shaped forms associated with this type of transformation. These strains occur around the growth centers of the facial bones. The basic explanation is that as something approximately spherical grows outward, under the influence of gravity it begins to take on a heart shape. The older something is, the more of a heart shape it will have.

In human faces, the growth upward from the head's center toward the top of the head is opposed by gravity, so upward growth is inhibited; but the growth downward toward the chin is in the same direction as gravity, so the forces combine and enhance downward growth. This result of this is that the older the face, the more elongated it appears in the bottom half, compared to the top. All the ratios measuring facial features also alter with time, in the same vertically asymmetric pattern.

If you create an object in an artificial world by using the force direction of gravity, the object's gravity counteraction strength, and force origins as creation parameters, then you cannot only age things such as faces, but you can also age any inanimate object in an anthropomorphic manner. In fact, one of the subsequent cardioidal strain experiments took a cartoon Volkswagen and applied the cardioidal strain. Viewers consistently reported the resulting cartoon as depicting an older Volkswagen. When the transformation was inversed, viewers perceived a caricature of a baby Volkswagen.

These transformational invariances extend much further than just aging; in another study at Brandeis [35], researchers attempted to find out if invariants related to facial appearances were responsible for perceptions of social affordances. It turned out that there was a strong correlation between the same parameters—the spacing of the eyes, the distance of the eyes from the top of the forehead and from the chin, and so forth. The same invariants of the cardioidal strain transformation that are used to perceive aging also apply to whether or not someone looks honest.

The studies show that there is a correlation; the hypothesized reason is that we have learned some correlation between age and honesty.

Young children are painfully honest—they say the darndest things. As part of growing up, they learn to lie and as they get older, they get better at lying. As part of our life experience, we pick up on such correlations, subconsciously forming generalized rules and stereotypes.

Whether or not someone is perceived to be honest can be tied to their perceived age and age-related features. In the same way that a stage actor might portray a dishonest character by hunching his shoulders, shortening the neck, narrowing his nose, and elongating his jaw, we can manipulate the gravity-related forces, counterforces, and parameters to control whether something is honest looking or not. Further, gravity and age-related effects on facial qualities are shown to affect the perception of such social affordances as warmth, submissiveness, honesty, physical strength, and naivete [35].

This demonstrates the usefulness of programming perceptual invariants into artificial worlds. As predicted by the ecological approach, they are heuristic in nature, not always correct, and sometimes quite overgeneralized, but they are commonly used by people in the real world. As rules for fuzzy logic operations, they are useful in building personae in artificial objects.

By building structural parameters into objects related to ecological forces, such as gravity and internal countergravity energies, I was able to write rules associating these basic parameters to some social affordances. These were simple rules about age, gender, honesty, and sadness. I began by applying these rules to human-like articulated forms, such as the trees, wooden mannequins, and the puppets of Puppets' World. I could then abstract the rules and, with rule inheritance, apply these rules to the top-level classes of objects and get just about any object to act.

The rule about sadness said that in order to look sad you had to look like you did not have enough energy to fight gravity. In the mannequins and puppets, this meant slumped shoulders, head hanging, and the like. For a tree, though, it might mean that there was not enough energy to hold up the branches. So, the tree would start to wilt. If the tree's constraints didn't prevent it, it might be reclassified as a weeping willow tree, through the appropriate calls to ASK. Objects could perform simple semiautonomous acting by using inheritable generalized rules that simply alter a few common base parameters.

In a way, this is not surprising. As with many problems in artificial intelligence, the parameters you pick in building your objects—what to pick as your representation—are going to make a great deal of difference in how effective they are and how easy the problem is to manage.

Acting in Motion

Acting is only partly the expression of innate character and affordances. What about the perceived motions of objects? The most obvious example of this is walking. It turns out that there are perceptual invariants involved with walking as well. One is that there are phase relationships between the body parts. For example, when you walk, the relationship between your arms and your legs is dramatically different from what it is when you run.

The biggest perceptual invariant on whether someone is walking or running is, interestingly enough, not the speed at which someone is moving, it is the phase relationship of the limbs. Imagine a slow runner and a fast walker. You might have a situation where someone was running slowly enough that he was actually moving more slowly than the fast walker. But in looking at the two of them you would still say the slower one was running and the faster one was walking.

The bipeds and quadrupeds of GenWorld all had rules about gaits, such as walking, running, and strutting. These rules were written relating the phase relationships between the joints and the resulting perceived gaits. Modifiers were added that worked like adverbs because there is, of course, a continuum in which one can go from a walk to a run or slow down from a run to a walk. During animation, these phase parameters are often smoothly interpolated as objects undergo changes in gait such as starting or ending a running sprint.

Also programmed were rules for the phase relationships of a horse's limbs. The four-legged gait rules were inherited by all quadrupeds, while the human rules of gait were inherited from the biped superclass. Legged objects could walk, run, stroll, and strut. Then, I did an informal experiment: I made the rules for the horse become the rules for the top-level object, so they were inherited by all objects, then tested what the perceived effect would be when watching bipedal figures move.

For walking this worked fine: the phase relationships were very close to human. Even for running there was no problem. Then, I changed the parameters to give the humanoid figures enough energy to gallop. The result was quite funny looking but, despite how amusing it was, it was still clearly perceived as a human galloping. This demonstrated the strong impact ecological invariants have on our perceptions, because something you had never seen before—a human galloping—was still perceived correctly.

In the end, I had a system that knew how to express a large number of personae based on a small set of rules. I could take simple humanoid figures—sculptor's mannequins—and give them gender traits by changing their centers of gravity. Perceptions as subtle as introvert versus extrovert could be created by using the rules and relationships of body parts to change postures. In combination with gaits, the object's movements could portray the object's implied intent, excitement level, and even some character traits.

A Glimpse of the Creator's Toolbox

Humans, like animals, perceive the world through ecologically based invariants. In creating artificial worlds, we must understand the human mappings of invariants to percepts and instill them into our tools. The building blocks underlying our artificial worlds require both physical and semantic representations that support, and directly relate to, the invariants of human perception. This combination of defining the issues and discovering their innate representations is often the key to solving any problem, and constitutes the theme of the work presented in this chapter.

With the evolving toolbox described, objects could also express a small range of emotions or, rather, they would be perceived as expressing these emotions by use of the perceptual invariants. Even inanimate objects could be made to visually embody emotions such as happiness and sadness, honesty and dishonesty, naivete, gloominess, excitement, age, or personal worth. I have implied that to build artificial worlds successfully, the creator must not only create objects, but also their affordances. To do this, the creator must be versed in the medium by which those affordances are communicated.

By putting rules into an inheritable object hierarchy, it was possible for any object to combine these rules to affect its own persona, under the creator's control. One could also invent objects, such as alien spaceships made of unidentifiable metals, yet get them to express recognizable properties, such as hardness, strength, and age. Additionally, one can alter familiar objects in new ways to achieve familiar percepts, such as creating a baby Volkswagen by inverse aging, getting humanoid figures to gallop, or instilling androgynous sculptor's mannequins with gendered characters.

Although it can be difficult to deduce the proper perceptual invariants and create the rules to express them, perceptual research and software tools exist to aid us in such endeavors. The technical tools used to support, manage, automate, and assist in the creation of artificial worlds have also been illustrated, through the Puppets' World and GenWorld examples. With the proper toolbox, it becomes much easier to create artificial worlds with objects that look and behave in ways we can understand and have natural interactions. The goal is to use the principles of the existing arts and sciences in the new art of creating artificial worlds.

In summary, the most powerful tools in the creator's toolbox are those of ecologically based perceptual invariants. Through skillful use of these invariants, the creators of artificial worlds cannot only construct more navigable worlds, but can sculpt the characters and moods of their spaces. As the worlds grow in their aesthetic sophistication, they will develop the need to convey things most meaningful to humans, such as emotions, feelings, relationships, companionships, and communications. Artificial worlds will evolve to become both a *medium* for communication and an *environment* for people.

While most people are unaware of how they acquire their perceptions of the world, the creator must become the expert of crafting of such perceptions. The tacit knowledge of perception which most of us take for granted, must be studied, acquired, and represented in our tools. We must be the masters of the gestalt, not just the masters of the components.

REFERENCES

[1] Troyen, Carol, *The Boston Tradition,* The American Federation of Arts, 1980, p. 65. Portrait of "Mrs. Ezekiel Goldthwait (Elizabeth Lewis)," 1771, by John Singleton Copley resides in Museum of Fine Arts, Boston, MA.

[2] Wertheimer, Max, "Untersuchungen zur Lehre von der Gestalt, II," pp. 301–350, *Psychologische Forschung,* **4,** 1923.

[3] Koffka, K., *Principles of Gestalt Psychology,* New York: Harcourt Brace, 1935.

[4] Isabella Stewart Gardner Museum, *Guide to the Collection,* Trustees of the Isabella Stewart Gardner Museum, Boston, MA, pp. 56, 58, 60, 62, 1987. Note: Prior to the greatest art theft in history, Rembrandt's 1633 painting "The Storm on the Sea of

Galilee" hung in the Gardner Museum. Several of Rembrandt's other works, including a self-portrait, can still be viewed there.

[5] Gardner, Brian R., Marek Holynski, and Rafail Ostrovsky, "Knowledge-Based Generation of Computer Images," in *Proceedings: Computer Graphics '86,* Fairfax, VA: National Computer Graphics Association, 1986.

[6] Holynski, Marek, Brian R. Gardner, and Rafail Ostrovsky, "Towards Intelligent Computer Graphics Systems," Technical Report, Boston University, 1986.

[7] Holynski, Marek, Brian R. Gardner, and Rafail Ostrovsky, "Meaning Oriented Generation of Computer Images," in *Proceedings: International Electronic Image Week,* CESTA/SIGGRAPH, Nice, France, 1986.

[8] Rafail Ostrovsky, Brian R. Gardner, and Marek Holynski, "Semantic Network Reasoning for Picture Composition," *Graphics Interface '86 Proceedings,* Vancouver: Canadian Information Processing Society, 1986.

[9] Gardner, Brian R., *Graflisp User's Manual,* Student Chapter of Association of Computing Machinery, Boston University, 1982.

[10] Gardner, Brian R., *Graflisp: A Graphics Package Design for Artificial Intelligence Applications,* Vols. I and II, Master's thesis, Boston University, January 1985.

[11] Shapiro, Stuart, "The SNePS Semantic Network Processing System," *Associative Networks,* N. V. Findler, Ed., New York: Academic Press, pp. 179–203, 1979.

[12] Michalski, R. S., and R. L. Chilausky, "Learning by Being Told and Learning from Examples: An Experimental Comparison of the Two Methods of Knowledge Acquisition on the Context of Developing an Expert System for Soybean Disease Diagnosis," *International Journal of Policy Analysis and Information Systems,* **4,** 1980.

[13] Holynski, M., M. Lu, and R. Garneau, "An Adaptive Graphics Analyzer as a Preference-Oriented Interface," *SIGCHI '87 Bulletin,* **19**(2), pp. 46–48, 1987.

[14] Holynski, M., R. Garneau, and E. Lewis, "An Adaptive Graphics Interface for Effective Visual Representation," in *Proceedings of Eurographics '86: The Computer Interface,* A. A. G. Requicha, Ed., New York: Elsevier Science Publishers B. V. (North-Holland), pp. 195–206, 1986.

[15] Gibson, James J., *The Perception of the Visual World,* Boston: Houghton Mifflin, 1950.

[16] Mandelbrot, Benoit B., *The Fractal Geometry of Nature,* New York: W. H. Freeman and Company, 1983.

[17] Barnsley, M. F., R. L. Devaney, B. B. Mandelbrot, H. Peitgen, D. Saupe, and R. F. Voss, *The Science of Fractal Images,* H. Peitgen and D. Saupe, Eds., New York: Springer-Verlag, 1988.

[18] Hagen, Margaret A., *The Perception of Pictures, Vol. II,* New York: Academic Press, esp. pp. 4–24, 1980.

[19] Marr, David, *Vision,* San Francisco: W. H. Freeman and Company, pp. 125–127, 1982.

[20] Gibson, James J., *The Senses Considered as Perceptual Systems,* Boston: Houghton Mifflin, 1966; reprinted by Waveland Press, IL, 1983.

[21] Gibson, James J., *The Ecological Approach to Visual Perception,* Boston: Houghton Mifflin, 1979.

[22] Bower, T. G. R., *Development in Infancy,* San Francisco: W. H. Freeman and Company, 1982.

[23] Bruce, Vicki, and Patrick Green, *Visual Perception: Physiology, Psychology and Ecology,* London: Lawrence Erlbaum Associates, esp. p. 139, 1985.

[24] Richards, W., "Selective Stereoblindness," in *Spatial Contrast,* H. Spekreijse and L. H. van der Tweel, Eds., Amsterdam: North Holland, 1977.

[25] Richards, W., "Stereopsis and Stereoblindness," *Experimental Brain Research* **10**, pp. 380–388, 1970.

[26] Richards, W., "Anomalous Stereoscopic Depth Perception," *Journal of the Optical Society of America* **61**(3), pp. 410–414, 1971.

[27] Foley, J. D., A. van Dam, S. K. Feiner, and J. F. Hughes, *Computer Graphics: Principles and Practice*, Reading, MA: Addison-Wesley Publishing Company, 1990.

[28] Wolberg, George, *Digital Image Warping*, Los Alamitos, CA: IEEE Computer Society Press, 1990.

[29] Johansson, G., "Projective Transformations as Determining Visual Space Perception," in *Perception: Essays in Honor of James J. Gibson*, R. B. MacLeod and H. L. Pick, Jr., Eds., Ithaca, NY: Cornell University Press, esp. p. 137, 1974.

[30] Magarshack, David, with chapters translated from the works of Stanislavsky, K. S., *Stanislavsky on the Art of the Stage*, New York: Hill and Wang, 1961.

[31] Thomas, Frank, and Ollie Johnston, *Disney Animation: The Illusion of Life*, New York: Abbeville Press, 1981.

[32] White, Tony, *The Animator's Workbook*, New York: Watson-Guptill Publications, 1988.

[33] Hayes-Roth, F., D. A. Walterman, and D. B. Lenat, Eds., *Building Expert Systems*, Reading, MA: Addison-Wesley Publishing Company, esp. p. 91, 1983.

[34] Todd, J. T., L. S. Mark, R. E. Shaw, and J. B. Pittenger, "The Perception of Human Growth," *Scientific American*, **242**, pp. 132–144, February 1980.

[35] Berry, D. S., L. Z. McArthur, "Perceiving Character in Faces: The Impact of Age-Related Craniofacial Changes on Social Perception," *Psychological Bulletin*, **100**(1), pp. 3–18, 1986.

Chapter 6

Full-Body Unencumbered Immersion in Virtual Worlds

(The Vivid Approach and the Mandala® VR System)

Susan Wyshynski and Vincent John Vincent

Vivid Effects

Toronto, Ontario, Canada

Our final artistic contribution comes from a talented pair of musicians/performance artists. I first met Susan and Vincent through the Computer-Human Interaction conference where I got my first look at their Mandala system. I was surprised at how easily they combined an artistic vision for performers creating new works with a business sense that has led their technology to be featured on television and in museums. In this chapter they give an overview of that system and show how artificial reality technology can make possible new kinds of performances and provide entertainment without reducing the audience to mindlessness.

—A.W.

The Mandala has appeared throughout humanity's history as a universal and essential symbol of integration, harmony, and transformation. It gives form to the most primordial intuition of the nature of reality, an intuition that inheres in each of us, giving us life.

The Mandala may be regarded as an engine of change, releasing energy to the extent to which the individual using it and concentrating upon it is capable of identifying themselves with it. Ultimately, the Mandala leads its user to a visualization and realization of the source of energy within themselves.[1]

—Jose and Miriam Arguelles

Introduction

"Any reality is an opinion. You make up your own reality! Wow." The words of Timothy Leary sampled against techno musical rhythms float through our downtown studio. A warehouse space decorated with posters and artifacts of Vivid adventures in the real world. Facing a chromakey blue wall are lights, TVs, cameras, computers, synthesizers, mixers, and a confusion of other toys of the trade. Our guests sit waiting to see what reality Vivid's Mandala® technology offers. "Will we get to try the glove and goggles?" one person asks. "No," we explain, "our current setup is a camera/TV-based type of interaction. Unencumbered. Great for location-based entertainment. Traffic in and out is instantaneous as the audience doesn't gear up first to view and interact. You will understand when you step into a world."

Throughout history, writers, visionaries, and philosophers have spoken of separate realities: Lewis Carroll took his readers "through the looking-glass" into a reality similar to yet separate from our own. Recent moviegoers stepped into an adventure within a computer reality in the film *Tron,* and ancient philosophers created pictures, called *mandalas* in the Sanskrit language, that could draw us into a separate reality, placing us within the center of a creative universe. Today the power of our electronic media offers us a whole new realm of experience. This technology has moved beyond being a medium that can enhance our visualization of concepts to one that encompasses the whole body in the experience.

Full-body interactive immersion in electronically generated worlds is the theme of this chapter. The concept of creative human interaction and communication through immersive technology is something The Vivid Group (Sue Wyshynski, Vincent John Vincent, and Francis MacDougall) has been exploring for more than 10 years. We named the product of our research the Mandala System, inspired by the ancient Sanskrit definition of a form that provides a gatepost between the many layers of reality. Our technology is a unique multimedia telepresence system. Its focus lies in the dealienation of the computer interface by empowering the user with freedom of movement and unencumbered interaction while ensuring precise, real-time response in highly visual computer worlds. Mandala provides the immersive playground for a kaleidoscope of interactive experiences.

In this chapter we discuss the reasoning behind pursuing an unencumbered full-body immersive technology, the flexibility of a camera-based approach, and the potential benefits it holds. We discuss how the Mandala VR System works; the various component configurations, the new emerging features, various Vivid projects, and the ever-expanding realm of applications.

The Start

The main concept behind creating the Mandala system was to use the power of computer technology to bridge the boundaries between the world of creative arts and communication. We wanted to offer users immersed in the computer world the ability to use their whole body to engage in levels of the traditional arts as well as explore whole new forms of creative communication. We wanted a tool that would offer engaging live presentations to an audience, as well as intense personal experiences. We envisioned a medium where the user would be able to pass instantly between roles, between being a dancer, actor, painter, musician, athlete, presenter, scientist, and more, or play a combination of roles simultaneously. Finally, we agreed that this technology would be a medium that could be used as a display device, video telephone, television, computer, and more at any given time.

Defining Mandala

In developing this technology, we were faced with two main problems. Our first was to create a wireless, remote, unencumbering technology so that the user would not have to wear, touch, or hold anything. Second, we wanted to make it nonhardware intensive and thus affordable to a large segment of the population. Our solution was to use the flexible nature of a video camera interface with affordable personal computers and peripheral hardware.

The technology today brings your image through the video camera into responsive computer and video worlds. You are placed in a virtual world where you see yourself and can interact with images to create sounds and music and control animation and video in real time. Through the camera you can use your whole body to interface into the worlds, without the need for gloves, trackers, or encumbering devices. Mandala frees the participant from conventional and potentially alienating interfaces such as keyboards, mice, and joysticks, because here the participant is the interface.

Why interface humans directly into computer-generated worlds? The answers are wide ranging. Imagine this possibility. You are away on a trip and you call home, thinking of your three year old. She really can't converse yet, but you miss interacting with her. In the VR pay phone you drop in some change and dial the number. Your child answers and you appear together in a virtual garden on the screen in front of you. Although you are in separate locations physically, you share the same viewing screen. Reaching down you pick up a virtual ball and throw it to her. She laughs and throws it back. It may not have the warmth of face-to-face contact, but it is high-quality contact that brings many communication factors into play. It allows for increased interpersonal relations, while allowing us to continue pursuing creative goals.

Vivid together with Bell Canada has been successfully experimenting with Mandala in teleconferencing situations, in which users on either end of the link see themselves in the same world and can interact together, even though they are in different cities.

How does the technology work? Many peripherals may be added to Mandala for special effects, higher end sound and video, and control of external devices such as lights, lasers, and robotics, which are discussed later. The core element of our system, however, revolves specifically around the software, the computer, a digitizer, and the camera. Briefly, the user's video image is digitized (at up to 30 frames per second), separated from the background, and the resulting image data are integrated into the computer animation and video worlds on the screen. By moving around in front of the camera you cause the digitized image of your body to move around inside the computer worlds. The software watches your movement through the video camera to see what you are doing in relationship to the graphic elements on the screen. These data are monitored on a frame-by-frame, pixel-by-pixel basis to establish interaction with animations. Hundreds of available events can be programmed into the animation world depending on the nature of your interaction. Through various contact techniques, animations (called *actors*) are transformed into any number of different states and simultaneously trigger any number of events—graphics, physics, sounds, sequences, and so on.

Our first successful experiment in developing a user-response system back in 1986 was an interactive grid: You could touch different squares on the grid with your image and cause it to change color. Then along came the "virtual drum kit," in which the drums surround your image and you play them by touching their animated drumheads. When triggered, a MIDI (musical instrument digital interface) note is sent to a slave synthesizer and you are immediately rewarded with the drum's sound. From these fairly simple but satisfying interactions, we moved toward controlling moving backgrounds and animation, such as flying birds that could land on your outstretched hand, fold their wings, and make sampled bird calls. We also developed interactive fast-moving sprites that can be used as balls and other high-speed objects. Sprites are extremely useful in game situations. Other developments to date include real-time control of video laserdisks, a full array of MIDI commands, control of external devices, and more.

The Technology

Our developments have been focused within six key areas that we felt would make Mandala a powerful world-building tool:

1. The user interface
2. Control of animation
3. Control of real-world video
4. A full array of MIDI commands
5. Control of external devices
6. New features: improved resolution, 3-D user tracking, and voice control.

The User Interface

Mandala is different from most other virtual reality tools in that you appear in the world with your full body, from a third-person point of view. The view is like an out-of-body experience because you see yourself in the world interacting. You are "through the looking-glass." We are familiar with this from our own dream states, where very often we watch ourselves from a third-person point of view. We also innately possess the hand/eye/screen coordination required in the Mandala system from the actions we perform daily in front of the mirror such as combing our hair and brushing our teeth.

You may choose from a number of options to determine how your image looks in the virtual world. The basic level allows you to appear as digital silhouette for which you may select a single color or grayscale effect. The more realistic approach uses genlock or chromakey to display the participant's full-color video image.

The nature of the video camera and the dynamics of the video image lend themselves well to the requirements of an interactive interface. A camera passively absorbs information about its surroundings; it does not need to emit anything or be touched. Its requirements are the same as for the human eye: some form of light differentiation.

Through its ability to adjust to different focal lengths, a camera easily analyzes a wide variety of different space configurations. This is extremely useful. When using the camera to view a space with a 6- to 20-foot radius, we are able to incorporate the participant's full body into the virtual world. Viewing a tighter space, say, a 1- to 4-foot radius, offers a magnified perspective and thus the ability to incorporate only hand movement or head and facial movement. When focusing on a much larger space such as a stage or arena, we can incorporate full-body immersion of multiple users through a single camera. Cameras can reach down into microscopic levels and out into macroscopic worlds. Multiple cameras can be layered to combine any number of space/participant configurations in a single virtual world. Remote- and motion-controlled cameras add an even wilder dynamic to the technology.

Sending serial information to a motion-controlled camera allows complete 360-degree scanning of the world surrounding it. Video cameras can send information long distances, even wirelessly, to a computer. A multiple-camera setup provides additional points of view to calculate depth of field along the x, y, and z coordinates of the user interaction space. With proper computational power the video camera can also be used for high-level image analysis.

On the digital level, we supply you with the ability to "mirror" or flip your silhouette image to avoid cross-cortexual problems. On the chromakey and genlock levels, our solution has been to attach an actual mirror to the video camera and angle the whole thing in such a way as to mirror the image in the world. This is a very important issue. We have all learned to brush our hair and teeth in the mirror, where lifting our right arm mirrors the movement on the right side. Without the mirror effect the video image would feel backwards, because your right arm would appear on the left side of the screen.

Control of Animation

Control of animation has evolved considerably since our first experiments. Today, graphics for our virtual worlds may be digitized from video or created from scratch. The software supports medium and low resolution, as well as overscan graphics. Mandala uses IFF pictures and brushes, and ANIM brush files (IFF and ANIM are Amiga computer graphic formats). It supports sprite animation and cell animation. It enables picture flipping sequences, moving picture backgrounds, and 360-degree world simulations. A simulated 3-D perspective may be achieved using animation that appears both in front and behind the user's image.

Each piece of animation is fortified with single-pixel accuracy of interaction; every pixel is potentially interactive. You may tell animation to respond to animation interaction, such as when animated objects collide. They may be endowed with multidimensional states and multidimensional command execution, capable of complex animation networking with real-time intercommunication between all animation. You may create animations with image transitions that occur over time. You may assign to animation both absolute and relative dimensional paths. You may define your animation as free-floating objects with manipulative laws of physics such as gravity, bounce, and friction.

Through animation interaction you may control scorekeeping and other global variables for databases (e.g., a video game highest score). The software gives you complete control over individual and group color transitions. A full range of instantaneous scene transitions and multicolor fades is available. Each piece of animation may be programmed to detect a wide spectrum of interaction: touching, pushing, redirecting, speed, angle and depth of animation contact, holding of animation, throwing of animation, repulsion and gravitational effects on animation, and many more.

Bodypaint capabilities allow the user's video image to paint the screen in multiple ways: fading and nonfading trails, painting with "held" animation, throwing paintbursts, and painting with transition animation brushes. The animation and environment changes can be controlled in parallel by user interaction and timed sequences.

Control of Real-World Video

A unique aspect of Mandala is its ability to incorporate and control real-world video into a scene. You are not limited to only computer animation in the worlds you create. This technology allows for complete control of laserdisk video footage and soundtracks for high-end background and audio.

Video is first gathered on tape and then pressed to video laserdisks. Once your video is on a laserdisk it is in a format that can be easily controlled by Mandala through serial port commands. A soundtrack may also be pressed along with your video footage. Video controls include going to any point on the video laserdisk, pausing the video, playing it slowly, or stepping it forward one frame at a time. Here is an example of how this is used:

With your camera you film a location that has a number of connected hallways:

1. Film going down the hallway *straight*.
2. Film going down the same hallway and *turning left* into another hallway.
3. Film going down the hallway and *turning right* into another hallway.

You have now documented three ways of traveling through the hallway on tape. Send the tape out to be pressed to laserdisk. Once on laserdisk you have three options at your command. Create three animated arrows and place them in the world. Using the laserdisk event types in Mandala, assign serial commands to each arrow so that when touched, each will send the necessary information to the laserdisk. For example, when the user interactively touches the right arrow in the world, it would tell the video laserdisk to jump to the point in the video where you filmed turning right; the left arrow would bring the user to the video of turning left, and so on.

At Vivid we use the interactive video capabilities extensively for in-house productions. Recently we completed an installation for Paramount Pictures and the Oregon Museum of Science and Industry (OMSI) that is a simulation of *Star Trek: The Next Generation*. Users step into an actual set of the transporter room in the real world and view themselves in the "Star Trek virtual world" on a large screen in front of them. They control where they wish to be transported and can interact with the scene when they arrive. For example, users could transport themselves to the surface of a planet, move around the location, and manipulate the objects there. Actual video footage from the television show is used for backgrounds and controlled via laserdisk.

A Full Array of MIDI Commands

Much time was spent in developing the "musical" side of our software, because one of the initial intentions was for use in stage performance. A full array of MIDI commands is now available that the Mandala authoring software supports. On an internal level, users have complete control of IFF sampled sounds on the Amiga for sound effects and synthesized speech. Although the software allows you to control internal computer sounds, it is fully geared for MIDI control of external devices such as synthesizers, sequencers, samplers, mixing boards, MIDI/SMPTE video controllers, light boards, and more (SMPTE is code used for tracking video).

The software allows users to drive MIDI devices through timed sequences or interaction. Controls include MIDI notes, patch and voice changes, internal transitions after interactions, pitch bend, volume control, and more. We also integrated control over sequencer programs such as Performer and Visions. With Mandala users can create multitimbral sound environments. Other MIDI-driven devices may also be controlled: MIDI soundmixers, MIDI video mixers, MIDI Starlight rigs, MIDI digital delays and effects boxes, etc. MIDI to SMPTE converters open up a whole new realm of multilever audio/visual control for stage and recording.

An example of a performance piece that is currently under development follows. The piece employs multiple levels of MIDI-controlled devices.

The stage is empty except for two cameras and two large video screens hanging above it. Jumping onto separate areas of the stage in front of two separate cameras, we find ourselves together in the same Mandala world in front of an elaborate "cyberdeck" displayed on the video screens above us. Touching and manipulating the correct series of virtual buttons, knobs, and faders, we open the cyberdeck and pass down the virtual hall into our central control bay. This area is like a live mixing studio; from here we can branch out to various pods to access control of all dynamics of the audio/visual presentation. We are both wearing wireless headset/microphones (covering only one ear) that are linked into our MIDI mixing board. The board is accessed through our virtual audio mixing pod. From that pod we can mix all levels of sound and control what the audience hears and what we hear in our headsets. We can talk into the microphones privately or let the audience hear what we are saying (singing, etc.).

At this point in the performance all channels are open and the audience hears us agreeing that we should temporarily part. The video control pod is accessed, a few switches are thrown, and suddenly the audience sees the two performers in separate but matching video control pods on the two large screens mounted side by side above the stage. There are, in fact, two Mandala systems.

The MIDI video switcher has complete control over the two stage cameras, including the merging of the two signals into a single Mandala system, as well as what is displayed on the two screens. The Mandala systems are linked serially as well. In this way, other relevant information can be passed back and forth between the two systems.

The first thing Vincent does is call up the sequencer pod (hooked up via MIDI to an external sequencer) and begin preparing a few tracks to be opened. Sue interactively calls up the lighting control pod (linked to a MIDI light control box) and sets the parameters for various lighting configurations. These configurations can then be accessed and played in real time at any time.

Instrument pods are individually accessed as we lay down the musical piece that will function as the initial sequence. First virtual drums, then bass, then keyboards (for chords) are called up and laid down separately on 10 or 12 different tracks. Having completed an initial track, Vincent carries on with other instruments, jamming to the looping track. Sue jumps back into the audio mixing pod and adjusts volume levels. Next, she enters the digital audio effects pod and starts to manipulate virtual faders for aspects of digital delay, reverb, decay, etc. A button marked "special stereo effects" brings her into a room with a ball on a pedestal and a menu panel for selecting tracks to be connected to the ball. Sue selects a few and retracks the menu. With a well-placed kick Sue sends the ball bouncing around the room, causing the connected audio to pan back and forth, up and around accordingly. Sue then grabs the ball, moving it about for more accurate control of the 3-D sound the audience is hearing around them.

Next Sue and Vince momentarily leave the stage only to have Sue return with a real violin and Vince return with a real guitar. Both instruments are connected to digital effects boxes that are controlled via the Mandala and we play along with a new sequence stored at a previous time.

This is just a small example of the combinations that could be created.

Control of External Devices

The Mandala system is capable of controlling multiple external devices simultaneously. The external serial port is often connected to synthesizers and other MIDI devices using a MIDI adapter. We use a multiport serial board to connect with other external devices such as a second Mandala system, a laserdisk video player, and other useful devices. Connecting two or more Mandala systems allows us to pass information back and forth between linked scenes in different systems. An example of this can be seen in the performance piece described in the MIDI previous section. At one point in the performance the two video screens placed side by side above the stage form one single video environment. In this world Sue and Vincent throw animation back and forth to each other and to animated characters. The connected computers update one another about appropriate locations and the dynamics of incoming and outgoing animation.

A second example whose video aspects were discussed earlier (under Control of Real-World Video) is Vivid's production created for the OMSI and Paramount Pictures for the two "Star Trek Transporter Room/Holodeck Experience" exhibits now touring North America. Synthesizers for sound effects are controlled via MIDI through one serial port. Video backgrounds that use the real footage from the show are controlled from another serial port via a video laserdisk player. The "beaming" in and out effect and other video tricks affecting the user and the background footage are controlled from a Video Toaster workstation by way of a third serial port.

A third example is The Vivid Group's Mandala "Alpha Deck Checkpoint Security Scan" simulator at the Tour of the Universe theme park. It is a good example of external control of robotics. Here robotic arms are opened and closed through parallel port commands from the Mandala allowing visitors to pass through a security gate only if they have performed the proper interaction.

Vivid has explored and utilized the external control capabilities for numerous other applications. Full room controllers via serial port commands have been set up to turn utilities on and off, control home entertainment centers, modems, printers, and so on.

New Features: Improved Resolution, 3-D User Tracking, and Voice Control

Currently, as the Amiga-based Mandala system software is being ported to the Macintosh II and PC platforms, it is undergoing a major shift in both depth and flexibility of its virtual environments, as well as the degree of analysis of the user's actions for all three platforms.

First, the computer graphics are being bolstered with higher resolution and hundreds of colors.

Second, free-floating 3-D rendered worlds are being added along with 3-D object-oriented imagery. This allows for a greater sense of depth of field and navigability of Mandala worlds and imagery. Real-world video capabilities are being expanded as CD-ROM is combined with current video laserdisk techniques and as more panoramic video footage is being incorporated.

Third, the integration of information from a second camera is now possible. One camera can be placed in front of the user and the second above or to one side of the user. This allows Mandala to sense movement in three dimensions rather than only along a 2-D axis. All movement along the *x, y,* and *z* coordinates in front of the camera can be integrated into the new 3-D worlds.

Fourth, levels of voice recognition are also being added along with more stereoscopic movement of sounds with the objects. An example of how this works follows.

The Physical Layout   You are in a room in the external world that is 20 feet long, 20 feet wide, and 15 feet high. The floor and one wall are painted blue. On the opposite wall is a huge video projection screen where you appear in a virtual world. There are two cameras, one above and one in front of you, and two large TVs on each side. By means of a video manipulation technique, the system has shrunk your virtual image to a proportion 10 times smaller than the camera is currently capturing you. As you approach a distance of 5 feet from the camera, the system gradually adjusts your image until it is at a 1-to-1 ratio display with your image in the external world. When you are at the back of the external room, stepping 2 feet forward could be arbitrarily set, depending on the nature of the virtual world, to represent maybe 6 times that or 12 feet.

The Virtual Layout   In the foreground corner of the virtual world is a pair of crystal electrode rhythm sticks. Since you are at the back of the external room, you appear in the back of the visible virtual landscape.

Images and obstacles are laid out on the landscape between you and the foreground rhythm sticks. As you move about in the real world, your video image moves about within the landscape. Since the computer knows exactly where you are in a 3-D space, you are able to interact with the appropriate images along the *x, y,* and *z* coordinates around you. You overcome the obstacles to get there: You jump the river, crawl through the fence, go around the fire pit, and avoid the powerful time hole that is circling above you. Arriving at the crystal sticks you are now in the corner foreground of the real world. As you grab the sticks, the full moon comes out, lighting up the landscape around you, and you find yourself surrounded by percussion instruments.

Now it is time to navigate your way across the landscape to explore these instruments. You have many options. One option is to use the voice recognition capabilities to use simple commands for the direction and speed with which you wish to move. This voice command level can also be used to turn the interactivity of animated objects on and off. Other options include simply calling up navigational instrument icons, such as interactive pointer arrows and speed faders. To move from the default Mandala third-person perspective to a first-person navigational view, your image is shrunk on command and delegated to a navigational control window on the side. (This command takes full advantage of the fact that the user's video image is a 24-bit full-color digital image that can be manipulated in size at any time.)

A new level of image recognition is also being developed. This will allow for many richer forms of interaction in the virtual world. Improved complexity analysis of hand tracking should allow more dexterous manipulation of virtual objects including 3-D rotation of objects. A good example of this was shown at the Chicago SIGGRAPH show in 1992 when we unveiled the first game on our new PC Mandala system. Here the user's image was reduced. To move about and navigate your way through the computer world, you simply pointed in the direction you wished to travel. The computer recognized this action and moved your image through the world accordingly.

Applications

The exploration of applications for this technology has been and continues to be an adventure in itself. The new types of VR technology have been rapidly influencing the boundaries of multimedia, video adventure games, music, live performances, education, television production, and current mediums of communication, such as teleconferencing and the telephone. It is hard to say how much this interactive technology could affect our everyday reality.

Games

We have found that this type of technology is very well suited to interactive game environments. Prohibitive costs have kept Mandala within the boundaries of "location-based entertainment," yet we have been working toward a solution for affordable home entertainment. A beneficial aspect to its introduction in large-audience public environments such as museums, science centers, and amusement parks has been to test out what works and what doesn't in the world of interactive gaming.

We have found that to capture the attention of today's demanding audience, the games must be highly interactive and make room for and respond instantly to the player's creative input, while simultaneously challenging them both mentally and physically. From the opening scene onward, the player must be totally immersed in the virtual game: he or she must use memory, creative processes, awareness, speed, strength, flexibility, agility, and other techniques commonly employed in real-world situations if the adventures are going to be extremely exciting and tangible. One of the virtues of these unique human interface games is that regardless of the theme or orientation, each one promotes physical fitness because the whole body becomes involved in the interaction. It's an "adventure sport" of the future.

During the last few years we have employed the technology in game categories ranging from sports to fantasy adventure games, games based on education and discovery, and those promoting positive concepts, such as environmental awareness and self-growth potential.

Imagine an adventure video game in which you are the central character, wandering through a maze with a multitude of doors, behind each of which lies challenges, dangers, and, ultimately, freedom. Snatch the animated golden key and use it to open a door, or find yourself juggling with an animated wizard. Take off in a spaceship and protect a planet from the destruction of a dangerous asteroid bombardment!

The following is an example of a game currently under development. The initial implementation was shown at SIGGRAPH '92 in Chicago in the VR Gallery.

"Free-Fall Cyberball" "Free-Fall Cyberball" is a virtual ballet in zero-gravity reality. It is a melding of virtual sports, dance, acrobatics, and video game experiences.

The Game The user steps into the dual-camera 3-D tracking configuration in real space. His or her full-color live image appears in the video monitor, one-tenth the size of the screen. The player is in a vast bubble-shaped "antigravity chamber" (the player's image is affected digitally with simulated qualities of zero gravity) and is surrounded by objects that look like pinball bumpers.

The object of the game is to get a ball into a net. The complication is that the net is moving around the screen, and the player must propel his or her image around the screen to score baskets. The ball itself floats within the space and bounces off the bumpers, changing in size according to its position within the space. The player's image is also affected by its position in the 3-D virtual room. The player must step back in order to contact the ball in the background, and forward to hit a ball in the foreground. The computer can alter the player's size by degrees (i.e., 1 foot back in the real world equals 5 feet back in the virtual world).

There are objects moving and floating around the screen. The player must avoid some objects while interacting with others. Some of the objects may be used to propel one's image around the screen by pushing off them, holding onto moving ones, and so on. Body contact with the bumpers prompts the player to experiment with the angle of their arms, legs, or entire body to bounce in the desired direction. They become involved in an acrobatic dance in virtual space, maneuvering around the environment.

The Scene/Setting: The antigravity bubble is very large. We can only see a part of its curving wall on the screen at once. The walls are very dark glass, ribbed with an organic metal frame. Coming close to the wall you can see out over a planetscape.

The objects floating in the bubble are imaginary futuristic items. Some have glowing/pulsing/flashing lights on them and are made of some tough material or metal. They are of reasonable size to allow for multiple units to appear on screen simultaneously with the user's image without seeming really crowded.

Among those currently using the technology for interesting game applications are high-profile sports organizations such as the NHL Hockey Hall of Fame. They have an interactive sports simulator, which is basically a goalie-training game device. The player stands in front of a virtual net and blocks incoming pucks. The final implementation of this game uses actual film footage of a hockey rink and net with actual hockey players who skate in to shoot pucks at the net.

Television and Film

During the last few years, this interactive VR technology has been finding its way into the worlds of television and film. Due to its strong "video" orientation, the Mandala is proving itself to be a great audio/visual production tool for TV and film studios. As an interactive blue screen technology, it can be a replacement for elaborate sets and can save much of the costly postproduction time of actor/animation overlays. One can create numerous interactive worlds that do not use physical space or concrete materials. Postproduction of actor/animation overlays can be eliminated using this technology because the scene takes place in real time, merging the actors and animation together on the set.

Among those using this new VR gear in the television broadcast arena is Nickelodeon channel. Their show "Nick's Arcade" is a kid's game show that takes place in Mandala worlds. Here is an excerpt from an article in *Compute Magazine* describing the weekly program:

Sunday afternoon in Cyberspace. The "Nick's Arcade" studio consists of a huge ground-floor sound stage and a second-floor control room. There's a tech table with the 3000s, a judge's table, and a scoring table with the CDTV units. The MIDI keyboard and all the computers for the Bonus Round are in the second-floor control room.

There are three special sets configured for the three final Interactive Bonus Rounds. These environments are designed like videogame worlds, with ladders, bridges, platforms, ramps, and other special features. The whole set is painted a video-invisible blue, so the real background drops out and is replaced by the computer-generated background when filmed by the Mandala system and the Live! board. When entering the game field, the contestant sees the empty set. The image displayed on the monitor is the contestant composted onto the Amiga background and interacting with the virtual world. Success depends on how well the contestant can integrate the two universes in his or her mind.

Before the game, the kids get a chance to orient themselves within the space. They get to spend 45 seconds on the one-player sets and 60 seconds on the two-player Wizard Level set. In that time, they learn how to move in the empty field, how to watch themselves on the video monitors, and how to integrate the video world with the real world so they can touch and dodge sprites. These trial sessions are played in front of a studio audience, who seems to love the test runs as much as the real thing.

There are 11 different games, ranging from futuristic worlds to ancient tombs to cafeteria food fights. Some are shot from the side, and some from overhead. In some games, the contestants run around in a static game screen; in others, the background scrolls past them. In the final Wizard Level, the two contestants must cooperate onscreen to win the game.

. . . The producers point out the advantage "Nick's Arcade" has over other virtual reality systems. Their show needs no helmets, gloves, or other restrictive devices. The players are completely free, and they use the most natural of all input devices—their bodies.[2]

Future Communications: The Virtual Phone

When envisioning the communication medium of the future, one's mind may jump to the idealized television-phone, such as the one so well depicted in the film *2001: A Space Odyssey*. This dream has been somewhat realized with the advent of teleconferencing and the Integrated Services Digital Network, and virtual reality players including Vivid have been working to take this dream one step further. During the past few years, with the help of Bell Canada, we have been using Mandala to conduct experiments linking numerous cities in a single virtual world.

Users in two separate parts of the world have been able to step into a single virtual reality together and interact with one another. They toss animation such as balls back and forth, walk through a virtual forest and pick flowers, or even challenge one another in an interactive adventure game! Language barriers can be overcome because long-distance interaction will no longer be restricted to speaking or writing.

On June 3, 1992, the Mandala was used on the Picturetel video-conferencing system linking Nice, France, and the McLuhan Program in Toronto. People on both sides of the Atlantic enjoyed playing music, moving images, drawing pictures, and interacting with each other. The Mandala effectively enhances video-conferencing technology. The Mandala was also featured in other McLuhan Program video-conferencing initiatives, notably November 5, 1988, in the Transinteractivity event between Toronto and Paris and April 8, 1989, in a three-way interactive test between New York, Atlanta, and Toronto.

Such transcontinental links are currently feasible in a business-oriented teleconferencing scene. In this case, attendees on both sides of the link are able to step into virtual world simulations—together or separately—and interact with key areas of interest, such as parts of a structure, or within a storyboard for a TV commercial or a movie under production. Their virtual touch empowers them to control and produce animation reactions: They can open the door and walk inside the virtual building, or reconfigure the virtual storyboard to their liking.

Interactive Advertising

If you have chanced on certain conferences or trade shows recently, you may have had the opportunity to "step into" the futuristic multimedia tool of interactive advertising. Companies such as BF Goodrich are using Mandala systems to draw people into a desired conceptual reality. It is different from any other multimedia tool. When you enter the virtual reality, the interactive experience actually becomes a personal link into ideas and concepts that the company is presenting.

Advertisers familiar with the new interactive technologies view the "media and the passive observer" as a thing of the past. Always looking for more interactive ways of involving the public in advertising campaigns, current uses include interactive Mandala system "billboards," video walls in malls and stadiums, etc., that will allow people to step right into and interact with an advertisement or commercial, which might be in a video game format, an interactive virtual wonderland, or even a scene from the latest hit movie or rock video.

A fun application is interactive "make-your-own rock videos." This was a concept picked up by Labatt's Breweries as part of their "Enter the Blue Zone" campaign for Labatt's Blue beer. Here, participants stepped live into an actual rock video of their choice, where they became the lead singer, as well as being able to play animated instruments such as drums, cowbells, and tambourines. After their interaction, the participant walked away with a videotape of themselves in the "Blue Zone" virtual reality as a rock star.

The Vivid Group has also created a number of interactive virtual worlds designed for product simulations. A good example of this is a production we recently finished for a pharmaceutical company. The interactive world provided a central focus for their trade booth where visitors could step into a controllable scientific visualization of their product. The visitors entered the microscopic world of the blood stream and various organs. Once there visitors could actively manipulate the product to experience and help understand how it works on particular viruses.

The Virtual Stage

The Mandala is a unique musical instrument. With it, a player holds the "keys" to innumerable instruments, to innumerable musical voices, and to doors into virtual wonderlands. By simple video touch, the player calls his or her virtual instruments into being and sends them away. Through gesture the performer is empowered to control lights and cameras and is empowered to take the audience on audio/visual journeys into virtual worlds, projected on giant video screens above the stage. Here the performer can escape physical restraints, setting free a new dimension of expression governed solely through movement and dance.

In the early 1980s, during the conceptualization period of the Mandala system, Vivid's dream was to create a very powerful performance tool. Being interested in expressiveness through creative dance forms and music, it seemed natural that in 1986 Vivid's technology made its first exciting debut on stage at the Tunnel Club in New York City before 4,000 viewers. The following quite from *Sentry Magazine* is a description of that unique, first virtual world performance.

> The Tunnel Club, New York City: Somewhere in this melee, at 12:00 midnight, there would be a multimedia performance by Vincent John Vincent using the Mandala. A very large video projection screen was set up in the middle of the dance floor. The tall graceful form of Vincent John Vincent appeared. Totally unprepared

for what was to come, the crowd held its breath. He began to dance, playing music and controlling graphics by his movement as scene after scene appeared.

A backdrop of a Mayan temple with brightly colored (interactive) fruits and birds was followed by a maze. . . . The scene changes, sounds and timing all were responding to the artistic expression of the dancer. He could as easily grab a handful of magenta to paint the sky, as play a hard drum riff.

When the performance was over, the crowd roared for more. This experience had been a first for everyone in the hall. Sound, sight, movement and artistic vision had been combined through computer technology into a new art form.[3]

This historical moment for the Vivid Group was to be the first of many such interactive, virtual world performances. Since then, the Mandala system has been appearing on stages throughout the world from Tokyo, Amsterdam, and Paris to San Francisco, Seattle, and other places throughout Canada, the United States, and Europe.

Vincent, the first performer to introduce this unique concept, continues leading the forefront of virtual reality performances. Accompanied in the virtual space by Susan Wyshynski, and often musically by the live band "Days of You," they step through the windows of their video cameras into the animated computer virtual world, inside which the Vivid Group has created many landscapes and images from natural, historical, mystical, spiritual, and futuristic themes. Audiences are taken on audio/visual journeys through virtual wonderlands that exist only within the computer and the mind of the beholder.

Amusement Parks and Virtual Reality (or VR Escapism)

Today global communication, global travel, and the information age have dramatically changed our daily lives, including how we spend our leisure time. We are expanding our awareness of the world around us, and just what there is to see, experience, and learn. Much more of our leisure time is being spent in this pursuit. Of course, we are limited. We can't really go everywhere, or do and learn everything. The development and creative use of technology and engineering are addressing this desire through the creation of safe adventures in the form of amusement park attractions. Today people can, for a time, escape their everyday reality and enter a magic kingdom, jump on a daredevil roller coaster, or be launched into space in a simulated rocket.

The questions addressed in the creation of these experiences revolve around how we progress from the "passive audience" state toward creating interactive audience-participation attractions that give every visitor a personal experience, and still continue to address mass audiences. Virtual world developers offer a few answers to these questions. Here is an example of one possibility:

> Imagine a virtual world roller coaster ride where just your torso is strapped securely to the "train," and you are free to move your arms and legs.
>
> As the train takes off, and you watch yourself on the huge video screens you pass, you travel through simulated outer space. A bombardment of 3-D comets comes whirling toward your train at a terrifying speed. You reach your arms and legs out in instinctual defense, repelling the comets. Later, streaking down a tunnel, your waving arms and legs leave rainbow-colored imprints on the walls.
>
> When the ride changes direction and suddenly drops, you fall down Alice's rabbit hole. You reach out and virtually touch the 3-D objects around you and manipulate them. "Grasp" an animated book and open its cover, or take hold of a key as it races by, or switch on the free-floating animated light that whirls around you.

This is not just a fantastic dream of the future; this example is truly not far from reach. In fact, utilizing the current state of the Mandala virtual world technology, much of this is possible today.

Here are a few brief ideas of what exactly is possible today utilizing Vivid's virtual world interactive Mandala system:

> Complex adventure games could be created where 100 visitors each step into a separate tiny room with a virtual world Mandala inside. As each person enters the virtual tunnels and opens the virtual doors, which they view on the screen in front of them, they will encounter some of the other participants (through the use of a video switcher) who are coexisting in another part of the same interactive adventure. The participants can choose to continue together, or travel their separate ways. This would truly be an adventure.

> Groups could embark together on an adventure into an actual maze, where the participants' interaction with virtual world animation would provide them with clues. Different virtual world interactions would open actual doors in walls where there appeared to be a dead end, allowing the participants to continue.

These ideas for interactive virtual world exhibits and attractions are currently being applied to museums, science centers, and galleries worldwide. Vivid has exhibits in Washington, D.C., at the Tech2000 gallery of the future; at the American Museum of History of the Smithsonian Institution; in Torino, Italy, at the gallery for the History of the Machine; in Montreal at Images du Futur; OMSI in Portland; St. Louis Science Center; and the Tour of the Universe, located at the base of Toronto's CN tower.

This early **Snowscape** world was generated with GenWorld. Here, an "invisible cameraman" agent has chosen the camera position and angle. Copyright © 1986 by Brian Gardner.

The fractal-based **Portrait of the Sky** depicts an artificial world by combining the elements we attribute to the sky — cold, vast, starry, alien, orbits, spirals, rising, setting, and movement — through the colors, shapes, and textures chosen for the environment. Copyright © 1987 by Brian Gardner.

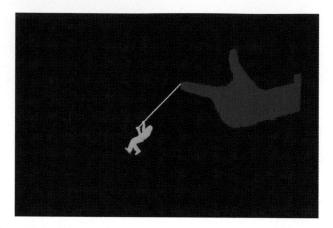

Hanging by a Thread. In this playful teleconference, the images of the giant hand and the tiny person can belong to individuals in different locations. As the small person moves from side to side, his image starts swinging back and forth. If he times his movements carefully, he can pump, so his image goes higher and higher. With considerable effort, it is possible to do a 360° turn. Copyright © 1988 by Myron W. Krueger, Vernon, CT. Reprinted by permission.

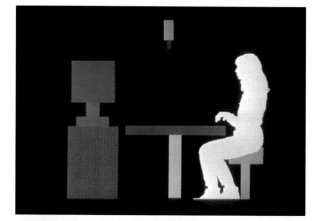

VIDEODESK Installation. A ceiling-mounted camera looks down on the user's hands as they rest upon a normal desktop. The image of the user's hands is then displayed on the computer screen over an application. The image of the hands can be used to perform functions such as menuing or drawing that are needed to operate the application. Copyright © 1986 by Myron W. Krueger, Vernon, CT. Reprinted by permission.

Virtual Valley and **Planetscape!!,** two of the virtual worlds constructed by young students from the Pacific Science Center at the University of Washington's Human Interface Technology Lab. Copyright © 1992 Washington Technology Center. Reprinted by permission.

A geologist virtually explores a digital terrain environment created from a composite of Viking orbiter data from Mars and 10 cm resolution laser rangefinder data from "Mars Hill" in Death Valley, California.

Synthetic view of Valles Marineris, the vast canyon system on Mars, created by the NASA Virtual Planetary Exploration system using data from the Viking orbiters. Synthetic color is based on elevation encoding. Elevation is unexaggerated.

Sharpening up reflexes on the NHL VR Goaltender Trainer. Copyright © 1991 by the Vivid Group. Reprinted by permission.

The Vivid Group's co-directors Susan Wyshynski and Vincent John Vincent interacting with on-screen microchips while co-director Francis MacDougall looks on. Copyright © 1991 by the Vivid Group. Reprinted by permission.

Interacting with the wildlife in a Mandala virtual video world. Copyright © 1991 by the Vivid Group. Reprinted by permission.

Conclusion

Through the coincidence of world development trends, our research throughout the 1980s was, as we were to discover, part of a growing movement toward immersive, interactive technology. As we began to market our system, we were pulled into the vortex of the rapidly emerging VR "hyperindustry." Currently we stand as a progressive alternative to standard virtual reality techniques. For us Mandala is a dynamic medium in itself, and we often joke that Mandala is the evolution of the television as we know it, the ultimate cure for the couch potato. Mandala takes us into the TV and removes the barrier between interaction and observation.

Virtual reality, the movement, continues to wash in with the flavor of a revolution, pulling thought out of the woodwork. Like a repeating fractal, humanity sits on the elusive cusp of change. It's the continuing episode of "Planet Earth Hurls Through Space while Humanity Grapples with the Riddle of Reality." One observes all the familiar elements: artists, thinkers, media, corruptible youth, government, and business types. It seems no small coincidence that, as many walls and established orders and economies are falling into obscure hands of the past, people around the world are opening doors into alternate realities and looking to establish new forms of communication. Could this be the fall of the Tower of Babel?

Building Technology to Bridge the Gap

Many are concerned that hands from the old establishments are striving to manipulate the media in its youth. The effects are worthy of attention. Just as the television has been jealously guarded by a select few and often used for propaganda and proliferation of violence, today's new medium are vulnerable to the same fate. We are already seeing the appearance of extremely violent, very real experiences in the VR marketplace. One example is a VR game that offers consumers the opportunity to virtually hack one another to bloody deaths with axes in a dual-participant head-mounted setup. What is most terrifying is the first-person experience, which has brought us one step beyond passive viewing. We no longer watch the experience, we are personally responsible for it and incorporate it into our psyche.

The following is a quote from Derrick de Kerkhove, codirector of the Marshall McLuhan Foundation, speaking about the impact of VR on the human psyche:

Every major technological innovation goes through several phases before it can be assimilated by a culture. At first it is externalized in an artificial setting such as a stage, a page, a screen, or any other display technology. Second it works its way into the psyche of the user even as its user interacts with it one way or another. When it finally penetrates the user during the course of the last stage of assimilation, it becomes a psychological reality, it becomes the normal way of being, of thinking, of feeling, of living. We can surmise from this pattern, which can be observed from the time writing was introduced in the west, all the way to our responses to computerization, that the end result of VR technologies will be to feed back and feed forward in our minds without intermediaries directly. The future of VR is to interact with our minds in such a way that we can organize our thoughts directly in flexible digital environments. Inversely, flexible digital environments will have a direct unmediated impact on our thinking processes.[4]

Vast creative potential is offered by the virtual experience to today's audience and we question the desire to bypass social responsibility for the "easy" profits of potentially destructive human addictions used in the past to market other technologies (e.g., fear, war, violence, sexual exploitation, etc.). We feel that there is no need to promote violence as a form of interaction with anything, especially other humans.

We can only hope that in this time of transition that more and more people view the virtual market with these perspectives and the will to pursue new and exciting creative applications. Fortunately, we are one of many in this growing field who are dedicated to using the powerful potential of these new technologies to enhance the quality of our lives here in the rapidly emerging electronic global community.

May there be a flowering in the virtual garden, and may the air fill with the peaceful sounds of digital birds singing to the morning sun.

NOTES

1. From MANDALA, by Jose and Miriam Arguelles. © 1972 by Jose and Miriam Arguelles and Shambhala Publications, Inc. Reprinted by arrangement with Shambhala Publications, Inc., 300 Massachusetts Ave., Boston, MA 02115
2. Reprinted by permission of COMPUTE, © 1992, COMPUTE PUBLICATIONS INTERNATIONAL, LTD.
3. Reprinted from an article entitled "Mandala, A Very Vivid Performance at the Tunnel" appearing in November 1987 Amiga Sentry Magazine, used with permission from publisher, Thomas E. Bucklin.
4. Reprinted with the permission of Derrick deKerkhove, Director of the McLuhan Program.

Part III
Softwhere in the World

The idea for this section came from one of the authors who asked me "Where in the world are you going to put this chapter?" The world is an important place; people working in virtual reality are often accused of trying to replace the real world, even as we simulate it. This is, of course, a false accusation. Virtual reality no more replaces the world than do things like telescopes or movies. They—and VR—are simply tools that allow us to look at our universe in ways not possible before.

In this section I present four chapters that relate virtual reality technology and ideas to real-world problems and suggest real-world uses for VR.

Chapter 7

An Easy Entry Artificial Reality

Myron W. Krueger
Artificial Reality
Vernon, CT

Myron Krueger is the acknowledged godfather of the whole field of artificial reality. He has been working in this area for decades, pushing ideas that are only now becoming accepted. I also owe him a personal debt because it was my experience with his Videoplace system seven years ago which opened my eyes to the possibilities of AR and set me on the path I'm now following.

Krueger's book goes into great depth on the field; in his chapter here he provides an overview and describes some of the real uses to which the technology has already been put.

—A.W.

The Ultimate Interface

As a graduate student at the University of Wisconsin in the late 1960s, I saw the encounter between human and machine as the central drama of our time. At that time, the human interface was just a veneer applied to the computer to make it a little easier for the human to use. It seemed obvious that the interface consisted of two elements: human nature, which was not evolving at all, and computers, which were evolving faster than any technology in history. It seemed clear that the focus of interface research should be on human nature, not on the transient computer.

In the ultimate interface, input should come from our voices and bodies and output should be directed at all our senses. Since we will also interact with each other through computers, the ultimate interface should also be judged by how well it helps us to relate to each other.

The logical consequence of this thought process was the concept of an artificial reality in which the laws of cause and effect were designed to facilitate the functions that interested the user.

What is Reality?

In our physical reality, we use our bodies to interact with objects. We move our bodies or turn our heads to see better. We see other people and they can see us. We have acquired a consistent set of expectations through a lifetime of experience. Any system that observes these conventions will be instantly understood by everyone on the planet.

What's So Great about Reality?

What is wrong with reality that we need the computer to rise above it? Reality often gets in our way. We spend much of our lives getting from one place to another. In addition, we are too large, too fast, or too slow to experience many aspects of reality. Finally, much of it is dangerous and dirty.

Of course, there are many aspects of reality that we would be loath to give up in order to use computers. We are mobile creatures, not encumbered or tethered. Why then, do many seem to expect artificial realities that require goggles, gloves, and body suits to be attractive? Or, is it that an unencumbered artificial reality is not possible?

Artificial Reality

More than 20 years ago, I decided to create an artificial reality that did not constrain people's movements. The computer would perceive participants rather than accept input from users. My early efforts, starting in 1969, used sensory floors that detected a participant's movements around a room. The computer responded through a video projection of a computer-generated graphic image. In 1970, an artificial reality called VIDEOPLACE was conceived and simulated. Actual construction began in 1974. It has been demonstrated worldwide since 1985.

VIDEOPLACE

In VIDEOPLACE, you are perceived by a video camera and the image of your body is displayed in a graphic world. The juxtaposition of your image with graphic objects on the screen suggests that perhaps you could affect the graphic objects. This expectation is innate. It does not need to be explained. To take advantage of it, the computer continually analyzes your image with respect to the graphic world. When your image touches a graphic object, the computer can respond in many ways. For example, the object can move as if pushed. It can explode, stick to your finger, or cause your image to disappear. You can play music with your fingers. The graphic world need not be realistic. Your image can be moved, scaled, and rotated like a graphic object in response to your actions or simulated forces. You can even fly your image around the screen.

You can be joined in this world by graphic creatures. The first of these characters is called CRITTER (Figure 7.1). He chases you around

FIG. 7.1.   CRITTER

the screen. If you extend your hand, he lands on it. If you remain still, he climbs up your body until he reaches the top of your head where he does a celebratory jig. He is a graphic pet. You discover that you can get him to dangle from your finger, or make him explode and momentarily disappear by surrounding him with your body and slowly constricting the space around him.

The image of another person who is in a similar VIDEOPLACE environment may also join you on the screen. When her image touches yours, the contact may cause a sound. In some interactions, her hand is greatly enlarged, enabling her to pick you up or shrink your image by pressing down on your head. When her giant hand touches your image, it may push you across the screen. If you push back, a video battle ensues that climaxes when she pokes you in the head, and your image is knocked over—only to pop back up again a moment later. If you have the presence of mind, you can shoot her with your fingers or retaliate with a karate blow that cuts off your tormentor's hand.

In another playful interaction the giant hand of the other person appears on the screen with a graphic string hanging down from the extended index finger (Figure 7.2). When you walk on the screen, your miniaturized image is dangling at the end of the string. You wonder if you can make yourself swing. By moving from side to side, you start your image swinging back and forth. You quickly learn that if you time your movements properly you can pump so that your image goes higher and higher. Now, you are racing back and forth. Both you and any observers start to wonder whether you can do a 360-degree loop. Past experience has shown that if you succeed, you may well be greeted by applause. This example illustrates how the medium can connect participants to those around them rather than cutting them off. It is one of 50 interactions that have been created within the VIDEOPLACE telecommunication environment.

VIDEOPLACE was conceived as an art medium, a designer world in which the laws of cause and effect could be defined by the artist and changed in composed ways from moment to moment. One of its themes has been the discovery of new ways for people to be together at a distance. Thus, it is a serious suggestion for informal visits in the future with distant friends and family. If a parent or grandparent wants to visit with a small child, the telephone is not very satisfying, because young children are often puzzled and put off by it. If all participants are visible on the screen, they could play a game together. The child's

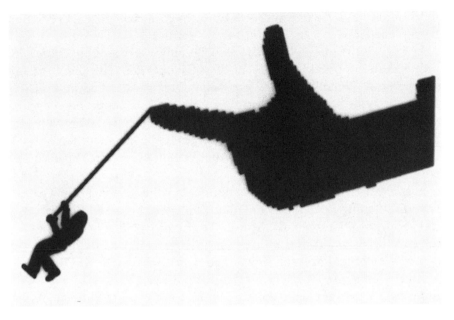

FIG. 7.2. HANGING BY A THREAD

image could be large and the adult's small—a child's fantasy brought to life. Telecommunication would no longer be limited to talk. You could do something together.

Education

It is always said that experience is the best teacher, but experience is an uncertain and inefficient teacher. However, if experience could make specific points, we would have a powerful opportunity to revolutionize what we teach, as well as how we teach it. VIDEOPLACE is such an experiential medium.

Education teaches as much by the means employed as it does through the content it attempts to convey. Contemporary education immobilizes the student and pits itself against the child's need for activity. It assigns meaningless exercises whose results are thrown away and never asks children to accomplish anything that is useful to others. Students are being prepared to operate in a busy-work world, in which nothing they do seems directed at any goal. Thus, when they enter the work force, they do not question why they must justify every action with reams of paper. Action itself is unfamiliar.

In artificial realities, the body can be employed as a teaching aid, rather than suppressed by the need to keep order. The theme is not "learning by doing" in the Dewey sense, but instead "doing is learning," a completely different emphasis. In 1976, I proposed a system whose goal was to teach students the process of being a scientist before requiring them to learn the jargon, memorize the names of famous scientists, or solve any of the mathematical puzzles that are normally taught in science classes.

In this VIDEOPLACE environment, students would be cast in the role of scientists landing on an alien planet. Their mission would be to study the local flora, fauna, and physics. The world would be deliberately unrealistic. It would operate by unfamiliar physics and would be designed to give children an advantage over their teachers. Each child would enter alone. Their unique behavior, as well as their size and perhaps even what they were wearing, would allow them to discover different things about the environment. Thus, no one child could dominate the class. The students would need each other.

After their individual sessions, they would discuss what they had observed under the supervision of the teacher. Since their experiences would be different, they would disagree. To convince each other, they would observe more carefully, communicate more clearly, and develop testable theories. Then they would devise critical experiments to resolve disputes. Note that unlike the traditional school experience, the students would do the talking, not the teacher.

Artificial realities could be composed for a variety of other educational purposes. For instance, the most successful foreign language learning occurs through total immersion in an environment where only that language is used and the student is required to speak. One method of achieving this goal is to employ a tutor who never uses the student's own language and simply starts pointing to objects and naming them. This process would be assisted by placing both student and tutor in an artificial reality that would provide a graphic context in which the instruction could take place.

A variety of graphic objects could be provided as props with which the teacher could illustrate concepts. For instance, the teacher could place a graphic hat on the student's head or throw him or her a graphic ball. Users could enter a graphic house and point to objects and demonstrate activities within it. Initially, this system would be an aid to the human teacher. Ultimately, it would evolve into a fully auto-mated language lab in which the student's pronunciation would be tested against the system's ability to understand. By placing the em-phasis on speaking, rather than on reading and grammar, the student would develop an operational skill. The fact that the learning experi-ence was real in its own terms would make the knowledge gained seem more valuable, especially to the students that are hardest for traditional education to reach.

VIDEODESK

VIDEOPLACE technology also exists in a more practical office format. The VIDEODESK is a conventional desk with a ceiling-mounted camera aimed down at your hands as they rest on the desk's surface (Figure 7.3). The image of your hands is displayed over the graphic and text information on your computer screen.

As in VIDEOPLACE, the computer can see your hands and knows where they are with respect to the objects and text on the screen. Thirty

FIG. 7.3.   VIDEODESK

times a second, the silhouette of your hands is analyzed and the location of the fingertips and their relationship to objects on the screen is determined. Basic computer functions such as menuing and positioning can be accomplished by using the fingers rather than a mouse.

One VIDEODESK operation that is delightfully natural is drawing. The image of the user's finger is used as a stylus. We have demonstrated this capability for years and have found that people can discover it or instantly pick it up by observing someone else draw. No explicit instructions are needed. When the drawing interaction was first implemented, we observed people waving their open hands over their drawings in an apparent attempt to erase them. This expectation was so universal that we incorporated it into the technology: the image of the artist's open hand is a signal to erase the entire screen.

In addition to replacing mouse functions directly, there are operations that can be done more efficiently using hand gestures. A mouse only provides control of a single point, whereas the VIDEODESK permits the user to specify several points at once. While it is awkward to use all 10 fingers simultaneously, the 2 forefingers can be used for separate functions quite comfortably. There are also cases in which it is natural to use the thumbs and forefingers in concert.

For instance, two fingers can specify the endpoints of a line, the opposite corners of a rectangle, or the size and position of a circle. Most impressively, the thumbs and forefingers of two hands can act as control points for a spline curve (Figure 7.4). Adjusting these four points simultaneously is far easier than the one-at-a-time techniques that have to be employed with a mouse. In fact, these adjustments are so natural that the user is not aware of which finger he or she is moving to get the desired effect. It is coordination rather than command.

Since the operations described are more than sufficient for duplicating the function of a mouse, we can assume that there is a useful class of applications that might be controlled in this way. Rather than rely on gesture for every function, we expect voice input to replace the keyboard. While speech technology is thought to be a distraction in the office, if management thought that such distractions were a problem, workers would already have individual offices. Whatever the distraction, point-and-talk is as natural a way to interact with computers as it is with other people.

In addition to its intuitive value and multipoint control, the VIDEODESK has other compelling advantages. First, an ongoing skirmish in the computer revolution is the battle for the desktop. For a time, the

FIG. 7.4.   SPLINE CURVE

computer appeared to be winning, completely supplanting the former uses of the desk. Users reacted by buying specialized furniture or dedicating a separate table to the computer. The additional floor space and furniture must be considered part of the expense of the computer itself. Recently, the tide has been reversed. Users are quite aware of what they have lost and are eager to recover the use of their desktops.

Furthermore, the VIDEODESK is completely compatible with traditional uses of the desk. There is nothing to hold, nothing to wear, nothing to wear out, and no wires. You can interact with the people in your environment exactly as you normally would. This would not be true if you were wearing contemporary data goggles. This fact is important because most people have a variety of responsibilities and perform many different tasks. Only a few might be full-time artificial reality personnel. The rest will have to choose, moment by moment, whether to operate in an artificial reality or in the real world. In fact, they will often want to be able to operate in both simultaneously. If considerable ceremony is required to enter or leave an artificial reality, there are fewer functions for which the technology will be used. Similarly, if the technology cuts you off from your local colleagues or makes you look foolish to them, you will think twice about using it.

Three Dimensions

As described so far, the VIDEODESK is strictly a two-dimensional interface. On the other hand, most existing applications operate in two
dimensions. In fact, the overwhelming majority of three-dimensional
applications are controlled with two-dimensional interfaces. They
have to be, because there are no widely used three-dimensional input
devices. Therefore, the VIDEODESK techniques can be retrofitted to the
world of existing applications.

The VIDEODESK can be extended to operate in three dimensions by
means of a sample plane that can be positioned anywhere in a three-
dimensional volume in any orientation. Once the plane is positioned,
the image of the user's hands is projected onto it and can point anywhere on the plane. In Figure 7.5, the user's hands appear on a sample
plane in a volume of gas in a combustion chamber of a jet engine. The
forefingers of the user's hands define a line. The flow of gas through
that line defines a surface that is deformed as it flows through the

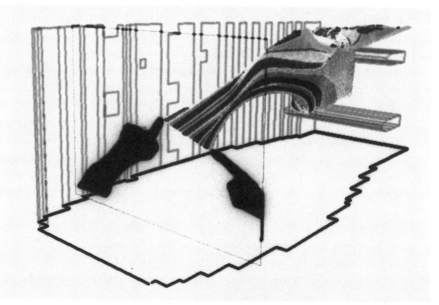

FIG. 7.5. COMBUSTION CHAMBER OF A JET ENGINE WITH USER'S HANDS PROJECTED BY
MEANS OF A SAMPLE PLANE.

FIG. 7.6.   VIDEODESK SCULPTURE SYSTEM.

volume. This application was originally developed for Pratt & Whitney and has recently inspired the development of a virtual wind tunnel at the National Aeronautics and Space Administration.

In our sculpture system, the user's fingers define a spline curve that is used as the aperture in an imaginary extruding device. If the user changes the shape of the spline curve as the graphic material is squeezed through the opening, a complex solid object can be created in seconds (Figure 7.6). While traditional computer-aided design tools are fine for shapes defined by engineering equations, they are too cumbersome for the creation of asymmetric shapes. In particular, they are unsatisfactory when the goal is styling, as is the case with automobiles and shoes.

Finally, it is possible to operate directly in three dimensions by perceiving the user's hands in three space. We implemented single-finger three-dimensional perception in 1987 using two stereo cameras mounted above the desk and by using a second camera that looked at the participant's hand from the side. With several cameras looking from different angles and more sophisticated image processing, it will be possible to get most of the information that a data glove provides without asking the user to wear anything on his or her hands.

While the research community assumes that three-dimensional input is superior, it is very uncomfortable to hold your hands in the air, without support, for any length of time. Raising your hand above the desk occasionally is acceptable, but protracted elevation of both hands would be difficult indeed. The advantage of the sample plane technique is that your hands are supported by the desk at all times.

3-D Displays

Unencumbering VIDEOPLACE input techniques can be combined with three-dimensional displays. For instance, Stereographics Corporation's Crystal Eyes glasses permit you to view three-dimensional images on a high-resolution monitor. These lightweight glasses block the view of one eye as the monitor displays the image intended for the other. Other displays are starting to appear that allow you to see a three-dimensional image on a computer screen without wearing glasses [1]. If these display techniques were combined with VIDEOPLACE technology, the three-dimensional image could change appropriately as you moved about a room in which all surfaces were used for stereo display. In fact, this approach immerses the participant in a three-dimensional world created with the full resolution of today's graphic workstations. For some applications, this approach would be far superior to head-mounted displays.

Teleconferencing

The term *VIDEOPLACE* refers to a shared visual space created by combining the live video images of geographically separated inviduals with computer graphics to create a telecommunication medium. This concept was demonstrated for both VIDEOPLACE and the VIDEODESK in 1970. In the last few years, it has been adopted by other researchers.

The idea is that when you call a remote colleague, it is increasingly likely that you want to discuss information that you have on your computer. The conversation will be more successful if your colleague can look at the same information on his or her screen. With the VIDEODESK, that communication can be enhanced by transmitting the image of your hands so that they appear over that same information on the other screen. Then, you can point to phrases in a contract, figures on a spread sheet, or components in a schematic exactly the same way you would if you were sitting together. In fact, it is easier than the common situation of being on opposite sides of a desk or table and having to turn papers upside down for your colleague to read. Naturally, your colleague's hands would also appear on both screens simultaneously.

VIDEODESK TeleTutoring

In Tomorrow's Realities Gallery at SIGGRAPH'91 in Las Vegas, we demonstrated VIDEODESK teleconferencing. Gallery visitors sat down at a VIDEODESK and saw the image of their hands on the screen in the context of the flow visualization application or the sculpture system described earlier. They also saw the image of the hands of another person who was sitting at another VIDEODESK. The second person, a student volunteer with 15 minutes of training, explained the applications while demonstrating how to use your hands to operate them. For the duration of the conference, we were consistently able to explain the use of a novel interface to control unfamiliar applications to SIGGRAPH visitors in just a few minutes. The fact that the entire interface was visible to the visitor made it possible to learn by imitation. Seeing a cursor controlled by a mouse in the hands of a remote colleague might seem to be equivalent, but the inferences required to interpret the cursor movements make learning how to use it much more difficult.

Since only the silhouette of the user's hands is transmitted, full video bandwidth is not required. The silhouette image can be compressed. The voice and gesture data can fit within an ISDN channel. (The Integrated Services Data Network is a combined digital voice plus data service.)

Gesture Messages

If your party is not there when you call, you could leave a voice message with your visual material, accompanied by animated hand gestures for your colleague's later perusal. This form of animated voice-plus-gesture documentation might also be useful in help mechanisms for any application. Many people would prefer a multisensory explanation to reading on-line documentation.

Synthesis

Since the goals of both encumbering and unencumbering technologies are similar, it is my expectation that they will coexist and merge. Data goggles the size of eyeglasses, or better yet, contact lenses will present little or no inconvenience, especially if you already wear corrective lenses. Rather than cutting you off from your immediate environment, these glasses will display virtual objects within the environment so that they can be seen by others.

The glasses will not change your appearance nor interfere with your view of your local colleagues. It is important that the displays not obscure your face, because the computer will use video cameras to perceive you. It will possess a detailed model of your body, facial expression, and clothing. This information will be used to generate a graphic image of you from any point of view. You will be able to converse naturally with people in your own environment and to make eye contact with a remote colleague whose image is projected into it.

As data glasses become less encumbering, there will be less resistance to wearing them. An additional factor that could make them more attractive is if they become superior to alternative displays. Although the resolution of current data goggles is inadequate for almost any application, they are certain to improve greatly in the not distant future. If, as I expect, their images become comparable to those seen in an Omnimax theater, the effect will be overwhelming.

Data goggles may also be the least expensive means of displaying high-resolution imagery. The cost of the high-resolution monitor is a significant component in the price of a graphic workstation, and small devices are inherently cheaper than large ones. The same argument applies to high-definition TV. Thus, there are powerful motivations, other than artificial realities, for developing these types of display devices.

Data goggles, without the accoutrements of data gloves and data suits, represent an important technology. To be able to look around a three-dimensional environment in a natural way is a very important viewing option and possibly preferable to any alternative. If data goggles could provide a sense of space, an architect could truly pre-experience a building. If participants could be realistically portrayed, meetings could be held in artificial realities not because they are the next best thing to being there, but because they are better than being there. A meeting of engineers convened to discuss a problem in a jet engine would be more intense if the participants found themselves literally surrounded by the engine. Sales might be a snap if you could literally take the customer to the mountaintop and show him the promised land.

One might assume that only three-dimensional applications will benefit from this type of visualization. However, the human interface is evolving toward more natural information. Three dimensional space is more, not less, intuitive than two dimensional space. Two-dimensional portrayal is the province of blueprints, schematics, and notation. Three dimensional space is what we evolved to understand. It is more primitive, not more advanced. Therefore, we can expect that three-dimensional representations will be used to depict what is now considered two-dimensional information. In addition, the trend toward representing conceptual information perceptually will continue.

Artificial realities are based on the premise that the perceptual intelligence that all men share is more powerful than the symbol manipulation skills that are the province of the few. Thus, the test is to translate the deliberately arcane into a form that our senses can understand. If we see it, we can know it. If we cannot, we can only talk about it.

REFERENCES

[1] Eichenlaub, J. B., A. Martens, and T. C. Touris, "3D Without Glasses Just Flat Out Better," *Computer Technology Review,* January 1990, p. 26.

[2] Krueger, M. W., "Computer Controlled Responsive Environments," doctoral dissertation, University of Wisconsin, 1974.

[3] Krueger, M. W., "Responsive Environments," AFIPS National Computer Conference Proceedings, AFIPS Press, 1977, pp. 423–434.

[4] Krueger, M. W., *Artificial Reality,* Reading, MA: Addison-Wesley Publishing Company, 1983.

[5] Krueger, M. W., K. Hinrichsen, and T. Gionfriddo, "VIDEOPLACE—An Artificial Reality, *SIGCHI Proceedings,* pp. 35–40, New York: ACM Press, 1985.

[6] Krueger, M. W., "VIDEOPLACE: A Report from the ARTIFICIAL REALITY Laboratory," *Leonardo,* **18** (3), pp. 145–152, 1985.

[7] Krueger, M. W., T. P. Gionfriddo, and K. Hinrichsen, "Real Time Perception of and Response to Actions of an Unencumbered Participant/User," U.S. Patent #4843568, 1989.

[8] Krueger, M. W., "New Realities for ISDN," *Network World,* pp. 59–61, November 6, 1989.

[9] Krueger, M. W., *Artificial Reality II,* Reading, MA: Addison-Wesley Publishing Company, 1991.

Pg 163
 → VR creates artificial...
user + the environment
 ... practical applin of
VR

Chapter 8

Virtual Reality
and Planetary Exploration

Michael W. McGreevy
National Aeronautics and Space Administration
Moffett Field, California
Ames Research Center
Human Interface Research Branch
Aerospace Human Factors Research Division
mcgreevy@eos.arc.nasa.gov

Michael McGreevy has been working in VR almost as long as Krueger. For years he has worked at NASA applying the ideas of visualization and inhabitable spaces to enable the planetary explorers to "be" where they could not physically go. I am especially pleased that his chapter shows how one can apply the ideas of VR and AR without needing fancy hardware—a central idea of this book.

—A.W.

Introduction

Virtual reality (VR) is a display and control technology that can envelop a person in an interactive computer-generated or computer-mediated virtual environment. VR creates artificial worlds of sensory experience, or immerses the user in representations of real spatial environments that might otherwise be inaccessible by virtue of distance, scale, time, or physical incompatibilities of the user and the environment. Virtual planetary exploration, whether in synthetic terrain within a computer, or using model-based telepresence to remotely operate a roving vehicle, is one of the practical applications of virtual reality.

The essential, defining characteristics of virtual reality systems are that they perceptually surround and include the user in the display

space; provide familiar, intuitive interactivity with depicted environments and objects; and potentially enable every informative characteristic of the environments/objects to be interactive, metamorphic,
malleable, and fluid.

The necessary components of a virtual reality system are captured
or designed models (typically digital) of environments/objects (and,
where appropriate, their behaviors); computer graphics systems capable of generating usefully detailed and sufficiently interactive envi-
ronments/objects; user interface devices (e.g., head-mounted displays,
gesture trackers, etc.) that support a sense of presence in a virtual environment; and strategies, metaphors, algorithms, and software defining
user-environment and user-object interactivity.

Considering the wide diversity of virtual reality applications and the
corresponding differences in acceptable trade-offs, a practical approach
is to focus on a specific set of users, understand their world, and design
to their requirements. To do this, it is useful to review the nature of the
user's enterprise as indicated by their operational experience, current
techniques and tools, and future requirements. In the area of videogames, for example, one might review the nature and characteristics of
historical and current games (especially real-world, nonelectronic
ones) and the unmet needs of players that might be addressed with further development. In the area of virtual planetary exploration, the strategy is to review mission operational experience, current techniques
and tools, and future mission requirements. This chapter surveys the
observations obtained with this approach.

Background

The National Aeronautics and Space Administration's (NASA's) lunar
mission simulator, built by General Electric (GE) in the early 1960s
and developed throughout the decade, was the first to use computer-
generated imagery. (At the time, imagery in the most advanced military
flight simulators was based on "flying" cameras over gigantic model
boards that looked something like glorified train sets.) In addition to its
originally intended use, this historic simulator was also used by Peter
Kamnitzer, head of the Urban Lab at the University of California at Los
Angeles (UCLA), to create an interactive city environment [1]. The user
could drive up freeway ramps and along freeways, ride up and down a

glass elevator, walk down corridors of buildings, look out windows, and fly in a helicopter over the city. The joint UCLA/NASA/GE project was documented in the 1968 film, *City-Scape*. This was the first time a simulator had been used to explore a digital model of a city. It is a surprisingly early example of the use of digital simulation techniques for general-purpose, interactive, spatial exploration.

In the 1960s, Ivan Sutherland created one of the pioneering virtual reality systems, incorporating a head-mounted display [2]. Unfortunately, the computer graphics systems (and thus the virtual environments) available to him at that time were exceedingly primitive. As a result, he and his colleagues were quickly diverted into inventing many of the fundamental algorithms, hardware, and software of computer graphics. While multimillion dollar military systems have used head-mounted displays in the years since Sutherland's work, the notion of a personal virtual environment system as a general-purpose user/computer interface was generally neglected for almost 20 years.

Beginning in 1984, McGreevy created the first of NASA's virtual environment workstations (also known as personal simulators and virtual reality systems) for use in human/computer interface research [3, 4]. With contractors Jim Humphries, Saim Eriskin, and Joe Deardon, he designed and built the Virtual Visual Environment Display system (VIVED, pronounced "vivid"), the first low-cost, wide field-of-view, stereo, head-tracked, head-mounted display. Clones of this design, and extensions of it, are still predominant in the VR market. Next, McGreevy configured the workstation hardware: a Digital Equipment Corporation PDP-11/40 computer, an Evans and Sutherland Picture System 2 with two 19-inch monitors, a Polhemus head and hand tracker, video cameras, custom video circuitry, and the VIVED system. With Amy Wu, McGreevy wrote the software for NASA's first virtual environment workstation. The first demonstrations of this virtual reality system at NASA were conducted by McGreevy in early 1985 for local researchers and managers, as well as visitors from universities, industry, and the military. Since that time, more than two dozen technical contributors at NASA Ames have worked to develop virtual reality for applications including planetary terrain exploration, computational fluid dynamics, and space station telerobotics [5, 6].

Currently, with continuing advances in the capability of affordable computer graphics systems, one of the key components of VR is developing well. But the other three components need substantial further development. Comparable advancements in capability and reduction of cost are needed for VR user interface devices (especially the head-mounted displays); for capturing/designing digital models of virtual environments and objects; and for VR software (based on improved strategies, metaphors, and algorithms).

To address these needs, an increasing number of academic, commercial, and government research and development efforts are appearing around the world, and new VR products continue to emerge [7–17]. Even a small selection of examples illustrates the breadth of the trend. Boeing in Seattle is working with the University of Washington to demonstrate VR-based marketing and engineering design tools for the new 777 transport. In Japan, widespread, serious efforts are being devoted to the technologies of virtual reality, which many Japanese refer to as *Tele-existence,* with an emphasis on its communication potential. The University of North Carolina, the University of California at Berkeley, and Cornell University are independently working on virtual architectural *walkthroughs.* The arts and entertainment communities are also advancing VR, with a variety of companies developing and marketing VR videogames, the first VR-based Hollywood movie succeeding at the box office in early 1992, and VR artwork appearing in popular technology magazines.

Amid this explosion of new interest, NASA continues to develop VR-related technology in directions suitable for planetary exploration, as it has done for more than 30 years.

Operational Experience in Planetary Terrain Exploration

NASA's operational experience is a valuable resource for understanding exploration behavior and the related user/system interface requirements for virtual reality systems. The following survey indicates that the desktop metaphor and the paperwork-oriented workstation based on that metaphor are inadequate for many planetary visualization situations. It also serves as a reminder that a more natural approach to spatial visualization has long been a fundamental part of planetary exploration. In particular, operational experience during the missions of Surveyor, Lunar Orbiter, Apollo, Mariner, and Viking indicates that planetary explorers seek to place themselves into a natural, direct spatial relationship with planetary environments. These exploration behaviors suggest that virtual reality systems are likely to be particularly useful in support of these applications.

Visualizing Earth's Moon

A significant aspect of the preparations for manned exploration of the moon involved simulations of vehicle operations, traversals in environments analogous to the lunar surface, and photo reconnaissance of the lunar terrain. In all of these cases, lunar explorers, which includes mission planners and analysts as well as astronauts, generally sought to place themselves into a natural, direct spatial relationship with the important aspects of the environment to be explored.

The generic operations to be conducted during manned flight to the moon and manned surface exploration (i.e., those not specific to the actual layout of the lunar terrain) were perfected in a variety of simulation environments. In each of these simulation cases, the visual, dynamic, and visceral components of realism were traded off as necessary to achieve the desired training and familiarization goals. In the early 1960s, NASA contracted with GE to develop the first simulator with computer-generated imagery for use in lunar mission simulations (the same one used by Kamnitzer). The evolving simulator was only capable of 240 edges (e.g., 80 triangles) at a cost of two million dollars by 1967. It was primarily useful for practicing rendezvous and especially docking between the lunar excursion module (LEM) and the command module (CM). For practicing final approach and landing, a unique, jet-powered, manned hovercraft, dubbed the "flying bedstead," was used. Use of this system provided the subtle cues that were vital to a successful landing. Walking in one-sixth gravity was simulated using a steeply tilted plane to represent the surface, and a set of pulleys and supports to suspend the nearly horizontal astronaut as he or she strolled along the walking plane.

Explorers also visited real planetary environments thought to be similar to those yet to be explored. The Apollo astronauts utilized the moon-like deserts of Arizona and Nevada to prepare for their exploration of the unfamiliar lunar surface. (Sometimes, when the terrain similarities were insufficient for the task, dynamite was used to create realistic looking impact craters.) These surrogate environments provided a firsthand sense of the environments to be explored, and stimulated thinking about systems and operations for lunar exploration. Geologist Harrison Schmitt, who was project chief of lunar field geological methods at the USGS Astrogeology Branch at Flagstaff, Arizona, had been the instructor of the astronauts on such field trips to analog environments. He was later to be the only geologist to explore the moon, as a crewmember of Apollo 17.

In addition to simulating the generic operations of flight and traversal, it was also necessary to visualize the actual surface of the moon so as to understand the nature of potential manned landing sites, and later to document the landing and traversal sites visited by the astronauts. These activities revealed that users attempted to integrate and visualize the terrain environment in a natural and direct manner.

On June 4, 1966, the unmanned Surveyor 1 spacecraft landed on the Ocean of Storms, near the lunar equator. Surveyor 1 was the first of NASA's five successful unmanned landings, between 1966 and 1968, designed to investigate the lunar surface environment. Each Surveyor had a video camera; some had manipulator arms for testing the soil. To image the surface, the single video camera pointed up to a pivoting and swiveling mirror, which sampled the surrounding environment as a collection of pictures. A total of 87,632 video images were taken by the five Surveyors. Surveyor 1 took more than 10,000 of them.

Technicians at the U.S. Geological Survey pasted the images onto the interior surfaces of 34-inch spherical shells (Figure 8.1). The mosaic panoramas imaged the entire environment surrounding the lander. These so-called "Surveyor mosaic spheres" were NASA's first virtual visual environment displays for planetary exploration [18, 19].

The Jet Propulsion Lab (JPL) enlarged the Surveyor prints and pasted them onto much larger spherical segments. When a person stood in the center of the display, he had the uncanny sense that he was on the moon [20]. It was NASA's second virtual visual environment display for planetary exploration. In effect, NASA had obtained more than a collection of pictures of the moon. It had captured environmental images of the moon.

Additional information was gathered with the five Lunar Orbiter missions from 1966 to 1967. These missions were designed to survey the lunar surface and to find suitable landing sites for the manned Apollo missions. The entire near side of the moon was mapped at a

FIG. 8.1 SURVEYOR MOSAIC SPHERES CREATED BY THE U.S. GEOLOGICAL SURVEY. Photograph taken by J. R. Eyerman.

resolution of 60 to 80 meters, while selected areas were mapped at 1 to 5 meters. The imaging system of the Lunar Orbiters was unique: 70-mm film was exposed and processed on orbit, and each negative was then scanned for electronic transmission back to Earth, where another negative was created.

Lunar Orbiter also provided the first close-up oblique views of the moon. For the first time, the vast crater Copernicus, for example, could be viewed from a low oblique perspective, making the mountainous terrain look almost familiar, and in a sense more interpretable. Certainly, this more familiar oblique view of terrain made the moon's surface seem to be more of a place, a location at which presence is possible, rather than merely an abstract disk in the sky. This development had a profound effect on the collective human conception of the moon. (Conversely, later Apollo images of Earth from the point of view of the lunar explorers made vivid and poignant the known, but until then not fully appreciated, sphericity of the Earth. Thus, the conception of Earth as a place and presence on it was also enhanced by imaging point of view.)

   To interpret nonoblique Lunar Orbiter images, mission analysts often found it expedient to cover large areas of the floor with enlarged, mosaicked prints representing the lunar surface. The resulting view of the surface was comparable to that of viewing part of a huge lunar globe from very close up. This provided an integrated, intuitive view of the moon as seen from low orbit. Clearly, desktop-oriented workstations would not be much help here.

   During each of the successful Apollo missions to the moon, between 1969 and 1972, astronauts routinely took 360-degree panoramic photographs as part of their environmental documentation. Typical of these is a dramatic panorama taken by Eugene Cernan at the crater Camelot during Apollo 17, the most recent manned planetary exploration mission. The panorama consists of 12 photos taken at approximately 30-degree intervals. The purpose of these panoramic images was to capture a sense of the environment for mission analysts and geoscientists, but the sweeping panorama also captures the stark beauty of the rocky surface. The view scans from the glare of the sun above deeply shadowed rocks, to sharply defined boulders lit from the side, to the brilliantly illuminated landscape down-sun, and around another 180 degrees back to the glare of the sun. A desktop-oriented workstation cannot do justice to such a dramatic panoramic image of the lunar terrain environment, nor can it recreate the sense of presence inherent in the integrated collection of views.

   Stereoscopic imaging during Apollo included hand-held stereo pairs obtained with a single camera. These were created by having the astronaut shift his weight onto one foot for the first image, and then, without rotation of the camera, onto the other foot for the second image. Another set of stereo pairs was obtained by using a specially designed surface close-up camera to image fine details of the lunar regolith. From orbit, a third set of stereoscopic images was taken using the panoramic camera, located in the service module which is attached to the command module.

   Clearly, spatial visualization was an important priority during the exploration of the moon.

Visualizing Mars

Mariner missions to Mars helped prepare for the Viking lander missions by sending back the first detailed images of the surface of Mars.

The only orbiter in the series was Mariner 9 in 1971–72. On November 14, 1971, it became the first man-made object to orbit another planet. Taking more than 7100 images, Mariner 9 mapped 98% of the surface of Mars at a resolution ranging from 1 to 3 kilometers, and 1% at 100 to 500 meters. The Mariner 9 photos were used to construct large, flat mosaics of the surface. For example, the full extent of Valles Marineris, the spectacular 3000-mile-long system of canyons named after the spacecraft that discovered it, was pieced together from a collection of orbital photos.

Of particular interest is the fact that the Mariner 9 images were also integrated to create four- and six-foot-diameter spherical models of Mars. The first photo-globe was completed in September 1973 by a team at JPL. The mosaicker was Earl Zimmerman. These globes were the first complete photomosaics of any planetary body. NASA had created the first physical model of an entire planet ever made from its images, providing an integrated representation of the planet. The desktop-oriented workstation cannot adequately display such a globe.

During the Viking mission to Mars in 1976, the orbiters imaged the surface of Mars for more than a month before landing sites were selected and certified. More than 50,000 pictures were taken, with 90% of Mars imaged at 100 to 150 meters per pixel, and large areas imaged at 7 to 30 meters. Images of the surface were pieced together right away for a quick look at the terrain. More exact mosaicking was also done by hand. It is interesting to note that walls and tables served not only as large display surfaces for orbital imaging mosaics, they also served as group decision-making displays. Given the format and use of the mosaics, a desktop-oriented workstation would not have met the users' needs.

Desktop electronic workstations were used as text-oriented command, control, and communication stations. Some could display, on a small monitor, the latest image from the lander as it was slowly built up from the transmitted bits. For example, such a console workstation was used by Jim Martin, Viking project manager, to observe the first color picture returned from the surface of Mars, and later, viewing another image, to verify that the pin restraining the surface sampler mechanism had indeed been worked loose.

Stereo imaging showed that apparently flat terrain was actually rolling hills and sand dunes. Because the two cameras on each lander were 82 centimeters (32.28 inches) apart, stereo views had to be synthetically altered so that the foreground terrain could be fused.

A tremendous computational effort went into the processing of stereo images, both for human viewing, and for stereophotogrammetric measurements of the terrain. This investment in stereo viewing is a clear indication that 3-D visualization was an important part of Viking mission operations.

The Viking landers were designed to capture panoramic images of the terrain surrounding the landers that, unlike the Surveyor mosaic spheres, did not have to be awkwardly pieced together. The facsimile cameras worked brilliantly, producing many detailed panoramas subtending 342.5 degrees of azimuth by 65 degrees of elevation. By making large photographic prints of these panoramas, the mission team had a wide "picture window" into the landing site.

When it came time to guide the sampler arm to manipulate the Martian soil, mission operations personnel resorted to the use of miniature and full-scale 3-D models. Occasionally, a lander photo of the surface would be specially processed so that the spatial relations shown were correct (to the extent possible) when the photo was laid flat next to a scale model of the lander. The model, along with such specially processed photos, helped planners to visualize the geometry of the surface sampling. The model and accompanying surface images also served as a group decision-making display.

One of the most interesting Viking mission snapshots [21] shows a planetary explorer at JPL crouched next to a full-scale mock-up of the lander in "the sandbox" (Figure 8.2). The scientist (holding a greatly enlarged panoramic photo) is trying to visualize the spatial situation from the point of view of the lander. This was so important to mission analysts that they used stereo images to pinpoint the locations and shapes of landmark rocks. They then created styrofoam models of the rocks for their full-scale model of the landing site. This is yet another example of the importance of 3-D visualization in Viking mission operations. When it came to manipulating the surface, a life-sized model of the local environment, based on three-dimensional imagery, was essential. While significant effort was expended to create this physical virtual environment for a static lander and its sampling task, the effort required to support a sampling rover will be far greater. A physical model would be too large and too elaborate, while a digital one would be ideal. For this application, a virtual planetary exploration system would be particularly useful.

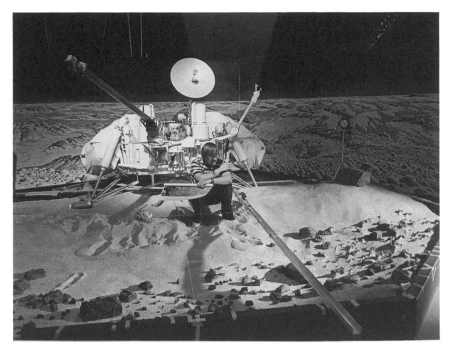

Fig. 8.2 A Mars-Viking scientist uses a model of the lander and landing site to visualize spatial relationships for mission operations. Photograph © 1977 by Hans-Peter Biemann.

Characterizing Unfamiliar Terrain Features

Planetary explorers have long used imaginative metaphors to characterize unfamiliar terrain features. In his book, *Countries of the Mind* [22], John Middleton Murry calls poetic metaphor "the analogy by which the human mind explores the universe of quality and charts the non-measurable world." Clearly, Murry saw the link between exploration and metaphor! He further refers to metaphor as "the means by which the less familiar is assimilated to the more familiar, the unknown into the known."

This use of poetic metaphor could be seen in the exploration behavior of Mars explorers. Mariner mission personnel informally named a network of canyons on Mars "the chandelier." Viking personnel referred to the moons of Mars as "potato-shaped." Rocks around the

Viking landers were colloquially known by such names as "Big Joe," "the muffler," or "Mr. Badger."

Voyager mission personnel also used poetic metaphor. Prominent features on Miranda, a moon of Uranus, were initially called "the chevron," "the racetrack," and "the pancake stack." Triton, the major moon of Neptune, is said to have large areas of "cantaloupe terrain."

Participants in the Magellan mission to Venus have described terrain features on Venus as looking like the clay-animation character "Gumby," like tiles, or even spider-like. They have described the highlands of Venus as so extensively deformed by geological forces that they are like bread dough that has been kneaded.

The heavy emphasis on food (pancakes, potatoes, cantaloupe, bread) as the known quantity in the metaphorical dyad is not unique to NASA people. IBM researchers recently imaged molecules of benzene and the caption on the photograph in a science journal said that they looked like "rows of freshly baked doughnuts."

Exploring Environments Analogous to Mars

Scientists and engineers explore Mars-like environments in order to develop an understanding of how to explore Mars itself. It is important to realize the extent to which planetary exploration relies on the use of Mars-like terrain on Earth. Unlike digital models of Mars, which capture the specific nature of that planetary environment, analog environments serve as general models, enabling the development of concepts, theories, and systems by analogy.

Learning How to Look for Life on Mars in Antarctica

Current preparations for the exploration of Mars reveal exploration behaviors that illustrate the value of presence in terrain environments. Just as in the missions of Surveyor, Lunar Orbiter, Apollo, Mariner, and Viking, explorers still seek to put themselves into a natural spatial relationship with the environments to be explored. They also seek to use the familiar to assimilate the unfamiliar.

A Mars-like environment can be found on Earth in the dry valleys of Antarctica. These remote and inhospitable valleys are cold, rocky, and without surface vegetation or animals. But the lakes in these valleys may help in the search for evidence of ancient life on Mars. Divers who have cut tunnels through the 18 feet of surface ice, have found living mattes of blue-green algae at the bottoms of these lakes. Current conditions in the dry valleys, including the lakes, are thought to be similar to those that existed on Mars 3.5 billion years ago when these algae first appeared on Earth. Could this form of life have appeared during that period on Mars, too? Scientists are exploring Antarctica to learn how to search for ancient life on Mars.

Scientists who dive under the ice of the Antarctic lakes also use remotely operated vehicles, or ROVs. In this case, remote control is used not to avoid the trip, but to extend their reach once there. But they want a greater sense of presence in the underwater environment than they can get with current ROVs. They want the ability to collect samples just as they would if they were physically present at the sampling site. They seek telepresence interfaces to put themselves into a natural spatial relationship with the remote environments to be explored. Further, these scientist/explorers believe that by demonstrating the utility of telepresence for real planetary science in Antarctica, they will improve the chances that the technology will be available for later application on Mars.

Current plans call for a central manned base on Mars with global access to unmanned rovers [23]. Thus, Mars explorers will also use remote control to extend their reach once there. Just as in Antarctica, these planetary explorers will want a vivid, first-hand sense of the remote environment. They will seek to put themselves into a natural spatial relationship with the environments to be explored. They will want the ability to collect samples just as they would if they were physically present at the sampling site.

Getting a Sense of Mars-like Terrain in Death Valley

Every year or so, a group of planetary mission analysts, designers, and geoscientists takes a field trip to personally experience Mars-like terrain in Death Valley and environs. The trip is for those who are engaged in the analysis and design of surface systems, landers, robotic imaging, and mission planning. Their objectives are revealing [24]:

1. Get a first-hand sense of natural terrain thought to be similar to candidate landing and roving sites on Mars.

2. Get a first-hand sense of a geological traverse in unfamiliar terrain.
3. Stimulate thinking on safe landing and roving techniques.

The behavior of these planetary explorers demonstrates that a first-hand sense of the environment to be explored is a very high priority for thinking about systems and operations for planetary exploration. These scientists and engineers wish to understand Mars as an environment by surrounding themselves with, and exploring, a similar environment.

As part of this effort, they typically compare surface views with aerial views of the Mars-like terrain. Thus, they attempt to learn to interpret orbital imagery of terrain as an environment consisting of paths and obstacles. These explorers intuitively understand that to appreciate the affordances of an environment, the environment must be experienced concretely and directly through personal experience.

Observing Geologists at Work in the Field

Since the presence of human geologists is held by some to be essential to the conduct of field geology on remote planetary surfaces [25], a field study was recently conducted to observe and characterize the nature of that presence [26]. The study was conducted in the Mojave Desert of Southern California at the Amboy lava field, a landscape that is analogous to terrain on Mars. Two experienced planetary geologists were interviewed and observed during the conduct of surface operations. Each subject then wore a head-mounted video camera/display system, which replaced natural vision with video vision, while attempting to conduct further surface explorations. As a result of this study, some specific field activities of these geologists have been characterized, providing more concrete guidance for the design of telepresence and terrain visualization systems.

A major advantage of presence is the opportunity to correlate willed self-motion and position with the resulting visual imagery so as to enhance one's understanding of the spatial arrangement of the environment and its constituent objects and their components. The geologists observed in the field exhibited and described exactly such behaviors. They moved themselves relative to the environment, and moved objects relative to themselves, in order to understand the terrain. They observed the environment from orbit (i.e., by studying orbital photographs), spiraled down from high altitudes in light planes to obtain dynamic oblique perspectives, climbed to high ground for a contextual view, measured terrain with their paces, accumulated mental models of the environment by visual scanning as they walked, oscillated slightly about a point in space to observe the glint of sunlight from crystals in rock faces, turned rock samples over in their hands, used magnifying glasses to view crystal facets, and differentiated between clay and silt by "tasting" samples (i.e., differentiating between smooth and gritty textures by putting a small amount of soil into the mouth and using the tongue as a tactile sensor). They observed the terrain at a wide range of scales and from many different perspectives.

Engineering in the Field

Planetary surface exploration systems are routinely tested in Mars-like terrain on Earth, typically the desert or volcanic terrain. Recently, a team of researchers went to a site in Death Valley known as Mars Hill to test a new laser imaging system that is being developed for future planetary rovers. This site is strewn with rocks and boulders in a configuration comparable to that surrounding the Viking 2 lander. This provided an appropriate test of the laser system.

The laser scans the terrain in a raster, that is, a parallel set of closely spaced horizontal scans. A stepper motor drives the laser along each scan, collecting a set of distance measurements along each scan line. Taking into account the position of the laser, and the precise direction and distance at each point on the raster, a 3-D digital terrain model is created.

Initial results of the test produced a vividly detailed model of the terrain, clearly showing the shapes and positions of individual rocks and boulders, the overall morphology of the terrain, and very detailed views of channels formed by water erosion. Observers familiar with Mars Hill have viewed various computer-generated perspective images of the terrain, and found that the laser-captured terrain model closely resembles the morphology of the site. (See the discussion of computed panoramas, and the stereoscopic illustration, in the section on "Demonstration Capabilities" later in this chapter.)

Digital Models of Planetary Terrain

While Mars Hill is used above as an analogical model of Mars, the digital representation of Mars Hill is a specific model of the real place. By exploring such a model, it is possible to gain a specific (as opposed to analogical) understanding of the place represented. Digital models of the planets are created by measuring the terrain with photographs, stereophotogrammetry, laser rangefinders, radar altimeters, synthetic aperture radar (SAR), and other means. The advantage of digital modeling over collecting images is that the model representing the planet may itself be explored. Vistas never before seen can be generated in color, in stereo, dynamically—enabling a dramatic expansion of exploration capability. Ultimately, all of the spatially correlated information about a planet could be accessed via such a model.

Comparing Orbital and Surface Views

If limited to orbital views of planetary terrain, planetary geologists are constrained from fully and naturally exploring the environment. To illustrate this, a Landsat satellite view of Wyoming might be compared with a surface view of Grand Teton National Park (e.g., as seen by a hiker). This would highlight the vast difference of interpretations associated with orbital views versus surface views. A satellite picture is perceived as a two-dimensional texture, not a habitat, not an environment. The surface view is the kind of view that human beings have evolved to perceive. It is difficult to view the satellite image and imagine the infinitude of surface views in useful detail. Yet even a static surface view is a pale shadow of the experience of presence in the environment. Without the capacity for freely moving about, one obtains a very diminished understanding of the environment.

A virtual reality interface would integrate the space in the picture with the space around the viewer, and it would enable the direct and natural exploration of the terrain. It would then be easy to interpret and interact with paths to traverse, obstacles to overcome, places too dangerous to tread, safe, sheltered areas, regions with resources, and useful or valuable objects—that is, all the affordances of the environment.

Synthetic Views of the Planets

Static imagery taken from the vantage point of orbit, or even from the planetary surface, cannot provide an unconstrained, interactive view of planetary environments. A solution, short of actual presence, is to create digital models of planetary terrain from the photographs and other measurements, and then to explore those models in a direct, natural, and intuitive way.

A digital terrain model can be created by taking several pictures: enough to cover an interesting area, enough to see all sides of the terrain features, enough to determine the elevations from stereophotogrammetry. That is precisely what the U.S. Geological Survey has done since the late 1970s with some of the Viking Orbiter views of Mars. By generating digital models of terrain shape and visual texture from the collection of pictures, views from any point can be computed as needed. Later topographic visualization work was done by Michael Kobrick and his colleagues at JPL, resulting in synthetic flights over digital models of terrain, including Olympus Mons and Mt. Shasta, as in the films *Topo Follies* and *Topo Follies II.*

More recently, Kevin Hussey and his colleagues at JPL have digitally explored a 3-D digital model of the entire Los Angeles area. They used a single Landsat picture and digital elevation data from the Defense Mapping Agency. They generated more than 3000 perspective images from the digital model and produced an animated virtual flight over the area. By allowing the eye to traverse the scene (albeit noninteractively), the interpretability of the terrain is distinctly enhanced. Digital models of Mars, Miranda (a moon of Uranus), and Triton (a moon of Neptune) have also been explored via animated virtual reconnaissance flights computed by Hussey's group.

The case of Miranda is particularly indicative of the power of digital modeling of the planets. Even though the Voyager spacecraft only had time to snap a handful of photographs of Miranda as it sped past, animation based on digital modeling makes it possible to fly virtually over the surface, flying low over the mountains, peering down into canyons. This kind of capability represents nothing short of a revolution in exploration.

The temperatures, pressures, and dense atmosphere of the planet Venus do not reward the actual presence of exploring humans or their machines. Thus, virtual exploration is the only practical way to explore the hostile planet. To make this possible, the Magellan spacecraft was sent into orbit around Venus on August 10, 1990. From orbit, through the dense clouds, the spacecraft has probed more than 90% of the surface using SAR, radar altimetry, and thermal emission radiometry.

The mission will generate approximately a trillion bytes of terrain data, more data than all previous planetary exploration missions

combined. Full-resolution SAR image mosaics, each covering a 5-×
5-deg square of latitude, will be produced with 0.075-km pixel spacing.
Each pixel value is interpretable as the radar scattering efficiency of the
surface. Mosaics of larger area and lower resolution will also be produced, for interpretation of contexts and more global processes. The
topographical and emissivity data products, resampled to a uniform
global grid, will have 5-km pixel spacing. Data are being distributed in
compact disk read-only memory format [27].

Magellan data are providing a detailed digital model of Venus for
virtual exploration on Earth. Already, dramatic virtual flights of exploration over the fascinatingly varied terrains of Venus have been computed by JPL. It is not widely appreciated, however, that in these
scenes the vertical scale is usually exaggerated by a factor of 22.5. This
has a serious potential to mislead the unwary, especially if the observer
has not first seen the unexaggerated terrain [28].

High-speed swooping over terrain to the accompaniment of dramatic
music, a hallmark of terrain animations since the early 1980s, is rapidly approaching the level of cliche already achieved by "flying logos"
in commercial television graphics. Further, the lack of interactivity inherent in animation limits its usefulness to planetary explorers. In the
near future, personal visualization systems will take advantage of advanced virtual reality technology and related multimedia hardware
and software. This will allow planetary scientists and engineers to explore directly and naturally Venus and other planetary bodies as they
would explore any other environment of interest, not as an animated
movie with parameters determined by the animator, but as a completely interactive virtual environment.

Comprehensive Planetary Models

In future terrain exploration missions, scientists, mission operators,
and crewmembers will be able to access highly integrated digital models of the planets and moons as explorations progress. These environmental models will incorporate many spatially correlated varieties of
planetary data, including geomorphology, resource distribution, tra-
versibility, atmospheric conditions, and habitability. NASA's Mission
to Planet Earth, for example, will generate an unprecedented amount of
such data for managing diminishing resources and tracking environmental concerns.

For manned exploration of Mars, environmental models are already under development. Tom Duxbury, a leading planetary cartographer, estimates that selected potential exploration sites will need to be modeled at a resolution of 20 centimeters per pixel. He also stresses that comprehensive 3-D digital models will be needed to support future terrain exploration missions [29]. Based on the exploration behavior observed during previous manned and unmanned missions and in analog environments, it is certain that users will seek to put themselves into natural spatial relationships with these integrated environmental models. This will allow users to readily interpret inherent relations in the environmental data. It will give users a natural, coherent framework for mastering the potentially overwhelming tidal wave of fine-grained, multidimensional, multiplanetary information. Beyond this utilitarian payoff, bringing the planets virtually down to Earth will democratize space exploration.

Designing Exploration Workstations

The activities of the people who participate in planetary exploration might collectively be called their exploration behaviors. The preceding overview of NASA's operational experience in planetary exploration, the use of analog environments, and the creation and use of digital terrain models highlights a wealth of exploration behaviors. It would be useful to distill these behaviors and apply them to the design of users interfaces for exploration systems.

This kind of distillation originally informed the desktop metaphor as well, but the behaviors of interest in that case were "desktop," paperwork-oriented behaviors. The desktop metaphor does not apply well to planetary surface exploration because many of the behaviors of planetary explorers are centered on achieving a spatial linkage with the environment being explored. This linkage serves to allow one's everyday, intuitive spatial sense to be applied to the new environment. Artificial means to create this linkage are at the basis of virtual reality systems.

Limitations of the Desktop Metaphor

The desktop-oriented workstation is generally considered to be the appropriate starting point of user/computer interface design, and most human/computer interface research and development emphasizes the desktop metaphor. In this view, computing is thought to be comparable to paperwork, and the objects and functions available to the user reflect this emphasis. Keystroke-oriented interactions and point-and-click interactions with icons representing objects such as documents, files, and paperwork tools are supportive of operations performed on text and simple pictures. This approach alone, however, is quite inadequate for planetary exploration.

NASA's experience in planetary exploration has demonstrated that the desktop-oriented workstation and the desktop metaphor are inadequate for many visualization situations. Operational experience during the missions of Surveyor, Lunar Orbiter, Apollo, Mariner, Viking, Voyager, and Magellan demonstrates that planetary explorers seek to place themselves into a natural, direct spatial relationship with planetary environments. Exploration of analog environments indicates that the behaviors of planetary explorers are not even remotely like doing paperwork. Instead, the important behaviors are locomotion throughout the environment, manipulation of objects in the environment, perception of shapes and spatial relationships, and a considerable amount of situational understanding to guide the explorations. Digital terrain modeling techniques, which have evolved dramatically during the last 30 or so years of planetary exploration, are making it possible to virtually recreate planetary environments from the accumulated terrain data. The desktop-oriented workstation will be sorely inadequate for exploring these digital worlds.

The Exploration Metaphor

Alternative user interfaces and metaphors are needed for planetary exploration and other interactions with complex spatial environments. These interfaces and metaphors would enable the user to explore environments directly and naturally manipulate objects in those environments. Personal simulators, virtual workstations, virtual reality systems, and telepresence user interfaces are systems capable of providing this integration of user space and virtual or remote task space.

The Exploration Metaphor [30], based on a distillation of observed exploration behaviors, is useful for guiding the look and feel of these interfaces. To apply the Exploration Metaphor is to assert that computing is like exploration and to support objects, operations, and contexts comparable to those encountered in the exploration of natural environments. The Exploration Metaphor is a user interface style that accommodates and augments exploration behaviors. In particular, it provides a useful sense of presence and direct interactivity with the terrain environment to be explored.

Rather than conceiving of a user/computer interface, the designer concentrates on the explorer/environment interface. The environment itself serves to structure access to pathways and layers of information and interactivity. Thus, for example, the user would directly query the terrain via naturalistic gesture, rather than type a query or click on an icon on a virtual desktop. No mechanism of interaction separates the explorer from the environment.

The Exploration Metaphor will contribute significantly to the look and feel of personal simulators, virtual reality systems, telepresence devices, and virtual workstations, in applications where complex spatial environments, real or virtual, are visualized, explored, and manipulated. Accordingly, the design of planetary exploration workstations should be based on the Exploration Metaphor.

Presence in Real Environments

The relationships between an ecological (or natural) environment and its inhabitants are central to James J. Gibson's theory of visual perception. This theory is probably best elaborated in his book, *The Ecological Approach to Visual Perception* [31]. Gibson, one of the greatest perceptual psychologists, argued that the study of vision must go beyond the study of the eye and brain. He wrote, "One sees the environment not with the eyes but with the eyes-in-the-head-on-the-body-resting-on-the-ground." He further observed, "When no constraints are put on the visual system, we look around, walk up to something interesting and move around it so as to see it from all sides, and go from one vista to another. That is natural vision. . . ."

To be truly effective, to accommodate all aspects of natural vision, the comprehensive visual interface must provide a sense of presence; that is, it must enable the user to observe and manipulate objects and explore environments directly and naturally. That is why the combination of the head-mounted display and the hand-mounted controller provides a compellingly realistic interface to a simulated environment [32].

Since the visual system involves, according to Gibson, the entire body and its relationship to the environment and the objects in it, then the user's self image is also part of visual perception. Gibson [31] wrote that the visual world is perceived ". . . by an exploring visual system, and the awareness of the observer's own body in the world is a part of the experience." Gibson further emphasized this point when he wrote, "To perceive the world is to co-perceive oneself."

Gibson hypothesized that by observing one's own capacity for visual, manipulative, and locomotor interaction with environments and objects, one perceives the meanings and the utility of environments and objects. That is the gist of his theory of affordances. It follows, then, that the ways in which the user is allowed to interact with virtual things in a computer-generated world will determine how well he or she can understand them. Thus, it is important to understand the kinds of interactions offered by real environments and the real objects in those environments.

What do natural environments afford the observer? Environments afford exploration. Environments are composed of openings, paths, steps, and shallow slopes, which afford locomotion. Environments also consist of obstacles, which afford collision and possible injury; brinks or cliffs, which afford falling off and possibly injury; water, fire, and wind, which afford life and danger; and shelters, which afford protection from hostile elements. Most importantly, environments afford a context for interaction with a collection of objects.

What do natural objects afford the observer? Objects afford grasping, throwing, portability, containment, and sitting on. Objects afford shaping, molding, manufacture, stacking, piling, and building. Some objects afford eating. Some very special objects afford use as tools, or spontaneous action and interaction (that is, some objects are other animals).

Clearly, natural objects and environments offer far more opportunity for use, interaction, manipulation, and exploration than the ones typically generated on computer systems. Also, a user's natural capacity for visual, manipulative, and locomotor interaction with real environments and objects is far more informative than the typically restricted interactions with computer-generated scenes. Although a virtual world may usefully differ from the real world, virtual objects and environments must provide some measure of the affordances of the objects and environments depicted in order to support natural vision more fully.

Presence in Virtual Environments

Connecting the user's space and the virtual display space is essential for creating a sense of presence in a virtual reality. Several strategies can be used to support this linkage by building a model of the user into the simulation system. Typically, however, the observer is hardly modeled at all, other than as a pinhole camera, the simplest model of the eye. Still, even the minimal pinhole camera model of the user can be used as a spatial link between the user and the depicted scene. At the very least, the center of projection should be located at the eyepoint of the user. This is rarely done, however, even though linear perceptive, the geometric theory that describes the nature of pinhole lens imagery, was specifically designed to link the observer to the pictorial space. Differences between the geometry of a perspective image and the geometry of the user's view of that image can have a pronounced effect on spatial perception by creating a mismatch between the user's space and the virtual display space [33].

Various means of providing different perspective images to each eye of an observer enable the creation of stereoscopic imagery. This adds the important cue of binocular disparity for improved spatial realism. Stereo provides an additional link between the scene and the observer by modeling the observer more completely, that is, as a *pair* of pinhole cameras.

In natural vision, static perspectives are rare. Moving the pinhole camera model of the observer through a computer-generated scene adds a number of spatial cues, including flow fields and the dynamic covering and uncovering of distant objects by near ones. Generally, however, this motion is presented to a passive and motionless observer on a display subtending a narrow visual angle. As a result, a sense of presence in the depicted scene is rarely achieved.

The dynamic visual effects that result from a user's actual self-motion provide a linkage between the user's space and the depicted space. This is accomplished by tracking the motions of the user and altering the imagery accordingly. By tracking head position and orientation, for example, a computer screen becomes more like a window. Moving closer to the screen provides a wider aperture of view. Moving left and right provides motion parallax proportional to self-motion.

A head-mounted display, with image geometry computed according to head position and orientation, enables the user to be virtually surrounded by a pictorial environment, and to move relative to depicted objects in a natural manner. By tracking hand-mounted controllers, the objects may be directly manipulated. This kind of interactive display was pioneered by Ivan Sutherland in the 1960s, although the field of view of his system was a narrow 40 degrees. By stimulating more of the peripheral visual field, the sense of presence in the depicted scene can be enhanced. Thus, wide field-of-view head-mounted displays, like the original virtual reality display developed at NASA Ames, can further increase the visual sense of presence.

Implementation of a Typical Virtual Reality System

A virtual reality system (or virtual workstation, or personal simulator) consists of the means to immerse a user in a virtual interactive environment created from digital models. Such a system is an integrated collection of body-ported input/output devices, computer and video hardware, and software to orchestrate the simulation. The user wears a head-mounted viewer. Typical viewers consist of a pair of video display screens (with their support electronics) and wide-angle magnifying lenses. The viewer is usually supported by a box of electronics for power supply, signal conversions, and functional adjustments and accessories. The viewer is generally designed so as to replace the visual field of the user, while some versions allow the imagery to be combined with the real visual environment of the user. Some researchers believe that eye-movement tracking is important, while others do not. The head-mounted unit generally carries a microphone, earphones, and a head-position and orientation sensor. Typically, the hands are fitted with shape, position, and orientation sensors. Ultimately, the entire body could be tracked, and otherwise instrumented.

A host computer integrates the (sometimes various) computing resources and the peripheral units and coordinates their interaction. A computer graphics system generates 3-D scenes for display in the viewer. The imagery is altered in accordance with the head movements of the user to provide, to the extent possible, a stable visual environment. Remote video cameras can be slaved to the motions of the user's head, providing a remote source of imagery for visual telepresence. Key peripheral systems convert voice commands to computer commands, convert computer output to synthetic speech or other sounds, and convert body movements to computer input. Hand gestures are interpreted as desired for alteration of the appearance of the scene, behavior of objects, or other interactions with the environment. Telerobotic systems can be controlled by the motions of the user's hands, providing remote manipulation. Force, tactile, and even thermal feedback can be used to allow synthetic or remote objects to feel more solid and real.

Digital models of various task environments, such as the space shuttle, space station, and planetary terrain, are created and stored in databases. They are displayed and manipulated by the software programs under control of the user wearing the virtual workstation. Video recorders can record what the user sees and hears for noninteractive replay later. Network links can enable a system to communicate with remote computing resources, remote task environments, and remote virtual reality systems.

The NASA Ames Virtual Planetary Exploration System

A virtual planetary exploration (VPE) system has been designed and developed at NASA Ames by the author and Lewis Hitchner of the Research Institute for Advanced Computer Science (RIACS). The system is a research tool for developing and testing concepts, methods, and user-based interaction strategies that may prove useful for the design of planetary exploration workstations based on the virtual reality paradigm and the Exploration Metaphor. Hitchner, with the assistance of David Koblas (late of RIACS), implemented the software. The effort is modestly funded by the Office of Aeronautics and Space Technology (OAST) at NASA Headquarters.

The approach has encompassed the following:

1. Review mission operational experience, mission constraints and opportunities, the state of the art in exploration technology, and future mission requirements.
2. Conduct field studies in analog terrain environments.
3. Work closely with the planetary exploration community.
4. Characterize user exploration behaviors and requirements.
5. Enlist interdisciplinary expertise to develop, implement, demonstrate, and evaluate advanced exploration workstation testbeds.
6. Place special emphasis on strategies for dealing with the inherent

conflicts between the high degree of interactivity associated with the virtual reality paradigm and the extreme complexity of planetary terrain environments.

Operational applications may ultimately include support for landing site selection and certification, as well as surface operations, including manned base construction and operation, manned and unmanned rover traversal planning and operations, and teleoperations between manned bases and remote unmanned rovers. Other potential applications include scientific data analysis, agency advocacy of planetary terrain exploration, and public affairs.

System Components

The VPE system was originally based on a Stardent (nee Stellar; Newton, Massachusetts) GS-1000 graphics workstation, which was later upgraded to a GS-2000. The upgrade provided a second independent graphics channel enabling full-color stereoscopic imagery. (Work is now in progress on the next generation VPE system, utilizing a Silicon Graphics, Mountain View, California, Skywriter with multiple Indigo workstations). The multistream instruction processor of the GS-2000 operates at up to 25 million instructions per second, while a pair of separate processors is capable of performing floating-point operations at a peak rate of 80 million floating point operations per second. Rendering is handled by a separate multiprocessor subsystem capable of producing up to 150,000 Gouraud-shaded, Z-buffered triangles per second. Maximum image size is 32,768 × 32,768. The data bus provides for a simultaneous data transfer rate of 320 million bytes per second between the processors and main memory. The VPE Stardent GS-2000 has 128 million bytes of random access memory and four disk drives, each with a capacity of 760 million bytes. Four input/output buses are available, each capable of transferring 16 million bytes per second.

The head-mounted display (HMD) currently used is the Flight Helmet by Virtual Research (Bruce Bassett, Sunnyvale, California), which is an extension of the design originated by the NASA VIVED HMD. It utilizes the same LEEP Systems optics (Eric Howlett, Waltham, Massachusetts), and it uses these lenses, as the VIVED sytem did, to view a pair of liquid crystal displays (LCDs). While the VIVED HMD was capable of presenting gray-scale NTSC television imagery, the Flight Helmet presents color NTSC television images. Although the pixel count of each LCD in the Flight Helmet is 360 horizontal by 240 vertical, it takes three pixels (one red, one green, one blue) for each full-color pixel. Two channels of composite video (red, green, blue, and sync) from the Stardent GS-2000 are converted to composite NTSC video by a pair of Folsom Research (Folsom, California) signal converters, and then input to the HMD. Prior to using the Flight Helmet, a VPL Research (Redwood City, California) Eyephones HMD was used. It, too, was derived from the NASA VIVED system and used the LEEP lenses.

A Polhemus (Colchester, Vermont) magnetic tracker detects head position and orientation, and a six-degree-of-freedom "space ball" (Spaceball Technologies, Lowell, Massachusetts) provides manual motion control. Two Exos (Burlington, Massachusetts) exoskeletons, interfaced via an IBM PC, provide left- and right-hand gesture sensing for interaction with human scale terrain data. A bank of Stardent rotary knobs is used for modifying parameters that can vary over a continuous range of values. A NeXT (Palo Alto, California) personal computer is used for its removable optical storage.

Demonstration Capabilities

The VPE system is capable of presenting interactive planetary terrain environments using digital terrain models (DTMs), digital image models (DIMs), Viking lander imagery, and laser rangefinder data from next-generation planetary rover imaging systems. Scenes may be computed on-the-fly, in stereo, enabling the user to explore the terrain freely, or a "panorama mode" may be used for presentation of very detailed environments.

Engineering trade-offs are being investigated that will allow the use of virtual reality techniques with exquisitely complex environments. One technique for dealing with the conflict between complexity and interactivity restricts the complexity of the scene during significant motions. Thus, the terrain essentially is reduced to a "cartoon Mars" when the user moves about. Then, whenever the user chooses a pause for a closer look, the terrain detail is increased. Currently, the complexity is reduced by a "dumb" algorithm that subsamples the terrain shape data, the DTM. Unfortunately, the "cartoon Mars" is sometimes so simplified that landmarks become unrecognizable. To deal with this, an effort is under way to compute "caricatures" of the terrain shape, which retain the essential features (i.e., those that are essential to a particular user) with a very small amount of terrain data. This should allow a reduction of shape complexity without losing the ability to navigate through the environment.

The VPE system is also capable of texture mapping a DIM onto a DTM. Typically, the imaging data (DIM) is of higher resolution than the shape data (DTM). The now standard technique of overlaying the image data onto the shape data provides the appearance of a very detailed 3-D scene with less shape data complexity. Thus, for example, the image data aids the user when navigating in "cartoon" mode. Once a site of interest is found, an extremely realistic and detailed view can be created by combining the full-resolution DIM and DTM (see color plate of Valles Marineris).

In addition to computing scenes on the fly, the VPE system may also be used in "panorama mode" to surround the user in a highly detailed terrain environment that may be viewed without rendering lag, regardless of scene complexity. In this case, the user is constrained from translating about in the virtual environment, but may rotate his or her head to any azimuth or elevation angle. This capability is a computer graphics version of the Surveyor mosaic spheres.

Panorama mode utilizes the Stardent's *virtual pixel maps* technique for storing large images in memory, and rapidly accessing subregions for display on the screen and in the head-mounted display. The technique enables the system to present a digital panoramic photograph, or precompute a 360-degree panorama of any complexity, taking whatever amount of time is necessary, and then to present this image to the user without additional computation. This provides a sense of being in a very complex and realistic environment, without the virtual reality system becoming compute bound. In most virtual reality systems, a mere few hundred polygons can unacceptably slow down the response to head movements because the scene must be computed on-the-fly over and over again.

In panaroma mode, an observer may, for example, be virtually present at the Viking 2 lander site on Mars, turning around to survey the surrounding 360-degree panoramic scene, and scanning from the distant horizon down to the pebbles near the footpads of the lander (Figure 8.3). To accommodate stereo fusion, given the 82-cm lander camera separation, the stereo pair is adaptively separated as the user looks down to the foreground. The VPE Viking panoramas are 8500 horizontal × 1800 vertical pixels.

This technique is also being applied to the Apollo panoramas. Unlike the Viking panoramas, these were captured on photographic

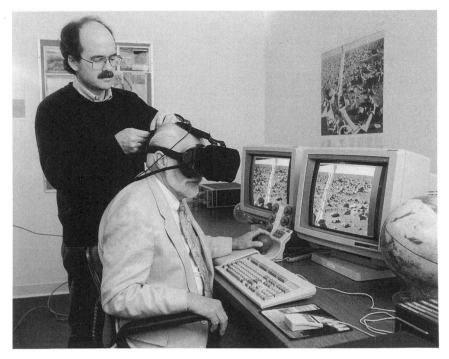

Fig. 8.3   The author adjusts the VPL headset worn by a geologist preparing to virtually explore the terrain surrounding the Viking 2 lander on Mars.

film as a collection of images, so they require mosaicking and conversion to digital form. That work is in progress.

In addition to displaying digital photographic panoramas, the VPE system can also compute arbitrary panoramic images from shape data, [i.e., DTMs] with or without visual texture [i.e., DIM] overlays. Thus, the observer can virtually stand on the floor of Valles Marineris, or anywhere else on Mars, and freely scan the entire 360-degree horizon, as well as look up to the peaks or down to the nearby surface. The resolution of these computed panoramas is only limited by the resolution of the terrain data. Given the "Mars Hill" DTM data from Death Valley laser imaging tests discussed earlier, whose resolution is 10 centimeters per elevation value, the detailed computed panorama can still be scanned at will, without rendering lag (Figure 8.4). The capability to compute a panorama from anywhere on or near the planet makes this technique far more flexible than the Surveyor mosaic spheres, which could only present the scene from the point of view of the lander.

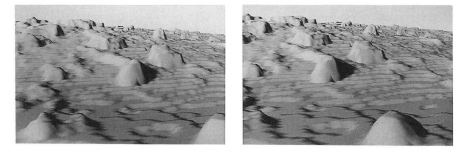

Fig. 8.4   SYNTHETIC STEREO VIEW OF MARS-LIKE TERRAIN IN DEATH VALLEY, CALIFORNIA, CREATED BY THE VPE SYSTEM USING LASER RANGEFINDER DATA. Left-eye image is on the left, right-eye image is on the right. Images may be fused by the method of uncrossed fusion, or by using a readily available and inexpensive stereoscope sold at most college supply shops. These images are part of larger panoramas.

To enable VR-based surrogate travel, a collection of panoramas could be photographed or computed for key sites of an interesting terrain environment, as we have done for Mars. We have come to call this approach the "Mars National Park" metaphor, because of its correspondence with a national park's collection of scenic overlooks, between which one must attend to driving rather than sight-seeing.

Plans call for investigation of the utility of integrating the panorama mode into the fully interactive 3-D environment. The user could navigate in real time through a caricature of Mars, then, on reaching a particularly interesting location, he or she could call for a panorama, rather than calling for great detail to be computed on the fly (with the corresponding loss of head-tracking responsiveness). If a panorama had not already been precomputed for the site, scenic detail might appear by progressive refinement, first filling in detail at the places toward which the user is looking. The result would be a vivid sense of visual presence within a highly detailed natural environment, with the ability to move about freely.

User-based Modes of Virtual Planetary Exploration

Current demonstration capabilities and other generic interactions serve as the building blocks of user-based interaction modes to be derived from experienced planetary explorers. For example, a recent study of exploration behavior in the field [26] revealed that planetary geologists routinely carry out intermediate altitude aerial reconnaissance, a capability supported by the VPE system. According to one subject:

> Doing this kind of field work, it's fairly common for us to start in the laboratory by looking at the available remote sensing data. And not just conventional air photos like this, but any other kind of data we can get, as well. And then going into the field, doing a reconnaissance of the field as a whole. And then overflying it. We commonly will rent small planes to fly over the area. It gives you a perspective that you can't get any other way. The air photos are not adequate. There are things that the eye can detect that remote sensing cannot. There are relationships that we can see from that low altitude perspective that you can't get, either on the ground or from orbit, let's say. And so that intermediate altitude aerial reconnaissance is an important part of the kind of field work that we do.

The subject was asked to elaborate on the utility of overflight in a small plane:

> It's difficult to describe, certainly in a quantitative sense, what one does on an aerial reconnaissance. It's the perspective of geometric relationships of different units that you can't appreciate when you're standing right on the surface. You don't have that overview. It's also because you're there. You're seeing it in color. You're seeing it with your own eyes. And from an oblique perspective. And from many different perspectives, because the plane can fly around and give you whatever geometry you want, to see the areas that you're interested in.

Such comments from users are particularly valuable to inform the design of VPE systems. The use of aerial reconnaissance, for example, cited in the preceding quote, clearly indicates that virtual flyovers of digital terrain are useful to the practical user and should be supported. Other user comments have indicated the importance of access to the original imagery data in conjunction with virtual recreations of the task environment [34]. Other users agree, and further assert the need for terrain-indexed access to related spatial data, maps, scientific papers, on-site videography, and accumulated observations of site experts [35]. As a result, the VPE system is being linked to multimedia devices, and work is under way to enable two-way access between the virtual terrain environments and the relevant multimedia database entries.

We are also investigating "ecological" manipulative behaviors, such as those associated with sampling outcrops during geological field work. As digital models of terrain progress to human-scale resolution, manipulative capability is being incorporated into the VPE system, particularly to support user-based telepresence research. Further, large area trackers are being developed to enable natural locomotive behaviors within virtual terrain environments.

In summary, we are working with experienced planetary explorers to characterize their exploration behaviors so that they may be supported by the VPE system. The system is iteratively exercised by these explorers and their colleagues in increasingly realistic mission-oriented tasks. During these exercises, we are conducting a variety of investigations regarding the specific sources of productivity or interpretation error, the nature and degree of presence and its utility, and the benefit of virtual reality techniques to specific tasks that support planetary terrain exploration.

Conclusion

Many of the fundamental concepts and techniques of virtual reality technology have been developed by NASA during a period of 30 years as a natural part of planetary exploration missions. This application-oriented development has made a substantial contribution to the field, which, along with parallel developments in other disciplines, such as medical imaging, builds a strong foundation for the further advancement of virtual reality technology. NASA is currently conducting research to apply this technology to areas that have a unique payoff to support its missions and goals, which are among the most technically challenging of VR applications. Planetary terrain exploration in particular will benefit from this research. Furthermore, virtual reality technology has the potential to democratize the experience of planetary exploration, which could have a profound effect on public perceptions of the U.S. space program.

VR is now being recognized as a major new paradigm in a broad range of applications, and it is already creating new commercial opportunities. It will greatly influence art, architecture, computer-aided design, communications, entertainment, education, scientific and medical visualization, simulation, training, and many other fields. Besides highly spatial applications, it will also have an impact on those that can be cast into a spatial context (e.g., 3-D libraries of text or other "dataspaces"). Further, it may be feasible to create virtual, dynamic 3-D worlds from inherently nonspatial data so as to ease interpretation and interaction. In general, virtual reality technology will dramatically alter human perception of the information environment.

Jacob Bronowski wrote in chapter 1 of his book *The Ascent of Man* [36]:

> Among the multitude of animals which scamper, fly, burrow, and swim around us, man is the only one who is not locked into his environment. His imagination, his reason, his emotional subtlety and toughness, make it possible for him not to accept the environment but to change it. And that series of inventions by which man from age to age has remade his environment is a different kind of evolution.

The personal simulator, an advanced user/computer interface, is one of the most recent of these inventions. When more fully developed, such devices will be able to generate synthetic perceptual environments that may be so compellingly realistic as to be worthy of being called virtual realities. The ability to capture and generate environments at will has the potential to provide vastly improved methods for exploring the Earth, the other planets, and synthetic worlds of one's own making. Virtual reality technology will thus provide another upward step along the exploratory path that Bronowski calls "The Ascent of Man."

Acknowledgments

This work is conducted within the Human Interface Research Branch of the Aerospace Human Factors Research Division, NASA Ames Research Center, Moffett Field, California, in the heart of Silicon Valley. The Virtual Environment R&D program continues to be funded by the Human Factors Research Program of NASA's Office of Aeronautics and Space Technology. The Office of Space Station's Advanced Development Program has also provided support. Funding for field studies came from the Office of Exploration.

On-site and off-site technical contributors to virtual reality research and development at NASA Ames include: Dov Adelstein, Romy Bauer, Randy Begault, Mark Bolas, Bill Briggs, Bob Brown, Steve Bryson, Joe Deardon, Steve Ellis, Saim Eriskin, Xin Feng, Cindy Ferguson, Scott Fisher, Dick Foster, Lew Hitchner, Eric Howlett, Jim Humphries, Rick Jacoby, Steffan Jeffers, Doug Kerr, Dave Koblas, Jim Larimer, Creon Levit, Ian McDowell, Michael McGreevy, Shigeru Morokawa, Ken

Musgrave, An Nguyen, Cordell Ratzlaff, Warren Robinett, Phil Stone, Ken Uhland, Beth Wenzel, Amy Wu.

Disclaimer

Commercial products, organizations, and individuals mentioned in this chapter are included solely to assist the reader in understanding the technical content. The author, NASA, and the U.S. government remain neutral concerning their merits, or the merits of others that are not mentioned.

REFERENCES

[1]Youngblood, G., *Expanded Cinema,* New York, E.P. Dutton, 1970.

[2] Sutherland, I. E., "A Head-Mounted Three-Dimensional Display," in *Proceedings of the Fall Joint Computer Conference,* Washington, D.C.: Thompson Books, pp. 757–764, 1968.

[3] McGreevy, M. W., "NASA Ames Virtual Environment Display: Applications and Requirements," internal technical document, Moffett Field, CA: NASA Ames Research Center, Aerospace Human Factors Research Division, September 1984.

[4] "NASA's Virtual Workstation: Using Computers to Alter Reality," *NASA Tech Briefs,* **12**(7), pp. 20–21, July/August 1988.

[5] McGreevy, M. W., "Personal Simulators and Planetary Exploration," Plenary address at CHI'89, Association for Computing Machinery Conference on Computer-Human Interaction, Austin, Texas, May 1989.

[6] McGreevy, M. W., "The Virtual Environment Display System," in *Proceedings of the 1st Technology 2000 Conference,* **1**, pp. 3—9. Washington, DC: NASA, 1990.

[7] Rogers, M., "Now, Artificial Reality," *Newsweek,* **111**(6), pp. 56–57, 1987.

[8] Meigs, J. B., "3-D TV Comes Home," *Popular Mechanics,* **164**(8), pp. 67–69, 88, 90, August 1987.

[9] Daviss, B., "Grand Illusions," *Discover,* **11**(6), pp. 36–41, June 1990.

[10] Ditlea, S., "Computerized Tour Guides," *Omni,* **13**(1), p. 26, October 1990.

[11] Jenish, D'Arcy, "Re-creating Reality," *Macleans,* **103**(23), pp. 56–57, June 4, 1990.

[12] Stark, D. E., "Journey Through Cyberspace: The New Frontier of Virtual Reality," *High Technology Careers,* **7**(4), pp. 6, 9, August/September 1990.

[13] "Cyberspace: Programmierte Paradiese," *Der Spiegel,* **44**(34), pp. 138–143, August 20, 1990.

[14] "Computerized Reality Comes of Age," *NASA Tech Briefs,* **14**(8), pp. 10–12, August 1990.

[15] Katayama, Ryuji, "Virtual Dynamite," *Business Tokyo,* **5**(2), pp. 22–27, February 1991.

[16] Rayl, S., "The new, improved reality," *Los Angeles Times Magazine,* pp. 17–20, 30, July 21, 1991.

[17] Stewart, D., "Artificial Reality: Don't Stay Home Without It," *Smithsonian,* **21**(10), pp. 36–45, January 1991.

[18] "From Surveyor: The Stark and Airless Beauty of the Moon," *Life,* **61**(1), pp. 62–67, July 1, 1966.

[19] Newell, H. E., "Surveyor: Candid Camera on the Moon," *National Geographic,* **130**(4), pp. 578–592, 1966.

[20] Steinbacher, R., personal communication, 1988.

[21] Biemann, H., *The Vikings of '76,* Cambridge, Massachusetts: Hans-Peter Biemann, 1977.

[22] Murry, J. M., *Countries of the Mind: Essays in Literary Criticism,* 2nd series, London: Oxford University Press, 1931.

[23] "Report of the 90-Day Study of Human Exploration of the Moon and Mars," NASA, November 1989.

[24] Bourke, R., personal communication, 1990.

[25] Taylor, G. J., and P. D. Spudis, "A Teleoperated Robotic Field Geologist," in *Proceedings of Space '90: Engineering, Construction, and Operations in Space II,* S. W. Johnson and J. P. Wetzel, Eds., New York: American Society of Civil Engineers, pp. 246–255.

[26] McGreevy, M. W. "The Presence of Field Geologists in Mars-like Terrain," manuscript submitted for publication.

[27] Pettengill, G. H., P. G. Ford, W. T. K. Johnson, R. K. Raney, and L. A. Soderbolm, "Magellan: Radar Performance and Data Products," *Science,* **252**, pp. 260–265, April 12, 1991.

[28] Brooks, F., personal communication, 1989.

[29] Duxbury, T., personal communication, 1990.

[30] McGreevy, M. W., "The Exploration Metaphor," invited presentation at Engineering Foundation Conference on Human-Machine Interfaces for Teleoperators and Virtual Environments, Santa Barbara, California, March 1990.

[31] Gibson, J. J., *The Ecological Approach to Visual Perception,* Hillsdale, NJ: Lawrence Erlbaum Associates, 1986.

[32] McGreevy, M. W., "Personal Simulators and Divergence from Realism," plenary address at SIGGRAPH Symposium on User Interface Software, Banff, Alberta, Canada, October 1988.

[33] McGreevy, M. W., "A Cognitive Engineering Approach to Spatial Information Display Design," doctoral dissertation, University of California, Berkeley, University Microfilms International 87-26297, 1987.

[34] Sullivan, K., and H. Moore, personal communication, 1991.

[35] Briggs, G., J. Moore, and G. Greene, personal communication, 1992.

[36] Bronowski, J. *The Ascent of Man,* Boston: Little, Brown and Company (1974).

Chapter 9

Summer Students in Virtual Reality

A Pilot Study on Educational Applications of Virtual Reality Technology [1]

Meredith Bricken and Chris M. Byrne
University of Washington
Human Interface Technology Laboratory
of the Washington Technology Center
Seattle, Washington
meredithb@aol.com

Meredith Bricken has spent more than twenty years working as an educator in innnovative learning. In addition, she has designed and modeled virtual worlds for Autodesk, the HITLab and Boeing. I had the privilege of first meeting her in 1990 and knew, after listening to her present her work, that I wanted her input into this book.

She has always been concerned about the appropriate use of technology in education and as VR makes its way into the classroom she stresses that we must be concerned with the way the technology is used. Will it promote outmoded dysfunctional teaching methods or will it help us recognize the situated nature of knowledge?

As you read this chapter, you should realize that the most important thing she and Chris Byrne have to say is not contained in their specific research results. Rather, they are talking about their efforts to set up a student-driven process that—unlike almost every other VR project you read about—gave the users (students) control over what they did with the technology.

—A.W.

[1] © 1992 Washington Technology Center. Sponsored by the US West Foundation, the Washington Technology Center, and the Pacific Science Center.

Introduction

Virtual reality (VR) is a new way to use computers. VR eliminates the traditional separation between user and machine, providing more direct and intuitive interaction with information. By wearing a head-mounted audio/visual display, position and orientation sensors, and tactile interface devices, we can actively inhabit an immersive computer-generated environment. We can create virtual worlds and step inside to see, hear, touch, and modify them.

Now that computing power has increased to meet the demands of real-time processing, VR technology has entered a period of public attention and wide industrial interest. Major corporations and companies worldwide are actively exploring the use of this technology for a variety of application areas, including telecommunications, arcade and home entertainment, production and assembly management, health care, digital design, and product sales and marketing.

A growing number of universities and research laboratories are doing the work necessary to develop more sophisticated VR systems. The production of cost-effective VR components is under way in America, Europe, and Japan. Within the next five years, a variety of affordable high-performance personal computers and workstations with networked VR capabilities are expected to be on the market.

In anticipation of the widespread availability of this technology, we took a first step in evaluating the potential of VR as a learning environment. We gathered two reciprocal kinds of information during the seven-week process. The primary focus was to evaluate VR's usefulness and appeal to students ages 10 to 15 years, documenting their behavior and soliciting their opinions as they used VR to construct and explore their own virtual worlds. Concurrently, we used this opportunity to collect usability data that might point out system design issues particular to tailoring VR technology for learning applications.

This chapter outlines the theoretical framework of our study, describes the research context, and outlines the students' VR activities. Both the pedagogical methodology in designing the students' learning experience and the observation methodology used to record and evaluate student responses are described. The discussion of these observations is followed by descriptions of the virtual worlds constructed by students. We conclude with a preliminary evaluation of the usefulness of VR for education.

Theoretical Framework

What we now call virtual reality has existed in various forms for three decades, and has already proved to be a useful learning environment for adults. The first head-mounted display was successfully devised to enable people to understand and manipulate computer-generated information more easily [1]. VR has been developed during the past 20 years to facilitate learning and performance in high-workload environments in the U.S. Air Force [2]. Flight simulators, which combine physical and computer-generated elements to create task-specific learning environments, have been highly effective in pilot training. Current VR systems provide new capabilities for perceptual expansion, for creative construction, and for unique social interactivity [3]. These characteristics of VR are relevant in three areas of educational theory: experiential education, constructivism, and social learning.

The experiential quality of VR provides a capability that is fundamental to the learning process [4–7]. A virtual world is a *place* where participants can have any number of different learning experiences. By including them within these three-dimensional multisensory environments, and closely coupling their natural behaviors to system functionality, participants feel a strong sense of *presence* [8]. Interacting in VR involves "purposeful movement that coordinates the cognitive, the psychomotor, and the affective domains" [9], engaging the whole learner in the task at hand.

Children actively build their own categories of thought about the world [10], and encouraging students to construct their own knowledge is demonstrably effective in learning [11–13]. Virtual worlds are constructive environments in which participants can create, manipulate, and edit any form of digital information. Objects, processes, and programmed inhabitants of the virtual world are elements for active problem solving. "In many instructional settings, students acquire only facts rather than acquire tools for problem solving. They often have not experienced the kinds of problems that make information relevant and useful, so they do not understand the value of this information" [14].

"Human learning presupposes a specific social nature and social process" [15]. Virtual worlds can be networked to provide shared environments that allow wide-bandwidth communication and collaboration between local or distant participants. The ability to exchange or share points of view *literally* in multiple-participant virtual worlds may intensify this social learning experience [16]. Cocreating virtual worlds for learning allows teachers and students to use computers in a cooperative group situation, where learners tend to be more productive [17].

Research Context

The Technology Academy is a science-oriented summer day camp, offered by the Pacific Science Center (PSC) in Seattle, Washington, to students from ages 5 to 18. The academy offers seven camp sessions, each one week long. Student activities center around hands-on exploration of new technologies. Academy "student researchers" are given a choice of focus areas such as robotics, MIDI digital sound interfaces, and multimedia. In the summer of 1991, in cooperation with University of Washington Human Interface Technology Laboratory (HITL) researchers and sponsors, students were first given the option to explore the area of VR.

The VR student research groups were limited to approximately 10 new students each week, ages 10 years and older. A total of 59 students from ages 10 to 15 self-selected to participate over the seven-week period. The average age of the students was 13 years, and the gender distribution was predominantly male (72%). The students were of relatively homogeneous ethnic origin; the majority were Caucasians, along with a few Asian Americans and African Americans. The group demonstrated familiarity with Macintosh computers, but none of the students had worked with 3-D graphics, or had heard of VR before coming to the Technology Academy.

One Technology Academy teacher and one teaching intern shared primary responsibility for the VR student researchers, along with support from other academy teachers and PSC staff members.

HITL scientists provided presession and ongoing training to Technology Academy teachers, which included experiencing VR using the laboratory's collection of virtual worlds. Teaching materials provided by HITL included videotapes describing the technology with examples of virtual worlds developed by HITL, the National Aeronautics and Space Administration (NASA), VPL Research, Inc., and the University of North Carolina. Teachers also received written virtual world design and modeling guidelines, modeling software documentation, pertinent HITL technical reports, and references for additional reading.

By agreement between HITL and VPL Research, Inc., a cost-free site license for the Macintosh modeling software package Swivel 3-D™ was granted to PSC for this study. The Technology Academy provided several Mac II computers for the students to use in constructing their virtual worlds at the center. HITL provided students with a Swivel file containing a "protoworld," which consisted of two basic elements of a virtual world. The first element was the participant's virtual body, represented by a graphic head and hand. The virtual head is the position-responsive point of view, and the virtual hand is the digital analogue of the participant's physical hand, used for gesture commands such as "fly" and "grab." The second element was a ground plane extended to the maximum size that the rendering software could handle, for scale and orientation reference.

Each student research group had access to five computers for eight hours per day. They worked in groups of two or three to a computer. They used a codiscovery strategy in learning to use the modeling tools. Students were clustered inside a circle of computers, making it easy for them to share ideas and techniques as they created different elements of their virtual worlds. Teachers answered the questions they could, but this software was new to them as well.

On the last day of each session, a PSC van took student VR researchers on the 15-minute ride to HITL. At HITL, students were able to get inside their worlds using VR interface technology. (We used RB2™ software on a Macintosh FX rendered by one Iris 320 VGX with a videosplitter; first-generation Eyephones™ were used for viewing and a right-handed DataGlove™ was used for gesture-command interactivity.) Directly after their VR experience, students were given a Polaroid photo of themselves wearing the head-mounted display and glove, taken as they explored their virtual world. They were then asked to fill out opinion questionnaires.

When evaluating the usefulness of VR, it is important to remember that commercial VR systems are currently at the "Kittyhawk" stage. They are awkward, limited in capability, and marginally reliable to use. A lag time exists between the participant's behavior and system update. The head-mounted display used in the study was very low in resolution; equivalent vision in the physical world is considered legally blind. Both the graphics and the sound elements are constrained by the power and expense of the system. Virtual worlds resemble cartoons compared to the animated computer graphics we see in movies and on TV. The 3-D acoustic environment of VR is currently limited to a small number of sound elements. Despite these limitations, researchers are beginning to collect valuable information about the usefulness of VR for particular tasks and applications.

Pedagogical Methodology

HITL researchers wanted to see what these students were motivated to do with VR when given access to the technology in an open-ended context. We predicted that they would gain a basic understanding of VR technology as we gathered personal response and usability information from them. We expected that in using the modeling software, this group might learn to color, cluster, scale, and link graphic primitives (cubes, spheres), to assemble simple geometric 3-D environments, and to specify basic interactions such as "grab a ball, fly it to the box, drop it in."

Building a virtual world is an exacting task, and the students had only one week to complete their project. We considered the possibility that they might become overwhelmed with the task and choose to *play around* with VR, rather than learn enough to use it effectively. However, we considered it more probable that they would be sufficiently intrigued by world-building to approach the task with directed energy.

The PSC's goal was to give kids access to interesting new technology. VR student researchers were given an opportunity rather than an assignment to build a virtual world. Their experience was designed to be a hands-on student-driven collaborative process in which they could learn about VR technology by using it and learn about virtual worlds by design and construction. Their only constraints in this task were time and the inherent limitations of the technology.

World-Building Process

Monday   Each new group of students began their training with an introduction to VR by the Technology Academy teacher, an experienced VR researcher formerly with NASA Ames. The students were also given a presentation by one of the HITL researchers that included slides and videotapes. After lunch, students met together with their two teachers to plan their world.

The brainstorming session lasted an hour or so, and included discussions of several aspects of world design and implementation. They addressed conceptual design (what kind of world do you want? what do you want it to look like? what can you do in there?), system constraints (polygon budgets and movement/interaction limits), and 3-D graphics modeling principles (the relationship of context and objects, shaping graphical objects, linking objects to form complex constructions, relative and absolute scales).

The decision-making process for including objects in a world was straightforward: if you want it, make it and put it in. Everybody wanted to make something. Division of labor was addressed: one or two older kids typically volunteered to construct a particular context that elaborated on the simple plane of the protoworld. All the students had ideas for particular objects to include in the world, and a list of graphical elements was made. The meeting adjourned, and everyone clustered around the computers to learn the modeling software.

Tuesday and Wednesday Everybody modeled something to include. They demonstrated a range of modeling skills, creating a variety of objects—from arbitrary blobs and blimps to objects such as a carefully crafted table with turned legs, a petaled rose, an interactive sculpture, and a set of wineglasses with carafe. Students continued to construct elements and import them from separate files into the shared virtual world context. The data structure underneath the objects was diagrammed and printed. They specified animation and interaction options (what could be grabbed, what would be animated) after the model was nearly complete.

Thursday Technical details, such as scale and link constraints, were double-checked. Students assembled printouts of their written world description, graphical data hierarchy and constraints, and views of their graphics file with the objects identified by name.

At noon, the word disk was delivered to HITL for programming, which involved importing the model into a separate dynamics programming package to add the specified interactivity and animation.

Friday Students explored their worlds one at a time, while other group members watched what the participant was seeing on a large TV monitor. Although this was not a networked VR, it was a shared experience in that the kids "outside" the virtual world conversed with participants, often acting as guides.

Student researchers also toured the laboratory's facilities, observing VR research in progress. Each student was given a demonstration of 3-D sound, and had the opportunity to informally discuss speech recognition systems, position-tracking systems, VR software programming, and artistic expression in VR with HITL scientists.

Each week followed roughly the same pattern, but there were discontinuities and exceptions. Successive student groups had the benefit of ongoing teacher training and experience, but they were also exposed to a decrease in teacher energy level over the course of an intensive seven weeks. The students' introduction to VR by different HITL researchers each week varied somewhat in form and content. Several technical difficulties arose with the VR system in week 4. The media was present twice during HITL site visits; while the kids seemed to take it in stride, it was perceived as intrusive by researchers. The Technology Academy teaching intern had sole responsibility for the students during the last two camp sessions.

Products: Seven New Worlds

The virtual worlds the students constructed are the most visible demonstrations of the success of the world-building activity. A brief description of each world is drawn primarily from the students' written world documentation:

Planetscape!! "A futuristic world of craters and critters . . . included is a flying fish, various hovering monsters, and a rocket inside of a crater." The flat, crater-strewn landscape lay under a pink sky, and also contained small towers and two characters named "Bob" and "Zeke" who could move along with the participant. (See color plate.)

Virtual Valley "The valley is enclosed by surrounding mountains on the Northern and Southern sides. The horizon is dotted by suspended geometric objects. In the center . . . is a cubelike surrene [sic] lake with seaweed and a modern block sculpture. The valley floor . . . is marked with green trees, multi-colored buildings, and an observatory. [3-D sound] will enhance our Virtual World . . . ." When entering the water a splash was heard; whenever something was grabbed, a metallic "klink" sounded; the students composed "eerie" music to hear while flying through the blue skies of the valley. (See color plate.)

Cloudlands "We wanted to have a group world, but we each had something different that we wanted to do. We made our own cloud, or we created clouds in groups. We each had a small, separate world of our own." One cloud was a western world with a colorful cactus, rocks, and a 10-gallon hat; one contained a shark and a starfish; one was an elaborate house; one was a pair of "tie fighters" (Star Wars spaceships).

Moon Colony "Our project . . . shows what we think the moon will look like in the future. It consists of many mountains, futuristic buildings and spacecrafts. The transportation is a monorail [animated to follow its track] . . . another is a spacecraft . . . and a blimp. Downtown is located in a clear dome shaped building." A black sky loomed above.

Neighborhood "[It] consists of four different styles of houses. . . . The first house is a futuristic house with one section below ground and two others above ground. All the rooms are furnished with 2-3 pieces of furniture. The second house is in the shape of a blimp, with the living quarters in the passenger section [where] there is a table with a rose and a vase. . . . The blimp is large and blue and holds the room high above the earth. The third house has three rooms . . . a coffee table where there are three glasses and a bottle of champaign . . . a table, six chairs, six glasses and a pencil. Lastly, there is . . . a regular house, with a spaceship in the back yard. There are three rooms: a dining room with a fancy table; a computer room with a computer, and a bedroom with a toy and a book."

Mid-Evil Space Station "Our world . . . consists of trees, flowers, mountains, cosmic objects, castles, insects, swords, stars, and a rocket. . . . We picked this idea because we will never be able to experience the past. . . . We also wanted to experience the future too, so we decided to make a mid-evil space station [shaped like a large castle high above the world] so we could have the experience of the past and the future together as one."

Mr. Mountain "Our world consists of a mountain with a nose, ears, and sunglasses [and a waterfall running out of the nose into a lake on the plain; inside the nose was a lake with a sunken treasure box containing money]. Inside of this so-called mountain we have a TV suspended in midair, a piece of dirty laundry, a farm with a pig, a cow, and an upside down farm house. We also have a very weird machine and a haunted house with a ghost [moving] outside. . . . These things all are nestled in a green forest."

Characterizing across these worlds, we find that they are complex, interestingly conceived, and well executed, as well as funny, imaginative, and very different from each other. The conceptual sophistication of the worlds clearly varied, ranging from a fairly standard moon colony, to "experiencing the past and the future together as one," to the addition of sound.

The most interesting feature of the students' worlds, for HITL researchers, was their peaceful nature. While there were powerful creatures in each world, their interactivity was not specified to be aggressive. There was no interpersonal conflict imbedded in these constructions, no guns or bombs.

Observations

In collecting information on both student response and system usability, we used three different information-gathering techniques. We hoped for both cross-verification across techniques and technique-specific insights. We videotaped student activities, elicited student opinions with surveys, and collected informal observations from teachers and researchers. Each data source revealed different facets of the whole process.

Videotapes

HITL videotapes consist of 14 hours of students' VR experiences. VR experiences at HITL are done while standing and moving within an approximately 4 × 4-foot area. The videos show the full-body movement of the students. Behaviors such as turning around, bending down, and reaching out are common. The impact of VR on kinesthetic learners deserves further research.

A view of what the participant was seeing in the virtual world could be seen on the large TV monitor. There were usually clusters of students nearby, talking with each other and with the participant while watching the monitor. The social behavior of participants varied widely: Some carried on running conversations with the other students during their VR experience; some were silent, reporting that they had been distracted by the sounds outside their world.

The students' worlds were not programmed with sound, with the exception of week two. In an isolated instance of returning students, two older boys who had attended the first session, along with the

17-year-old Technology Academy teaching intern, spearheaded the second session's highly successful extension into 3-D sound. One of these boys had reported external distraction during his VR experience, and tried an experiment in the first week's world: he wore his Walkman into VR. In the second week, he not only participated in creating the specifying sounds to Virtual Valley, but attempted to use graphical elements (mountains) as sound buffers. This example of transferring knowledge of the physical world into assumptions about virtual objects is one of the few conceptual errors noted by researchers; he realized his mistake during a discussion of sound-masking techniques.

Including 3-D sound was substantial additional work both for students and for HITL programmers and was not attempted by students in the following weeks. However, several students added their own sounds while in the virtual world by verbalizing motion noises as they flew, calling and talking to virtual characters, and making object-collision sounds.

The videotapes captured the sustained concentration of the students during their 10-minute VR experience, whether or not they verbalized. Their intensity of focus is more striking in review than it was at the time. Most of the videotapes do not display the high level of enthusiasm that was expressed in the student opinion questionnaires; participants were fairly serious during their immersion.

The videotapes were an important source of system usability information. The students were far more active while exploring VR than adult participants tend to be. Frustrations included getting wound up in the cables and having to hold the heavy headmount in place when bending over to look down.

On most of the tapes, the students' conversations are clearly audible. Those who addressed other students were most often asking questions: "What's that? Where am I? Where is . . .? The students outside the virtual world were usually able to answer the participant's questions without hesitation; they were seeing the same view on the high-resolution monitor. This indicates that the low resolution of the head-mounted display was inadequate for object identification and location recognition.

Despite these system constraints, the videotapes documented the students' remarkably fast accommodation to VR. They were adept at moving around in their worlds within the first minute or two when the system was working optimally. Interacting with objects was more difficult. Depth perception is difficult in low-resolution VR without the redundant cues that experienced world designers embed in their environment. Adaptation to the immaterial nature of virtual objects seemed quite easy for some students. One girl who seemed particularly at ease in VR bent over to fly down and tried to put her finger below her feet, through the floor of the lab; she seemed surprised that it was solid.

In looking at the tapes of different worlds, noticeable patterns could be detected in the students' ability to orient themselves and navigate through each world. It was easier for students to figure out where they were and to locate particular objects in some worlds than it was in others, apparently as a function of the design of the models [18]. Worlds with clearly discernable landmarks around the periphery of the world (*Virtual Valley, Moon Colony*) were easier for students to orient themselves in than the world with many similar craters and one central landmark (*Planetscape!!*). It was difficult for student to know where they were inside houses where closed cubes were used for rooms (*Neighborhood*), and hard to locate objects set among a thick forest of uniform trees or nested inside of other objects (*Mr. Mountain*).

The Technology Academy provided a videotape documenting the students' brainstorming process while designing *Mr. Mountain,* as well as shots of the students using computers to build objects with Swivel.

Opinion Survey

The 59 students answered opinion surveys about their experience in virtual reality. The surveys include redundant questions designed to elicit reactions both to world-building tools and to the VR experience. Three types of questions were asked: scaled (1–7); binary (forced choice); and open-ended.

The questions concerning students' personal responses to the experience of VR and the average scores are as follows (On questions where a seven-point scale was given, several students chose an answer higher than the allowed number. We counted those answers as sevens, but we wish to convey the enthusiasm with which the students responded.):

How did you feel about experiencing VR?	(1: did not enjoy; 7: enjoyed extremely) 6.5
Do you want to experience VR again?	(1: not at all; 7: very much) 6.8

Would you rather:	(forced choice)
Go into a virtual world (1)	
See a virtual world on a computer screen (0)	0.95
Go into a virtual world (1)	
Play a videogame (0)	0.98
Go into a virtual world (1)	
Watch TV (0)	0.96
Go into a virtual world (1)	
Use your favorite computer program on screen (0)	0.98

The students were overwhelmingly pleased with VR technology. The raw averages are incredibly high and show the students' appreciation of the VR experience. We believe that general student acceptance of this technology will be high.

Questions relating to world-building tools measured students' comfort with Swivel 3-D and with programming in general:

	(1: did not enjoy; 7: enjoyed extremely)
How did you feel about building Swivel worlds?	5.8
Do you want to learn more about building Swivel worlds?	5.7
Do you want to learn to program VR worlds?	5.6
Would you rather:	(forced choice)
Build a Swivel world and go into it (1)	
Go into a world that has already been built (0)	0.76

These responses were not as unabashedly positive as the ones concerning overall feelings about VR. However, the average scores were still very promising and certainly positive enough to continue to explore the possibilities of world creation in an educational program. We feel that this response shows some frustration with the tools or process of world building. Future studies can help indicate whether this reaction was due to the short amount of time the student had to use the tools, something inherently uncomfortable about the process, or some other reason.

We checked our assumptions about the redundancy of questions by looking at the correlations among the groupings that we had made. We found that the responses to the questions relating directly to liking or disliking VR were highly correlated and that the responses to the questions relating to world building were also mutually correlated.

We asked other questions that indicate directions for future usability studies:

	(1: not good; 7: good)
Do you think VR would be a good learning environment?	5.7
Do you think VR would be a good place to play?	6.0
Do you think VR would be a good place to work?	5.0
	[1: extremely disoriented; 7: not disoriented]
Do you feel disoriented (dizzy or nauseated) inside the virtual world?	5.7
Do you feel disoriented (dizzy or nauseated) after leaving the virtual world?	5.5
Which is easier:	(forced choice)
Seeing different views of the virtual world on the computer screen (0)	
Seeing different views of the virtual world in VR (1)	0.38
Moving Swivel objects on the computer screen (0)	
Moving objects in VR (1)	0.22
Getting to a chosen location in a Swivel world on the computer screen (0)	
Getting to a chosen location in a virtual world inside VR (1)?	0.53
Would you rather explore:	
A new place in VR (1)	
Explore a new place in the physical world (0)?	0.42

The questions concerning dizziness and the question about exploring new places are of particular interest. Dizziness can be related to specific aspects of the technology or to particular individual differences. It was not significantly correlated to attitude toward the VR experience. Nearly half of the students expressed a preference to explore new places in VR rather than new places in the physical world. This response was far higher than we had predicted, and needs further investigation.

We also asked several questions that allowed for open-ended answers:

- What was the one thing you liked best about VR?
- What was the one thing you liked least about VR?
- Now that you've been inside the virtual world you built, what would you change or add (if anything)?
- If you could go into any virtual world that you can imagine, what would it be like?
- What are the most important things you've found out about VR during your visit to the laboratory?

We found patterns in the answers to the open-ended questions. With regard to what people liked best about VR, many of the students mentioned enjoying activities within VR such as being able to move and fly and pick up objects in the world ("flying without wings"; "you get to go anywhere"; "picking up objects"). Many others commented positively about the experience of being immersed in a virtual world ("experiencing a new place without going far"; "I felt like I was in space floating through the world I created"; "being *in* it, not seeing it just on a screen"). Since this project also included the building of the worlds, we saw quite a few answers relating to the experience of world building ("we built our own world"; "going into my house and seeing my table"; "making your own world and going into it").

The answers to what the students liked least about VR verified our videotape observations, and perceptively echoed complaints by many professionals in the field. The resolution ("the screen was kind of fuzzy"), the hardware ("too many wires to get tangled in"), the software ("Swivel 3-D"), the lack of control ("couldn't move the right way"), and being dizzy ("feeling dizzy at the end") are all issues that are being actively explored in the development of improved VR systems.

The overwhelming answer to what students would change about VR is *more*. They want more objects, more movement, more color, more sound, more detail, and everything bigger ("more space and more buildings to pick up"; "more moving objects"; "more color and music"; "more").

We found the students' VR fantasies a fascinating part of the survey. Many students imagined utopias ("A pollution-free, evil-free, sadness-free, tree-filled world, like a almost perfect world"), historical worlds ("a medieval world with castles and towers"), outer space ("a forest on Mars"), water worlds ("underwater where I could swim alongside the dolphins and whales"), the physical world ("Virtual L.A."), games ("a world of stunts like bunjee cord jumping, sky diving, etc."), and elaborate visions that are difficult to categorize ("I would like to go inside a volcano, travel the lava tube and get blown out when it erupts"). The variety of answers showed tremendous imagination and indicated the VR appeals to the students' sense of adventure.

The students' responses varied on the most important things they found out about VR. Many commented on learning about what the VR state of the art was ("with a few more years of development it could be used for almost anything"; "it needs work"; "that technology is that advanced"). Others talked about how much fun it was ("it was really fun"; "it's *awesome!!*"). The most common comment was that they learned that world building and VR take a lot of work, with many students also commenting that the effort was worth it ("how hard people have to work to gain such an experience, and how fun certain work can be"; "your hard work definitely pays off well"; "how much work it takes").

Informal Observation

Informal observations were useful for seeing social behavior and broad patterns of student response to VR. The following comments, collected from the notes of teachers and researchers, indicate directions for future research:

It was difficult to assess how representative the reactions of these students were of the American school population. The group as a whole consisted of computer-literate, predominantly white males, who had access to this relatively expensive summer camp. Further studies on more diverse populations are required.

The students learned enough about the modeling software in 10 or 15 minutes to start creating objects. This is a much shorter learning curve than most adults demonstrate, an indication of students' ability to learn VR dynamics programming. Developmental differences were noticed in preferences for modeling particular elements of the virtual world: ages 10 to 12 were more comfortable with object construction; ages 13 to 15 were more comfortable with context design.

Both boys and girls seemed equally successful in creating elements of the world. Gender differences were noticed in the world design process during the one week that females outnumbered male students. The design approach in predominantly male sessions was goal-oriented; they made an initial decision on the content of their world and constructed objects according to plan. The predominantly female group (who created *Mid-Evil Space Station*) was process-oriented; they decided on a concept and then constructed a variety of items, choosing which ones to include in the world spontaneously.

Collaboration between students was highly successful, and resulted in strong group bonding. One week's group named themselves the Black Light SimSense Group, and submitted an additional survey reflecting their consensus on each answer. It seemed significant that everyone contributed something to each world, and that we did not hear any negative comments from the students about each other's work.

Summary

These students were fascinated by the experience of creating and entering virtual worlds. Across the seven sessions, they consistently made the effort to submit a thoughtfully planned, carefully modeled, well-documented virtual world. All of these students were motivated to achieve functional competence in the skills required to design and model objects, demonstrated a willingness to focus significant effort toward a finished product, and expressed strong satisfaction with their accomplishment. Their virtual worlds are distinctive and imaginative in both conceptualization and implementation. Collaboration between students was highly cooperative, and every student contributed elements to their group's virtual world. The degree to which the student-centered methodology influenced the results of the study may be another fruitful area for further research.

Students demonstrated rapid comprehension of complex concepts and skills. They learned computer graphics concepts (real-time versus batch rendering, Cartesian coordinate space, object attributes), 3-D modeling techniques, and world design approaches. They learned about VR concepts ("what you do is what you get," presence) and enabling technology (head-mounted display, position and orientation sensing, 6-D interface devices). They also learned about data organization: Students were required by the modeling software to link graphical elements hierarchically, with explicit constraints; students printed out this data tree each week as part of the documentation process.

Researchers learned which of the present VR system components were usable, which were distracting, and which were dysfunctional for this age group. Our conclusion is that improvement in the display device is mandatory; the resolution was inadequate for object and location recognition, and hopeless for perception of detail. Another concern is with interactivity tools: manipulating objects with the DataGlove™ was *not* natural; discrete gestures triggered particular commands but there was no actual manipulation of objects. The head-mounted display has since been boom-mounted for lighter weight and less intrusive cable arrangement.

Students, teachers, and researchers agreed that this exploration of VR tools and technology was a successful experience for everyone involved. Most important was the demonstration of students' desires and abilities to use VR *constructively* to build expressions of their knowledge and imagination.

Our preliminary conclusion from this study is that VR is a significantly compelling creative environment in which to teach and learn. Over their years in school, students could create a universe of learning worlds that reflected the evolution of their skills and the pattern of their conceptual growth. Evaluating comprehension and competence would become experiential as well as analytical, as teachers explored the worlds of thought constructed by their students.

REFERENCES

[1] Sutherland, I., "Sketchpad, A Man-Machine Graphical Communication System," Ph.D. thesis, Massachusetts Institute of Technology, 1963.

[2] Furness, T., "Visually Coupled Information Systems," presented at ARPA Conference on Biocybernetic Applications for Military Systems, Chicago, Illinois, April 1978.

[3] Bricken, M., "Virtual Reality Learning Environments: Potentials and Challenges," *Computer Graphics Magazine*, **25**(3), pp. 178–184, July 1991.

[4] Dewey, J., *Democracy and Education*, New York: Macmillan, 1916.

[5] Bruner, J., *Actual Minds, Possible Worlds*, Cambridge, MA: Harvard University Press, 1986.

[6] Silberman, C., *Crisis in the Classroom*, New York: Random House, 1970.

[7] Papert, S., *Mindstorms*, New York: Basic Books, 1980.

[8] Zeltzer, D., "Virtual Environments: Where Are We Going?," in *Proceedings 12th International IDATE (Institut de l'Audiovisuel Telecommunications en Europe) Conference*, Montpellier, France, 1990.

[9] Harrow, A., *A Taxonomy of the Psychomotor Domain*, New York: David McKay, 1972.

[10] Piaget, J., *The Child's Conception of the World*, New York: Harcourt, Brace and Comapny, 1929.

[11] Duffy, T., D. H. Jonassen, *Instructional Principles for Constructivist Learning Environments*, Hillsdale, NJ: Lawrence Erlbaum Associates, in press.

[12] Jonassen, D. H., "Objectivism Versus Constructivism: Do We Need a New Philosophical Paradigm?," *ETR&D*, **39**(3), pp. 5–14, 1991.

[13] Spiro, R. J., and J. C. Jehng, "Cognitive Flexibility and Hypertext: Theory and Technology for the Nonlinear and Multidimensional Traversal of Complex Subject Matter," in *Cognition, Education and Multimedia: Exploring Ideas in High Technology*, D. Nix and R. Spiro, Eds., Hillsdale, NJ: Lawrence Erlbaum Associates, 1990.

[14] Bransford, J. D., R. D. Sherwood, T. S. Hasselbring, C. K. Kinzer, and S. Williams, "Anchored Instruction: Why We Need It and How Technology Can Help," in *Cognition, Education and Multimedia: Exploring Ideas in High Technology,* D. Nix and R. Spiro, Eds., Hillsdale, NJ: Lawrence Erlbaum Associates, 1990.

[15] Vygotsky, L., *Mind in Society: The Development of Higher Psychological Processes,* Cambridge, MA: Harvard University Press, 1978.

[16] Brown, J. S., A. Collins, and P. Duguid, "Situated Cognition and the Culture of Learning," *Educational Researcher,* **18**(1), pp. 32–42, 1988.

[17] Belkin, G. S. and J. L. Gray, *Educational Psychology,* Dubuque, IA: William C. Brown, 1977.

[18] Bricken, M., "Virtual Worlds: No Interface to Design," in *Cyberspace: The First Steps,* Cambridge, MA: The MIT Press, 1991.

BIBLIOGRAPHY

Clark, R. E., "Reconsidering Research on Learning from Media," *Review of Educational Research,* **53**(4), pp. 445–459, Winter 1983.

DeVillar, R. A., and C. J. Faltis, *Computers and Cultural Diversity, Restructuring for School Success,* Albany, NY: State University of New York Press, 1991.

Johnson, D. W., and R. T. Johnson, "Interdependence and Interpersonal Attraction Among Heterogeneous Individuals: A Theoretical Formulation and a Meta-Analysis of the Research," *Review of Educational Research,* Spring 1983.

Kozma, R., "Learning With Media," *Review of Educational Research,* **61**(2), Summer 1991.

Wittrock, M. C., "Students' Thought Processes," in *Research in Teaching and Learning,* Vol 3, New York: Macmillan Publishing Company, 1990.

Chapter 10

Visualization of Information Flows: Virtual Reality as an Organizational Modeling Technique

Charles Grantham
University of San Francisco
San Francisco, California

Charlie Grantham is another of those "finds" I talked about in the introduction. I've known him for years because we are both involved in the CSCW field. So I was surprised to see him at a VR conference where he showed real applications of his ideas using visualization technologies. I think it is extremely important that VR move beyond the scientific and engineering community if it is to have its maximum impact. In this chapter, Grantham shows how the ideas of VR and AR can be of use to anyone who has to manage a business or organization in our rapidly changing world.

—A.W.

Introduction

This chapter reports the results of developing a dynamic modeling process based on the cybernetics theory of J. W. Forrester and the metaphysics of John Bennett. A software model of organizational functioning based on the pattern of information flows within the organization is detailed and presented as a methodology for surfacing and verifying assumptions about organizational effectiveness such as productivity and investment in training. Visualization of organizational functioning is a very promising application of virtual reality technologies because it fits with how people cognitively process complex information.

The model used here has been constructed using IThink™ software and represents the continuous process of *Comflow* (i.e., communications flow) [1]. The model is designed to indicate visually development of pathologies [2] within the living organizational system. The results of the application point to the value of using model development in an interactive, iterative structured process as a management decision-aiding tool. This potential application of virtual reality can provide an avenue for managers to break the consensual trance that exists in business management and "wake up" to become self-observing [3]. Simply stated, virtual reality presents an opportunity to simulate complex business decisions without actually implementing them, thus lessening the chance of making disastrous business decisions.

Visual analysis of information flows in organizations will become a standard accepted business practice within 10 years for successful business firms. Recent advances in technology (mostly integration of technologies) have brought us to the point of being able to use computers to simulate business decisions, in real time, as a new technique of management. The core idea of this chapter is to move the reader from a traditionally static model of business to a dynamic one. Central to this is the idea of simulation with the aid of computers. We believe this is a significant application area for virtual reality technology to provide new analytic tools for the business community.

Computer-based visual simulation techniques can be a valuable part of a methodology to design information environments that characterize organizational functioning. In a recent article in *Byte* magazine, we see that "research from many fields is being synthesized to create a design philosophy of information environments" [4]. These information environments represent a place for the increased use of modeling environments. The particular technique we describe here may be termed one of "participatory design" and as such represents a shift in the dynamic modeling process from *expert* to *partnership* with people who have the necessary subject matter expertise.

We now have the capacity to construct dynamic models of an organization that link hard variables, such as financial data, to softer variables, such as levels of trust and commitment. These modeling processes meet all the requirements for adequacy outlined by Dur and Bots [5]. Moreover these techniques are extensions of earlier work done by Forrester [1] and others.

This chapter is intended to push organizational analysis into this new realm of dynamic computer-based models of functioning.

Organizations can be characterized in many ways. Traditionally, we have done this with financial models. However, these have not always worked well in information-intensive environments. Further, there is some evidence to indicate that "groupthink" has emerged as a tendency in large organizations, making it difficult for a manager in a system to perceive what is actually occurring. New models of organizational functioning are needed as a thinking tool to do this.

Many contemporary management consultants are trying to do this: Peter Senge [6] with organizational learning; Michael Hammer with "business re-engineering" and David Nadler and "organizational architecture"[1] are only a few. A theoretical basis for those ideas is presented here in a way that allows managers to quantify what is going on in their businesses and use virtual reality technologies to make that functioning visible.

This chapter extends an organizational analysis model developed by Bennett [7] by turning his theory into measurable information flow patterns. These flows are then transferred to the modeling environment by constructing a complete equation simulation model using commercially available software. The chapter concludes with a discussion of how computers can be used to model complex information environments, dynamically, and the implications of this for managers and organizational designers.

Dynamic Modeling

Modeling of an organizational process has traditionally been done through financial modeling. The advent of the spread sheet in the mid-1970s ushered in a whole era of examining the impact of alternative courses of organization action. However, those models assumed that all important processes of the firm could be reduced to cash flow equivalents. As computer technology becomes more and more the mediator of communications within large, complex organizations, new methodologies for analyzing them become necessary. Many approaches have been developed such as the sociotechnical method [8]. However, all of these have difficulty capturing a complete, systemic picture or image of the organization [9].

---

[1] See *Business Week,* August 31, 1992, for an excellent overview of these approaches.

What is the rationale, then, for developing advanced ways of thinking about how the firm functions? Dur and Bots [5] offer three cogent reasons:

1. Organizations develop over long time spans and much knowledge about functioning is tacit knowledge, not reflected in past financial records.
2. Organizations allow for many points of view, which are continually negotiated.
3. Organizations often grow rapidly so that no one individual can have a reliable picture of the entire organization at any one time.

This means that our current business environment is moving quicker, with a larger span of control and changing so rapidly that old ways of analyzing them have reached their limits of utility. Therefore, model-·ing of the organizational process can overcome these problems by making the tacit knowledge explicit, can relate various vantage points, and can provide a cognitive bridge between complexity and local rationality. From a psychological perspective, modeling helps managers surface assumptions about behavior and do it in a way that makes these assumptions visible.[2] Visible assumptions are more easily interpreted, modified, and agreed on. Last, this process allows people to get the "big picture" and not be bounded by their everyday experiences and limited scopes.

Going about this process is not easy. It is best attempted when guided by experienced facilitators who can manage the conflict, interpretation, and political interests involved. This process must promote the active participation of all involved. It must also be necessary to represent points of view (i.e., world views) without initial regard to consistency of all parts of the model.[3] The techniques should also be aimed at reducing the cognitive distance between current mental models and reality. This lets the real mental models people are using surface and *does not let any of the participants assume they know what others are thinking.*

Dynamic modeling must make explicit use of time dimensions. In this case we usually refer to linear time as a first iteration. An effective

---

[2] We all have assumptions about what goes on around us. It is very difficult to get outside that mindset with the tools we use everyday because we use them in old ways. New psychological tools are needed.

[3] This often involves just getting the picture in front of people *before* asking how different sectors of the model affect one another.

analytical tool will let you move forward and backward in time. It is also helpful to have a time scaling feature, which allows you to extend the analysis over long time periods to examine relative short- and long-range impacts. Further, you must be able to specify the sequence of events in this time domain. Last, the modeling technique must permit, even encourage, investigation of the model from different viewpoints—the ability to play "What if?" This can be a very playful aspect in which participants mentally "walk around" the model, "get inside of it," and examine it from all angles while communicating among themselves about what they see and what they're experiencing and believe.

This dynamic modeling process has a rich history. Forrester [1] was one of the first to demonstrate the utility and power of dynamic modeling. His own work in organizational analysis led to the identification of several types of flows that could be used to model an organization. For example, *Matflows,* which are materials; *Enflows,* energy; *Monflows,* money; and *Comflows,* communications. The model presented here is analogous to these *Comflows.*

This type of work gained some popularity in the 1970s and was most evident in the publication of the Club of Rome's report "The Limits to Growth" [10], which predicted dire consequences for world population. In the intervening decades, simulation using computers has been extended to various design problems in nuclear physics and most evidently in weather prediction. Now systems analysis is gaining ground in several applied disciplines and computer simulation is being used more extensively. Elsewhere in this book you have read about some of these examples. This chapter is devoted to looking at how a line manager could make use of virtual reality.

Current Approaches

Organizational simulation has been around for some years and takes many forms. However, we are now beginning to see a dramatic surge in its use as a management analysis technique. This has been brought about by increased computer capacity, which allows simulation using graphical interfaces, rapid processing for real-time analysis, and networked personal computers so many people can experiment with the same model over separations in time and space. Brevity prohibits a complete discussion of different approaches, but the main modeling techniques are discrete event simulation, conceptual data models, mathematical optimization, and equation simulation [5].

All of these techniques aim at the same general cognitive target: Make complex systems understandable. The most basic system process model we use is a *dialectical model.* It is a three-part model that contains a force toward change, a force restraining that momentum, and a force that reconciles these two opposing forces. Karl Marx's classic formulation of thesis, antithesis, and synthesis is perhaps the most famous of these three-term system formulas. The dialectic model resolves a certain tension that exists in matters of "relatedness."[4] This is a difference between knowledge and understanding often stressed by information environment designers. Awareness of all the facts can be seen as knowledge, but seeing the connections between the facts—their relatedness—is understanding. It is this relatedness that we are trying to get at in simulation models: How is this proposed action related to an outcome and further how does *that relationship* connect to another possibility?

But, again, constructing models is one thing; making them visible is another. Herein, lies the potential power of virtual reality technologies. If we have a sound theoretical basis for constructing the models and can use a technology to make the visible to more than one person at a time, we have constructed a virtual business model.

Computer technology is now allowing us to run through business operation simulations very quickly and compare results by means of sensitivity analysis. Previously the technology limited the number of iterations that could be conducted because of slow processing speeds and memory limitations. In some cases, various scenarios that were run on mainframes required day-long intervals. This time lag destroys the cognitive ability of analysts to hold different scenario results simultaneously in their minds. We cannot discuss the utility of dynamic modeling or use of computer technology to support consideration of the cognitive factors involved in this type of decision-making.

Visualization and Cognition

We live in a visual culture [11]. More than 60% of our mental processing power is devoted to visual processing. Once complex images are made visual they can then also become mobile, immutable, and reproducible [12]. McNeil [13] contends that this visualization process

---

[4] *Relatedness* and *connectedness* are important parts of Bennett's metaphysics also. The point is that everything is related within an organization, but oftentimes not connected. Visualization is a very good technique for making this distinction explicit.

was the key to allowing the ancient Chinese government bureaucracy to develop because of its use of ideograms to symbolize complex organizational processes. Visualization allows us access to an alternative method of analysis.

TenHouten and Kaplan [14] present two main theories of inquiry that the Western scientific (and by extension managerial) world uses. The primary mode is analytical and is based on numerical data. In fact, Latour's paper [12] makes the point that people go to great lengths to take complex visual data and transform them into something that can be quantified and turned into a comfortable cognitive artifact. But there is another way of knowing and understanding: knowing through synthetic inquiry [14]. This type of inquiry makes use of complex images that present several people with the same image of reality. This reduces the "veiledness" [5] of the data and allows them to be interpreted with assumptions of meaning clarified. The utility of this is very clear when you view several managers or executives sitting together and viewing the ubiquitous profit chart on the viewgraph. The meaning of the direction of the profit line is quite clear to everyone and has a particular implication for action, which is the topic of discussion. *Displaying critical information in visual form has cognitive impact beyond that of mere listings of numerical data.*

Visual images are very dense. That is, they contain quite a bit of information. It is not only the elements themselves (which may be words, symbols, etc.), but their relationship to one another that is important. For example, a chart or graph displays the same information contained in a table—but the chart or graph produces much more information in the mind of the viewer. Currently, the visual display of scientific information is receiving increased interest as our ability to assemble very large databases increase [15]. However, application of visualization techniques to organizational analysis is only now beginning [16, 17].

Some very interesting work is also taking place in the cognitive sciences related to visualization. Varela, Thompson, and Rosch [18] suggest that there is no absolute objective measure of the visual process. In other words, there is no objective, outside picture of the world that is simply perceived. Indeed, their analysis shows that cultural factors and psychological states can have an impact on defining visual images—and their perception. This means that two business managers from two cultures could look at the same financial data and come to vastly different conclusions about the relative health of the firm. The

---

[5] Strictly numerical data can convey quantity or amount, but is severely limited in conveying a sense of complexity or how *this* is related to *that.*

implications are that a virtual reality of a business can be, and really is, a socially negotiated process. If these images are made visually available, we will create a new cognition of the enterprise with implications for changing organizational behavior.

Organizational Functioning

Several technologies are integrating themselves in a way that makes real-time simulation possible and engaging. In the past we have had large mainframe computers, complicated algorithms, and paper output of numerical data to simulate processes. These have been expensive and results have been hard to interpret—especially in a holistic, non-quantifiable manner. Telecommunications and computer software have been coming together for some time now. It is almost impossible to distinguish today where computers leave off and networks begin. So now we have a suite of technologies that allows us to manipulate (and design) communications. We can change content, form, style, and channel. This is the necessary and sufficient set of communication technologies that allows us to simulate organizational processes robustly in such a way that they become believable and real.

Bennett's Hexad Structure

As we said earlier, our approach to organizational analysis bears a strong resemblance to Forrester's view of comflows within organizations. However, we would like to extend that approach by using an even more complex model of organizations. One popular organization design technique involves the use of a variety of visual frameworks to symbolize various organizational processes [17]. These frameworks have been developed through use of the metaphysical writing of John Bennett [7] and are visual symbols of complex processes—blueprints of a sort.

Organizations process information to manage uncertainty and puzzling situations [19]. The way in which they manage the flow of information can indicate the relative health of large, formal complex organizations. We are proposing that an organizational design model based on information flows can be used as a diagnostic tool, as well as a design template for an organizational development practitioner. In common practice physicians use a similar approach in medical diagnosis and prescription.

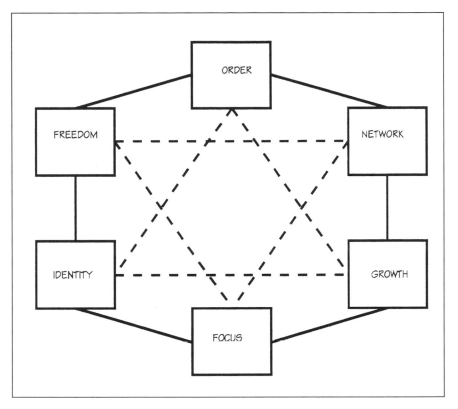

FIG. 10.1.   BENNETT'S MODEL OF ORGANIZATIONAL FUNCTIONING.

Bennett [7] sees a multiterm system composed of six elements as a model that describes a concrete "event," that is, something which has come into existence and is complete. A six-term system becomes the basis for describing a work organization, because it does exist and is complete. In systems theory terms, the organization has a boundary, requisite variety, and constituent parts that are connected to one another.[6]

Bennett's work provides the basis of this model by relying on structural aspects of organizations. Figure 10.1 is a diagram that identifies these elements of organizational health. This figure is meant to convey the interconnectedness of the six elements. The dark lines that form the outer border signify that all elements must be viewed as a complete whole. The dotted lines inside the figure form two triangles, which are two subsets of the entire process. Freedom, Network, and Focus unite

---

[6] There are many models of healthy organizations. The sociotechnical approach of Passmore [20], the diagnostic approach of Kotter [21], the cybernetics model of Beer

TABLE 10.I

DIMENSIONS OF ORGANIZATIONS AND INFORMATION FLOW ANALOGS

Organizational Dimension	Operational Definition	Information Flow Analog
Growth	Measure of organizational scale coupled with rate of change	Normalized volume First-order derivative
Focus	Efficiency of operation Output variance reduction	Variation in output types Standard deviation
Autonomy	Rate of innovation Measure of creative ability	Creation rate of "objects" Second-order differential
Order	Measure of sequencing of operational steps	Degree of indexing of objects Log-linearity: entropy
Identity	Measure of uniqueness Boundary permeability	Self-references Degree of translation
Network	Measure of interaction pattern Density and reciprocity	Density of communication Ratios of frequency and direction

to build potential for action. Identity, Order, and Growth are the manifestations of that potential. So elements can be examined as unique things, in sets of three or as a whole. The point here is that the business enterprise must be considered in its totality to be truly understood. Each of these structural elements has an analog of information system flow, which is outlined in Table 10.1.

Each of these structural elements is therefore characterized by an information flow. By definition, we can diagnose the relative functioning of an organizational element by examining the associated information flow characteristic. This principle becomes the basis for the creation of our unique diagnostic (and design) paradigm.

The purpose of developing a model of organizational functioning that can be operationalized and used as a basis for dynamic computer modeling is to assist in the diagnosis and intervention of business enterprise. Miller and Miller [2] offer an analysis of organizations as living organisms that contain various subsystems. They break down organizations into some 20 subsystems, which can be analyzed for variances in

---

[22], and the comparative approach of Morgan [9] are some of the most popular in use today in the practice of organizational design. We do not attempt to argue the validity of their model or our model of organizations. We are much more concerned with the idea of reliability in the use of the model for comparative analysis. Our model is an application of Bennett's work to our own information flows, extended into the process aspects of organizational interaction.

functioning. When any of these subsystems is out of balance, the organization can be characterized as possessing a pathology that needs to
be corrected. We use the same logic in the application of Bennett's
theoretical constructs and our interpretation of information flows to organizational modeling. That is, we can examine variations in function
of these six elements in the dynamic model to locate "organizational
pathologies."

Computer Modeling of Organizational Functioning

Traditional models of organizational functioning have been limited to
financial and statistical analysis. This way of simulating possible scenarios of business are very helpful when the processes are based on
cash flows, balance sheets, and income statements. The advent of computerized spread sheets changed the way in which managers made
many decisions. They had a tool to examine possible effects of business
decisions before they were actually made. "What if" analysis became a
standard tool of business managers. However, not all business processes fall into these categories.

The business environment is becoming more complex, dynamic, and
sensitive to impacts from outside firms and markets. To understand today's complexity completely, managers need to look at feedback loops,
time lagged effects, and "softer" variables, which cannot be easily
translated into dollar measures. Management science has also discovered that people can often comprehend very complicated numerical
relationships visually. Truly a picture is worth a thousand words—
or a few dozen spread sheets.

Software tools are becoming available that allow business leaders
to model these complex processes quickly and easily and display the
results in a visual dynamic format [23]. Figure 10.2 is an example of
what a simple business model relating firm growth to organizational
learning rates looks like. The boxes in the model represent reservoirs
where quantities are collected such as learning and size. The circles
stand for valves that control rates of flow. Arrows are pipes and the
little clouds are boundaries of the model. This model states in explicit
form the following: We assume that an organization's ability to focus
on the production process is a function of its experience modified by a
knowledge conversion factor. Further, a firm's expansion rate is a function of this learning and ability to focus. Finally, a firm's ultimate growth,

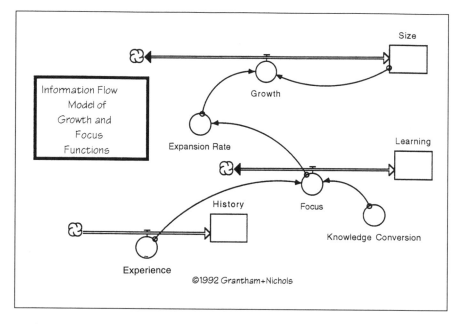

FIG. 10.2.   INFORMATION SYSTEM FLOW MODEL OF GROWTH AND FOCUS FUNCTIONS.

or size, is determined by this expansion rate. Once we have diagrammed this process, the software automatically generates the mathematical equations that relate all parts of the model. The code generated
by this model is listed in Appendix A.

A typical graphical output for this model is given in Figure 10.3. The
interpretation of this model is that as learning decreases over time
(curve 2), there is a corresponding lagging decline in firm size (curve 1).
The power of this modeling technique is that you can instantly return
to the model, change the assumptions,[7] and rerun the simulation to
compare projected results. For example, if we return to the model
and change the Knowledge conversion factor to be positive, reflecting
an assumption of increased expenditure for employee education, we
get the results of Figure 10.4. As you can see, a simple change in one
variable has a significant impact on how the model behaves. We can
now go back and extend the time scope of the model and insert the
assumption that learning increases and then decreases in a cyclical

---

[7] The process of changing assumptions relates to knowledge acquisition from participants in the modeling design process. See the conclusion for methodological comments.

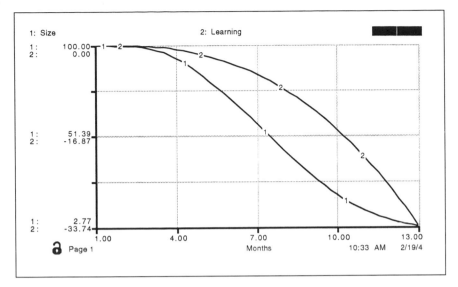

FIG. 10.3.   DYNAMIC MODELING OUTPUT.

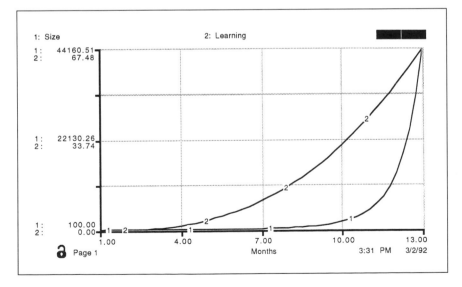

FIG. 10.4.   MODEL OUTPUT WITH POSITIVE EDUCATION ASSUMPTION.

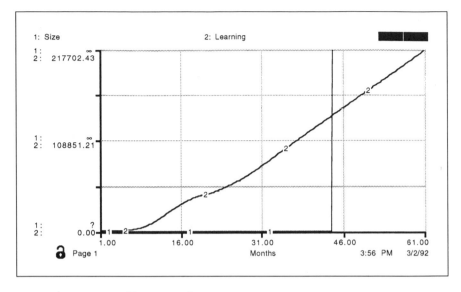

FIG. 10.5. LEARNING FUNCTION OVER TIME.

fashion during a three-year period (Figure 10.5). We can model this assumption as a graph. We now see that learning reaches some sort of threshold level at about 44 during a five-year simulation. Take-off occurs after more than three years of increased effort to build learning in an organization.

The use of models such as this decreases the learning time for managers. This simple illustration of modeling environments takes approximately five minutes to demonstrate. We have found that the computer becomes a very effective teaching tool in these dynamic modeling situations.

This result has high intuitive appeal for practitioners. We all know that organizational change, and especially learning, is time sensitive. It takes a long time to realize positive effects. The next step in the modeling process would be to perform a series of sensitivity analyses to see just what occurred in the interaction of variables between month 31 and month 46.

Application

We have extended this modeling process to incorporate all of the elements of Bennett's organizational health model. Each of the six elements is paired with those which represent its opposite in functioning, thus yielding three segments to the model. Each of these segments can then be interactively linked to determine the effect pathologies in one sector have on another sector.

We use this general model to develop a baseline example of organizational health. This process is conducted in a small focus group setting with a skilled group facilitator and a systems engineer. Once the baseline case is established, the model is then used in an interactive fashion to examine the relative impact of different decisions, much as we outlined in the preceding two-element example. The complexity of the model grows rapidly and there are cognitive limits of comprehension.

The functionality of the underlying application development software can be exploited to manage this problem. The model is constructed in sectors with the algorithms connected in a dynamic linking process. We have included a partial listing of the algorithms as Appendix A. These modeling equations are an operationalization of the assumptions about "relatedness" of the elements of the organization. The basic metaphor of information flow is manifested in the model with flows, valves, and reservoirs. This is a very good representation of the dialectical model. Forces toward creation (flows) are restrained (valves) and yield a unity of opposites, which are accumulated (reservoirs). Therefore, the application of the dynamic modeling process using computer technology and visualization techniques meets the methodological test of validity, which we sought by employing a dialectical model of inquiry [14].

Conclusions: Organizations that Wake Up

Dynamic equation modeling of organizational processes offers a new management tool to examine the effects of a range of management initiatives in today's complex business environment. Virtual reality technology carries with it much promise to develop this application. Further, the real value of this process is to make *implicit* assumptions about organizational behavior *explicit,* model them over time, and make this process visible to participants so they may conduct the natural negotiation process among themselves as purposeful managers.

Our mental capacity to model these complex systems is built with a number of rather simple submodels, which are capable, in combination, of mimicking very complex organizational processes. The new models we will need to use in the future are dynamic, systemic, and evolving. As our horizon of concern extends into what used to be other systems, we need to develop the corresponding capacity to generate more complexity from simplicity. Just as a hologram contains all the information to replicate a complex image in any one part, so do organizations when viewed as viable systems. Our modeling tools, through use of a constrained set of simple primitives, need to be able to self-generate more and more complexity.

Finally, "Successful information environments express a high degree of virtuality: a good fit between the external worlds they are intended to represent and the virtual worlds they actually produce" [4]. We believe that future research pathways in dynamic modeling, at least of organizations, should stress development of fidelity between the model and reality.

Virtual reality has been labeled by some as a hallucination or having a psychedelic quality. Well, perhaps it does, but we would like to stand that idea on its head. Virtual reality simulations of business enterprise functioning can break us out of the existing consensual trance that business managers exist within. Charles Tart [3] submits that our enculturation processes have put us into a consensual trance, which is not an accurate reflection of reality. I suggest that the same applies to the way we manage most businesses today.

One technique that Tart recommends for "waking up" from this trance is a process called *self-observing*. Self-observing involves becoming increasingly aware of, and sensitive to, our internal physical, emotional, and intellectual states. I would like to suggest that virtual reality technologies, along with a sound model or organizational functioning, can provide a tool for large organizations to wake up, break the consensual trance, and become self-observing.

REFERENCES

[1] Forrester, J. W., *Industrial Dynamics,* Cambridge, MA: The MIT Press, 1961.
[2] Miller, J. G., and J. L Miller, "A Living Systems Analysis of Organizational Pathology," *Behavioral Science,* **36,** pp. 239–252, 1991.
[3] Tart, Charles, *Waking Up: Overcoming the Obstacles to Human Potential,* Boston: Shambala, 1987.
[4] Jacobson, Robert, "The Ultimate User Interface," *Byte,* pp. 175–182, April 1992.
[5] Dur, R. C. J., and P. W. G. Bots, "Dynamic Modeling of Organizations Using Task/ Actor Simulation," in *Proceedings of the Second International Working Conference*

on *Dynamic Modeling of Information Systems,* Washington, D.C., July 18–19, 1991, The American University, pp. 15–35, 1991.

[6] Senge, Peter, *The Fifth Discipline,* New York: Doubleday, 1990.

[7] Bennett, J. G., *The Dramatic Universe,* Vol. II, Charlestown, WV: Claymount, 1987.

[8] Cummings, T. G., "A Concluding Note: Future Directions of Sociotechnical Theory and Research," *Journal of Applied Behavioral Science,* **22**(3), pp. 355–360, 1986.

[9] Morgan, Gareth, *Images of Organizations,* Beverly Hills, CA: Sage Publications, 1986.

[10] Meadows, D. H., D. L. Meadows, R. Randers, W. Behrens, *The Limits to Growth,* New York: Universe Books, 1972.

[11] Alpers, S., *The Art of Describing: Dutch Art in the 17th Century,* Chicago: University of Chicago Press, 1983.

[12] Latour, Bruno, "Visualization and Cognition," in *Knowledge and Society: Studies in the Sociology of Culture Past and Present,* Vol. 6, pp. 1–40, New York: JAI Press, 1986.

[13] McNeil, W., *The Pursuit of Power, Technology, Armed Forces and Society since A.D. 1000,* Chicago: University of Chicago Press, 1982.

[14] TenHouten, W. D., and C. D. Kaplan, *Science and Its Mirror Image,* New York: Harper and Row, 1973.

[15] Tufte, E. R., *Envisioning Information,* Cheshire, CT: Graphics Press, 1990.

[16] Grantham, C. E., "The Virtual Business: Evolution of a New Organizational Form," *The Journal of Organizational Computing,* Norwood, NJ: Ablex Publishing, forthcoming, 1993.

[17] Grantham, C. E., *The Digital Workplace,* New York: Van Nostrand-Rienhold, 1993.

[18] Varela, Francisco, E. Thompson, and E. Rosch, *The Embodied Mind: Cognitive Science and Human Experience,* Cambridge, MA: The MIT Press, 1991.

[19] Daft, R. L., and R. H. Lengel, "Organizational Information Requirements, Media Richness and Structural Design," *Management Science,* **32**(5), pp. 554–571, May 1986.

[20] Passmore, William, *Organizations: The Socio-technical Systems Perspective,* New York: John Wiley and Sons, 1988.

[21] Kotter, John, *Organizational Dynamics: Diagnosis and Intervention,* Reading, MA: Addison-Wesley, 1978.

[22] Beer, Stafford, *Diagnosing the System for Organizations,* New York: John Wiley and Sons, 1985.

[23] Feiner, Steven, and C. Beshers, "Worlds within Worlds: Metaphors for Exploring *n*-Dimensional Virtual Worlds," in *Proceedings UIST '90,* New York: ACM Press, pp. 76–83, 1990.

Appendix A

Code Listing (Partial)

Direction
History(t) = History(t − dt) + (Experience) * dt
INIT History = 5

INFLOWS:
Experience = GRAPH(TIME*Product_Development)
(1, 0.5) (2, 0) (3, 3.5) (4, 9) (5, 14.5) (6, 17.5) (7, 25) (8, 30.5) (9, 39.5) (10, 50) (11, 56) (12, 65.5) (13, 69.5)
INFLOW TO:
Learning(t) = Learning(t − dt) + (Focus) * dt
INIT Learning = 0

INFLOWS:
Focus = Experience*Knowledge_Conversion
INFLOW TO:
Size(t) = Size (t − dt) + (Growth) * dt
INIT Size = 100

INFLOWS:
Growth = (Size*Expansion_Rate)/Identity
INFLOW TO:
Expansion_Rate = (.1*Focus)
Knowledge_Conversion = .02+(Interaction_Density/.6)

Appendix B

Definition of Terms

Growth: Realization of greater range in terms of absolute size or market penetration; a measure of scale. Growth can also be realized as combination with other entities in symbiotic form.

Focus: Development of efficiency in operation; a measure of variance reduction in output. Concentration of effort to eliminate waste is process.

Freedom: Rate of innovation; a measure of creation. An opening to possibilities to develop ideas, products, or processes that currently do not exist in the organization.

Order: Relationship of steps within a productive process; a measure of sequencing. A measure of internal efficiency.

Identity: Definition of uniqueness; a measure of salience to environment. Also related to definition of boundaries of the organization.

Networks: Interaction pattern, both internal and external; a measure of pace and density, connectedness and reciprocity.

Index

Other Academic Press Professional Titles of Interest

Modern Image Processing: Warping, Morphing, and Classical Techniques
by Christopher D. Watkins, Alberto Sadun, and Stephen Marenka

Image Processing has applications to numerous disciplines, and with the availability of powerful and inexpensive hardware, it is now an area being implemented and investigted by all levels of computer users. *Modern Image Processing* contains both practical and theoretical information regarding techniques for processing images that are scanned or take through a CCD (camera arrays-digital cameras). It instructs the reader about how to enhance, manipulate, and extract information from the images which have been acquired. The book also includes the source code required to perform all of the image manipulation.

ISBN 0-12-737860-X

August, 1993; $49.95 (tentative)

Multimedia Production Handbook for the PC, Macintosh, and Amiga
by Tom Yager

This handbook is a comprehensive resource guide for selecting an appropriate multimedia system from among the many currently available. It focuses on three of the best platforms for Multimedia applications: IBM, Macintosh, and Amiga. Author Tom Yager brings two years of experience as director of Byte Magazine's Multimedia Lab to this exciting new text. By using this book, managers, developers, and end-users can more effectively map out their time and capital for resources and development.

ISBN 0-12-768030-6   8/93; $35.95 (tentative)

Usability Engineering
by Jakob Nielsen

Written by the author of the best-selling *Hypertext & Hypermedia*, this book offers an excellent introduction to Usability Engineering. Practical guidelines for addressing usability considerations in the software engineering process are covered throughout the book. It also provides concrete advice and methods that can be systematically implemented to ensure a high level of usability in the final interface.

ISBN 0-12-518405-2 $29.95

Other Academic Press Professional Titles of Interest

T$_E$XHelp: The On-Line T$_E$X Handbook
by Arvind Borde

This innovative package gives T$_E$X users access to on-line help with most aspects of the program. It supplies explanations of all T$_E$X commands, and it discusses a large range of typesetting topics.

The program:

- is a useful tool for the beginning and advanced T$_E$X user
- is completely menu driven and is very easy to use
- works like a HyperText tool: entries contain highlighted words that users can choose in order to directly access further information
- allows users to save entries in files, which can be processed with T$_E$X and printed or previewed
- permits, on some systems, direct T$_E$X previewing of entries by pressing a sigle key.

The package provides a data file which contains descriptions and explanations of T$_E$X commands, as well as discussions of may commonly-used typesetting terms and techniques. It also provides a file of new T$_E$X commands that allows the processing and previewing of saved entries.

This program was developed by Arvind Borde with the assistance of Tomas Rokicki.

ISBN 0-12-117640-1 $49.95 (tentative)

Using C in Software Design
by Ronald Leach

Using C in Software Design provides a creative approach to learning C by emphasizing software engineering. This text is designed for beginners or those learning C as a second language. ANSI C is used throughout the book and thought-provoking problems are included at the end of each chapter. The book is divided into two sections; the first emphasizes the simpler software engineering aspects of C, allowing the reader to begin writing interesting programs quickly. The second part discusses advanced C topics, such as pointers, structures, and the design of larger C programs which extend over several source code files.

ISBN 0-12-440210-0   August, 1993; $39.95 (tentative)

Other Academic Press Professional Titles of Interest

FRACTALS EVERYWHERE
Second Edition
Michael F. Barnsley

ISBN 0-12-079061-0 $49.95

June 1993   560 pp.

About the Second Edition:

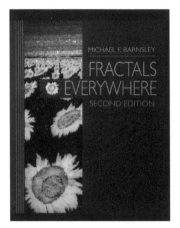

"The material contained in the second edition is quite obviously more extensive in detail and scope....the style of writing is technically excellent, informative, and entertaining....the material in this book will make an excellent university-level course."

— Robert McCarty

"The problems and examples are well-chosen and interesting....difficult concepts are introduced in a clear fashion with excellent diagrams and graphs."

— Alan E. Wessel
Santa Clara University

This volume is the second edition of the highly successful *Fractals Everywhere*. The focus of this text is how fractal geometry can be used to model real objects in the physical world. The new edition features:

• A new chapter on Recurrent Iterated Function Systems, including Vector Recurrent Iterated Functions (V-RIFs)™

• Problems and tools emphasizing fractal applications

• An all-new answer key to problems in the text, with solutions and hints.

This edition of *Fractals Everywhere* is the most complete and up-to-date fractal textbook available today.

Fractals Everywhere may be supplemented by Michael F. Barnsley's *Desktop Fractal Design System* (version 2.0) with IBM or Macintosh software. *The Desktop Fractal Design System 2.0* is a tool for designing Iterated Function Systems codes and fractal images, and makes an excellent supplement to a course on fractal geometry.

Other Academic Press Professional Titles of Interest

Radiosity and Realistic Image Synthesis
by Michael Cohen and John Wallace

Radiosity and Realistic Image Synthesis is the first comprehensive look at the radiosity method and the tools required for creating visual experiences via the computer. Basic concepts and mathematical fundamentals underlying image synthesis and radiosity algorithms are covered thoroughly (a basic knowledge of undergraduate calculus is assumed). Discussions are based on algorithms developed to implement the radiosity method, ranging from environment subdivision to final displays. Successes and obstacles in implementing these algorithms are highlighted. Over 100 illustrations and 16 pages of full-color images explain the developments and results of the radiosity method.

ISBN 0-12-178270-0   July, 1993; $49.95 (tentative)

HYPERSTAT
Macintosh Hypermedia for Analyzing Data and Learning Statistics
by David M. Lane

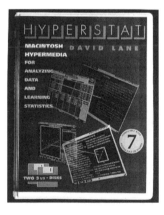

HyperStat is a unique hypermedia software package for the Macintosh. It serves as an integrated combination of a program for data analysis, a hypertext in statistics, and a set of interactive simulation/data exercises called "explorations." It is both a statistics book that can do calculations and a statistical analysis system with a tremendous amount of on-line help. A 120 page user manual is also included.

HyperStat's statistical procedures cover simple as well as more sophisticated analyses. For instance, *HyperStat* has procedures for multiple regression and complex analysis of variance. The latter procedure can compute an analysis of variance with up to four between-subject variables. Other procedures emphasize graphics such as box plots, stem and leaf plots, scatterplots, frequency polygons, and histograms.

HyperStat uses hypertext to provide over 2,000 links between related concepts and between results of statistical analyses and explanatory material. The combination of hypertext and *HyperStat's* electronic index makes looking up information extemely easy.

July, 1993, c. 120 pp., ISBN: 0-12-436130-7   7/93; $59.95 (tentative)

ORDER FORM

To Order: Return this form with your payment to Academic Press, Order Fulfillment Department, 6277 Sea Harbor Drive, Orlando, FL 32821-9816, or **call toll-free 1-800-321-5068.**

QUANTITY	AUTHOR/TITLE	ISBN	PRICE

Subtotal

Sales Tax (where applicable)

TOTAL

☐ Payment enclosed (please include applicable tax)

☐ Bill me directly (We cannot ship to a P.O. box)*

☐ Bill my company (purchase order attached)*

*Shipping, handling, and tax will be added to billed orders. Tax will be added to credit card orders.

Charge card #_____   Expiration Date _____

Your Signature_____

Name_____   Telephone _____

Address _____

City_____   State/Country _____

Zip/Postal Code_____